Legacy of the Dog

THE ULTIMATE ILLUSTRATED GUIDE TO OVER 200 BREEDS

TETSU YAMAZAKI
TOYOHARU KOJIMA

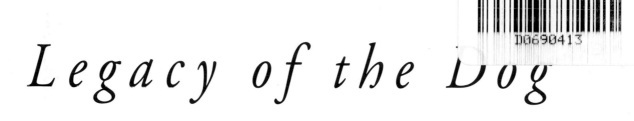

CHRONICLE BOOKS

SAN FRANCISCO

First published in the United States by Chronicle Books in 1995.

Photography copyright © 1993 by Tetsu Yamazaki.
Text copyright © 1993 by Toyoharu Kojima.

First published in Japan by Yama-Kei Publishers Co., Ltd., in 1993.

Printed in Singapore.

Library of Congress Cataloging-in-Publication Data:
Yamazaki, Tetsu.
    [Sekai no inu zukan. English]
    Legacy of the dog / by Tetsu Yamazaki.
       p. cm.
    Includes index.
    ISBN 0-8118-1069-0 (pbk.)
    ISBN 0-8118-1123-9 (hc)
    1. Dogs—Encyclopedias.   2. Dog breeds—Encyclopedias.
I. Yamazaki, Tetsu, 1949– II. Title.
SF422.K6413   1995
636.7'1 '03—dc20   95-2059
                        CIP

Translation: Yuh Nagano and Isao Tezuka with Neal M. Teitler
Cover design: Desne Border
Cover photograph: Tetsu Yamazaki
Typography: Suzanne Scott

Distributed in Canada by
Raincoast Books
8680 Cambie Street
Vancouver, B.C. V6P 6M9

10 9 8 7 6 5 4

Chronicle Books
85 Second Street
San Francisco, California 94105

Web Site: www.chronbooks.com

Contents

Dogs Forever

Of all animals, dogs have the longest history of friendship with humans. If dogs had never been part of our world, the human race may never have reached its present state of civilization. Dogs have protected our lives and property from enemies, have helped us hunt for other animals that provide sustenance, and have helped us out of trouble, sometimes sacrificing their own lives. Few other animals have been as important to humankind. The love for dogs is as universal as the desire for world peace. This book is dedicated to our beloved dogs and to the readers who want to know more about them.

Many books have been published about how to raise puppies and how to keep and train dogs, but very few are illustrated to show the appearance of each breed. This book includes photos of prize-winning dogs of more than two hundred breeds from all over the world.

As a lover of dogs from early childhood, especially rare breeds, I read innumerable books about them as I grew up. Until recently, there were very few rare breeds of foreign dogs in Japan;

such dogs could only be seen in illustrations and photographs. So although I had an image in my mind of each type of pedigreed dog, I grew up wondering what they actually looked like. Later, given the opportunity to see these breeds in the flesh, I realized that my earlier impressions were often quite different from reality. Probably this was because the dogs in the illustrations and photographs were not very close to the recognized standards.

In this book, I have been careful to select photos of dogs that are as close as possible to the current standards. As many photographs as possible have been included to provide visual enjoyment while showing readers at first glance what each breed really looks like. To assemble these photos of the world's best dogs, photographer Tetsu Yamazaki and I spent over three years going to major dog shows and visiting well-known kennels throughout Japan and around the world.

This book classifies the major breeds into seven groups. When talking about "pure breeds,"

we must remember that although some breeds evolved naturally over a long period of time, most were developed by careful selection from successive generations of crossbred progeny. In this way, characteristics such as hunting or working ability, speed, and sociability could be emphasized, while negative traits could be eliminated or minimized. Likewise, physical traits that best suited these attributes and tasks were selected, resulting in the conformations we now recognize as "fixed breeds." No doubt newer breeds will be developed in the future, while some of the presently recognized breeds may face extinction if their popularity declines. I believe we must try to avoid losing any of these breeds, so that they may be enjoyed by future generations.

My heartfelt thanks are offered to the officials of the many kennel clubs in each country I visited, and to the dog owners and handlers for their infinite cooperation in helping us to select and photograph the magnificent dogs shown in these pages.

—*Toyoharu Kojima*

The History of Domesticated Dogs

Classifying the Dog

The question of the dog's original ancestor is fascinating, but the answer remains highly speculative. Dogs are placed within the order Carnivora, a division of the larger class Mammalia. Carnivores are usually divided into eight families: Canidae (dogs), Procyonidae (raccoons), Felidae (cats), Mustelidae (weasels), Ailuridae (pandas), Ursidae (bears), Viverridae (civets), and Hyaenidae (hyenas). Domestic dogs are classified under Canidae. The Canidae are generally divided into four groups: the dog group (genus *Canis*), the fox group (genus *Vulpes*), the culpeo group (genus *Dusicyon*), and the bush dog group (all other genera).

The bush dog group includes the bush dog, crab-eating fox, bat-eared fox, raccoon dog, and gray fox, while the fox group covers almost all species of foxes except the gray fox and a few others. The culpeo group contains in-between species of dogs and foxes, such as the Falkland wolf, culpeo fox, striped-tail dog, Andes wolf, and maned wolf.

Included in the dog group are the dhole, African wild dog, and canis. The first two genera have only dholes and African wild dogs, respectively. The Canis group includes coyote, jackal, wolf, dingo, and the domestic dog.

All in the Canis group have the same skeletal structure, including five digits on the front paws, and four on the rear paws, and have a circular contracting iris. These shared characteristics indicate that the domestic dog may find its ancestor in this genus.

Prehistoric Roots

Members of the genus *Canis* appeared about a million years ago, first in Asia or Eurasia, later migrating back and forth between these continents and the Americas, mainly within the Northern Hemisphere. At that time, the Eurasian continent and the Americas were not yet separated. As no fossils of dogs have yet been discovered in Australia, it is presently believed that dogs evolved well after this continent separated from the others.

Because the oldest fossil of a dog is reputed to be from the Mesolithic, discovered in Yorkshire, England, with the remains of a civilization, it is currently believed that some 500,000 years ago, during the Paleolithic, humans had not yet developed a bond with dogs. Many early dog breeds evolved into their present form by adjusting to their habitat. Breeds with ancient bloodlines, which often resemble wolves in appearance and jackals in habit, are said to be less aggressive than wolves as they were often scavengers, surviving mainly on the remains of other carnivores and animals.

Wild Dogs and Domestic Dogs

Dogs resemble wolves more than any other animal. Wolves are distributed mainly in the Northern Hemisphere: Europe, North America, and Asia. Generally, those inhabiting the colder climates are larger, lighter in color (probably for protection), and more aggressive, while those found in warmer regions are smaller, with a yellowish fawn coloring that becomes lighter towards the abdomen, and are less aggressive. This latter coloring is the one most often seen in the domestic dog. Although wolves are often believed to be enemies of humans, in reality the opposite is more often true; they very rarely attack, but rather easily become accustomed to people.

Wolf

Jackals often hunt in groups; however, they mainly survive on carrion left over by other carnivores. The coyote, with its pointed muzzle, large ears, and thick tail, closely resembles the wolf, but lives on the grasslands of North America; hence it is also called the grassland wolf. It has sharply declined in number due to misdirected eradication efforts on the part of people seeking to protect their livestock. South America has wild dogs such as the crab-eating fox and the zorro. Zorros have big ears, thick tails, and thickset bodies. Progeny of crosses between these wild dogs and domestic dogs were highly treasured by the locals for their hunting ability. The wild dog of Australia is the dingo, which rarely barks in the wild, but readily starts barking once it is domesticated.

All of the above are members of the so-called dog group, and are thus considered relatives of today's domestic dogs. In appearance, habits, and expression, they are all quite similar. Even though there are some exceptions, such as short-faced bulldogs, toy Chihuahuas, bent-eared setters, and spaniels, generally they have shared characteristics. These include the type and total number (42) of teeth; skull shape, although size differs; total number (50 to 52) and type of vertebrae: 7 cervical, 13 thoracic, 7 lumbar, 3 sacral, and 20 to 22 coccygeal (tail); irises circularly contracting; a keen olfactory sense, with prey being sought by smell; similar physical ailments and illnesses such as distemper, rabies, and heartworm; manner of howling, growling, and expressing pain; facial expressions; method of expressing delight (ears pulled back and tail wagging), anger (hair stands up and canine teeth are displayed), and submission (rolling over on the back and/or tail being placed between the legs); nocturnal habits; a propensity to dig; a nine-week gestation period; and the opening of eyes at about two weeks of age.

Despite such similar characteristics, it is considered dangerous to cross domestic dogs and other *canis familiaris.* The offspring, although they can reproduce, not only have odd physical appearances but often prove to be shy.

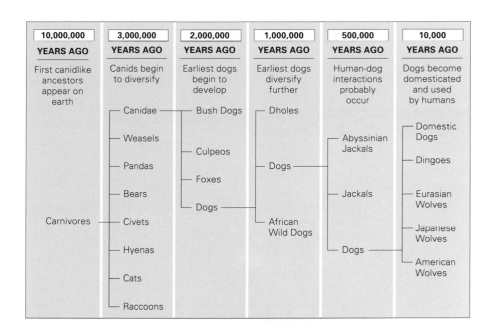

10,000,000 YEARS AGO	3,000,000 YEARS AGO	2,000,000 YEARS AGO	1,000,000 YEARS AGO	500,000 YEARS AGO	10,000 YEARS AGO
First canidlike ancestors appear on earth	Canids begin to diversify	Earliest dogs begin to develop	Earliest dogs diversify further	Human-dog interactions probably occur	Dogs become domesticated and used by humans

Carnivores — Canidae — Bush Dogs — Dholes
Weasels — Culpeos
Pandas — Foxes — Dogs — Abyssinian Jackals — Domestic Dogs
Bears — Dogs — Dingoes
Civets — African Wild Dogs — Jackals — Eurasian Wolves
Hyenas — Dogs — Japanese Wolves
Cats — American Wolves
Raccoons

Dingoes

German family and spaniel, Cologne

The remaining kinds of wild dogs seem to be irrelevant to today's domestic dogs.

Even today, some wild dogs are completely devoid of human contact, and live as they have for tens of thousands of years, allowing us to observe phenomena that give us clues as to how early wild dogs behaved tens of thousands of years ago.

Humans and the Dog

Ancient humans, wearing virtually nothing, must have shivered in the cold while hunting animals such as mammoths, deer, and boar with hand-held weapons. They also caught fish and collected shellfish from rivers and along seashores, foraged for roots, and picked fruits and edible leaves from plants. Probably, at this time, humans competed with wild dogs for food and even ate them. Later on when people banded together to form tribes and moved into caves, they began establishing and guarding territories. While human hunters likely most often prevailed over dog packs, both creatures probably began learning of the mutual benefits of establishing a relationship: Carrion leftovers were easily available wherever humans settled, and dog packs would begin barking when unknown humans or other animals approached. As dogs moved in

to live closer and closer to humans, people probably began to attempt taming them. We know that in northwest Europe during the Mesolithic period some twelve thousand years ago, humans began keeping dogs and other animals.

During the Neolithic, humans moved out of caves and established early settlements of thatched huts near water, engaging in agriculture and sheep raising. A complete fossil of a dog that had been neither killed nor eaten was discovered in a settlement in Europe from this period, and is believed to have been a domesticated dog. Neatly laid-out dog bones from Neolithic burial sites recently excavated in Europe also show that at this time dogs were already greatly treasured by people.

From the time humans realized that domesticated dogs could be useful and started to catch wild puppies, selection for desired physical and behavioral characteristics began in order to make the dogs better suited to certain tasks. Over centuries, these manmade modifications resulted in a number of recognizable dog breeds with distinct characteristics. Today, some 350 dog breeds are recognized by the Federation Cynologique Internationale (FCI), headquartered in Belgium, but considering that a number of national kennel clubs still

are not FCI members, the total number of recognizable breeds probably approaches five hundred. Each fixed breed has an official set of standards, which demonstrates the amazing degree to which the original wild dogs have been modified to produce the great variety we recognize today. Generally the standards set by each breed's recognized parent club, by which this type of dog is judged, covers its history and lineage, use, general appearance, temperament, conformation (head, body, tail, limbs, coat, coloration, and so on), gait, size, and faults.

Seven Groups

Following is an overview of the seven groups (herding, working, sporting, hound, terrier, toy, and non-sporting) into which the dog breeds in this book have been divided.

Herding Group

Humans used to catch wild animals and corral them for food or livestock farming. In order to keep the animals from running away and to protect them from predators, people started keeping dogs, thus originating sheepdogs. Consequently, human life improved enormously, as food and materials for clothes were always close at hand.

Working Group

Dogs sense an approaching enemy and warn their master. This was the origin of the many kinds of guard dogs. Today they include brave and loyal military dogs; pack dogs pulling heavy packs; big but gentle life-saving dogs; enormous and competent guard dogs; fighting dogs that once battled other dogs and animals; police dogs; companion dogs serving the deaf and the blind; sled dogs, and so on.

Sporting Group

Dogs of this group have a keen nose for prey. They will tell their master where the birds are and retrieve the birds when they are shot. Some retrievers like the water and are good swimmers, so it is easy for them to get the prey from the water.

Hound Group

There are two types of hounds: sight hounds and scent hounds. Sight hounds spot their prey from a very far distance and chase it until it is exhausted, while scent hounds find their prey by smell. Scent hounds work with police, searching for drugs and bombs. Dogs of this group can run at more than thirty-five miles per hour. The powerful and graceful body of a hound running at its maximum speed is a work of art. Many hounds are used as show dogs or racing hounds.

Terrier Group

The name terrier comes from the Latin word *terra*, which means "soil" or "ground," and these dogs are so named because they hunt prey hiding in burrows. Big hunting dogs are generally called hounds and small ones terriers. Every terrier is endowed with an excellent sense of smell, agility, a fighting instinct, and intelligence. Terriers are classified as long-legged, short-legged, long-haired, short-haired, or rough-haired. Today they are gaining popularity as domestic dogs and show dogs rather than as hunting dogs because of their good appearance, agility, and cuteness.

Toy Group

Some dogs from the hound group, sporting group, and terrier group are grouped into the toy group. These are distinguished by their small size, cuteness, and desirability as pet dogs and have become indispensable companions to many people.

Non-Sporting Group

Dogs that are suited for specific work and others that are not related to dogs of other groups in appearance or lineage are classified in the non-sporting group. Some are suitable for circus acts, as they have an attractive appearance and an excellent understanding and memory. Others are better rat catchers than terriers are, or are excellent guard dogs as they don't bark unnecessarily. It almost seems wrong to call them "non-sporting," as they are all, without exception, wonderful dogs.

Habits

Dogs have an exceptional sense of direction that is distinct from their keen senses of smell, hearing, and sight. They have an uncanny ability to return home from a long distance by the shortest route, without any landmarks that humans can recognize. When I was a young boy, I acquired a one-year-old Shiba Inu in Shinshu (on the Japan Sea side of the main island of Honshu), and brought it back to Tokyo by train. On the third day, it chewed a hole through the wooden kennel fence and escaped. Ten days later it had made its way back to the previous owner in Shinshu, some 155 miles away! Many similar episodes have been reported all over the world.

There are many theories about why dogs dig, try to sleep in dark hidden areas, and why, before they sleep, they usually walk around their resting spot. None of them have been proven conclusively, however.

Dogs like to keep themselves and their living area clean. This begins at the time they are born, when the mother cleans her puppies. Once they are able to walk on their own, puppies will defecate a good distance from where they sleep and eat. At this time they also start to fetch and hide things. Males will demarcate their territory (a trait believed to be a throwback to their wild canid roots) by urinating at various points within and outside their perimeter.

Dogs are legendary for their loyalty and protectiveness, although some breeds are better guard dogs than others.

Dogs help us psychologically, too. Tests have shown that walking a dog, or just having one as a companion, effectively helps speed recovery from an illness and aid in rehabilitative efforts. For everyone, but especially for children and the elderly, a dog can be a best friend, one that people can talk to about anything and who will help improve the quality of human life.

Dogs, no matter how we look at them, are lovable animals.

A busy dog show

Herding Group

This group harks back to when humans first began employing dogs to guard livestock, and has inherited many of the instincts and traits of its ancestors. The ancestral stock is believed to have been largely fierce guard dogs. The spiked collars we associate with such dogs were used to protect their throats from the attacks of wild animals.

From these dogs, a number of different strains were selectively bred to enhance the characteristics of today's herding group. For dogs that live in cold climates and must protect livestock from wolves or bears, thick coats (some-times double), as well as large size and strength, were of the greatest importance. Their coat protects them from both the cold and from predators, by making their skin difficult to grip. These dogs become instinctively more alert at sunset. Komondors and Anatolian sheepdogs fit into this category.

For managing livestock on big farms or ranches, dogs were selected for quick obedience to commands, plus the ability to assemble and herd as well as to retrieve missing livestock. The mudi, for example, is known for its extreme patience in chasing straying sheep and cows. Such breeds include collies, Shetland sheepdogs, bearded collies, Welsh corgis, and Border collies. Before cars and trains, the Bouvier des Flandres and the Australian cattle dog were developed to help drive livestock over long distances from isolated farms to big town markets.

The emphasis in developing herding group breeds has been on effectiveness and performance, such as endurance in bad weather and the ability to keep running at maximum speed, rather than on looks.

▶ Collie (Rough)

▶ Collie (Smooth)

▶ Shetland Sheepdog

▶ Pyrenean Sheepdog

▲ Border Collie

▲ Bearded Collie

▲ Catalonian Sheepdog

▼ Schapendoes

► Old English
Sheepdog

▲ Polish Lowland
Sheepdog

► Bouvier des
Flandres

◄ Kuvasz

▼ Briard

► Maremma Sheepdog

▲ Anatolian Sheepdog

▼ Bergamasco Sheepdog

◄ Komondor

▲ Puli

12

▲ Australian
Cattle Dog

► Australian
Stumpy Tail
Cattle Dog

► Belgian Shepherd
(Tervuren)

▲ Belgian Shepherd
(Groenendael)

▲ Australian Kelpie

▲ Belgian Shepherd (Malinois)

◄ Welsh Corgi
Cardigan

▲ Welsh Corgi Pembroke

▲ Belgian Shepherd (Laekenois)

▲ Mudi

▲ Pumi

▲ Sarplaninac

◄ Saarloos Wolfhond

▲ Dutch Shepherd (Rough)

◄ Dutch Shepherd (Smooth)

Working Group

Sharing sheepdog origins, this group has its roots in the ancient dogs that not only guarded livestock, but while the master was away also fiercely stood watch over the women and children. In wartime, they even fought as four-legged soldiers, often attacking an enemy much larger than themselves, many times laying down their life for their mission. This instinctive sense of duty and devotion was further refined in a number of breeds that could perform distinctive tasks. Principally guard dogs, the group also includes police,

watch, rescue, and working breeds. Of universal popularity is the German shepherd, well known not only for its dedication as a seeing-eye dog, but also in police-dog roles such as drug and bomb detection. Likewise brave, sturdy, tireless, and possessing a good memory are other police dogs such as the Doberman and boxer. Some, the mastiff being an early example, have been bred to be competitive fighters.

The St. Bernard, Great Pyrenees, and Newfoundland are well known for their search-and-rescue successes in snowy

mountains following avalanches and during natural disasters such as earthquakes. Likewise well suited for severe cold and snowy weather, the Samoyed, Alaskan malamute, and Siberian husky are sled dogs renowned for incredible stamina. Also included in this group is the Akita, one of which, Hachiko, is legendary in Japan for her fierce dedication. Such characteristics make the members of the working group extremely useful companions.

► German Shepherd

◄ Alaskan Malamute

▲ Siberian Husky

► Laika (West Siberian)

◄ Karelian Bear Dog

▲ Iceland Sheepdog

◄ Jamthund

◄ Samoyed

▶ Great Pyrenees

▲ Newfoundland

▶ Mastiff

▶ Landseer

▲ St. Bernard
(Smooth)

◀ Bernese Mountain Dog

▲ Russian Sheepdog (South Asia)

▼ Appenzeller
Mountain Dog

▲ Hovawart

◀ Russian Sheepdog
(Central Asia)

▲ Swedish Vallhund

15

▶ Bullmastiff

▼ Bordeaux Mastiff

◀ Tosa

◀ Rottweiler

◀ St. Bernard (Rough)

▶ Spanish Mastiff

▲ Leonberger

▲ Neapolitan Mastiff

▼ Tibetan Mastiff

▼ Russian Sheepdog (Caucasus)

▲ Australian Shorthair Pinscher

▼ Great Dane

▼ Doberman

▼ Pinscher

▼ Boxer

▼ Dogo Argentino

◄ Podengo Portugues (Standard)

► Podengo Portugues (Miniature)

▲ Akita

▲ Kishu

▲ Kai

► Hokkaido

▲ Shikoku

► Shiba Inu

Sporting Group

Members of this group are considered to be among the most attractive and picturesque of dog breeds. Equally at home while moving through grasslands, marshes, and waters, they were originally developed as companion dogs to catch and retrieve game birds long before guns were invented. Dogs were used to spot these birds, after which a falcon or eagle was released to scare the game into preset nets, and the dog gently retrieved the game. Once limited to preserves set aside for the nobility, game hunting today is a common sport,

and gundogs are an integral part of this quest.

Short-haired breeds such as the weimaraner, vizsla, English pointer, and German pointer were developed for game-bird hunting in the mountains. The German pointer sniffs around for game, such as pheasants. When the game is located, the dog goes into a point posture with its nose and upraised bent front limb. Then, once given the command, the dog makes the game fly up so that the hunter can shoot it down. Setters, on the other hand, bend

down to show prey location and to give the hunter a clear line to the target.

Spaniels have a sharp sense of smell, are tireless, and are capable of easily turning on a spot (something large setters can't do). They maneuver rapidly around swamps, wild roses, and bramble bushes, hunting out wild birds and fearlessly retrieving them. Some, like English and American cocker spaniels, have made the transition to highly popular household pets renowned for their gentle nature.

▼ English Cocker Spaniel

► American Cocker Spaniel

◄ Field Spaniel

► Clumber Spaniel

◄ English Springer Spaniel

▲ Brittany Spaniel

◄ Welsh Springer Spaniel

▲ German Spaniel

► Kooikerhondje

◄ Sussex Spaniel

18

► English Pointer

▲ German Pointer
(Short hair)

► German Pointer
(Wire hair)

► Weimaraner

► Vizsla

► English Setter

► Irish Setter

► Large Munsterlander

◄ Gordon Setter

► Irish Red and
White Setter

► Golden Retriever

▲ Flat-coated Retriever

▲ Labrador Retriever

▲ Nova Scotia Duck Tolling Retriever

▲ Chesapeake Bay Retriever

▲ Curly-coated Retriever

▲ Wetterhoun

► Italian Spinone

▲ Portuguese Water Dog

► Irish Water Spaniel

► Pont-Audemer Spaniel

Hound Group

Basically hunting dogs, these animals are classified by the prey they chase and are divided into bird and animal hounds. The former are mainly placed in the sporting group, and the latter, except for the terriers, in the hound group. These animals can then be broadly classed as sight, scent, or in some cases, sound hounds.

Sight hounds, such as greyhounds, Afghan hounds, and Irish Wolfhounds, spot the prey from far away and chase it at incredible speed until it becomes exhausted. This style of hunting was popular prior to the development of shotguns. Some large breeds, although speedy, make too much noise once sensing the prey, and thus scare it away.

Scent hounds, such as basset hounds and elkhounds, sense prey by smell, then run them into a corner and signal the hunters. Small, gentle Tiroler brackes and Schweizer laufhunds are not so speedy, but show great skill in cornering prey. Beagles instinctively know that a hare habitually returns to where it started, and so chases it into the hands of the hunter waiting at the starting point. Dachshunds, on the other hand, are humorous-looking, but determined short-legged hounds that hunt animals out of their nests. Dogs within this group have been trained to use their keen sense of smell for drug and bomb detection.

In olden times, some nobles maintained kennels of fifty to one hundred large hounds like foxhounds, as well as an entourage to care for them. A favorite hunting pastime was the "running of the hounds," when the whole pack of dogs would run in pursuit of a fox or deer, followed by noblemen on horseback. A number of breeds were also developed for competitive racing.

▼ Otterhound

▼ Bloodhound

▼ Beagle

▼ Dachshund
(Standard
long)

▼ Dachshund
(Standard
smooth)

▲ Dachshund
(Miniature smooth)

▼ Basset Hound

◀ Dachshund
(Standard wire)

▲ Petit Basset Griffon
Vendeen

▼ Basset Fauve
de Bretagne

▲ Dachshund
(Miniature wire)

▲ Drever

◀ Dachshund
(Miniature long)

► Saluki

▲ Afghan Hound

▲ Borzoi

► Hungarian Greyhound

◄ Whippet

▲ Greyhound

► Ibizan Hound (Rough)

▲ Windhund

▲ Ibizan Hound (Smooth)

► Pharaoh Hound

◄ Cirneco dell'Etna

▲ Elkhound

◄ Basenji

▲ Deerhound

▲ Irish Wolfhound

▲ Hamilton Stovare

▲ Erdelyi Kopo

▲ Rhodesian Ridgeback

▲ Foxhound

▲ Tiroler Bracke

▲ Bemer Laufhund

► Sabueso Español

▲ Black and Tan Coonhound

▲ Schweizer Laufhund

▲ Bavarian Mountain Hound

Terrier Group

Generally, dogs used to hunt large animals are called hounds, while those used to hunt small game are known as terriers. Some breeds, although called terriers, are included in the toy and nonsporting groups.

The unique character, intelligence, and neat appearance of terriers have gained them a wide popularity as both household pets and show dogs. The combination of strong limbs supporting tight musculature, along with a usually wedge-shaped head, makes this group of scrappy breeds especially well suited

for digging underground for burrowing animals. Further, the skin on the head is quite tight and the mouth is surrounded by hard hairs, all to prevent this digger from being bitten by the small animal it is pursuing.

This group can be divided into long- and short-legged breeds: Airedale, Irish, Bedlington, and Lakeland terriers in the first category, and Dandie Dinmont, Sealyham, and Scottish terriers in the second. Alternatively, they can be classified as short-, long-, or rough-haired terriers. Smooth fox and bull terriers fit

in the first, Skye terriers in the second, and cairn, wire fox, and West Highland white terriers in the last. These all came from a small number of terrier breeds that were crossed within this group or out-crossed to local nonterrier breeds. Many of the breeds were named for the location where they originated. Most of these breeds came from the United Kingdom; others include the Australian, black Russian, and German hunting terriers.

▼ Welsh Terrier

◄ Lakeland Terrier

▲ Fox Terrier Wire

► Soft-coated Wheaten Terrier

▲ Fox Terrier Smooth

◄ Irish Terrier

► Jack Russell Terrier (Rough)

▲ Airedale Terrier

▲ Kerry Blue Terrier

▲ Jack Russell Terrier (Smooth)

► Jack Russell Terrier (Broken)

▲ Parson Jack Russell Terrier

► German Hunting Terrier

▲ Cairn Terrier

▲ Scottish Terrier

▼ West Highland White Terrier

► Norwich Terrier

◄ Norfolk Terrier

◄ Sealyham Terrier

► Cesky Terrier

▲ Skye Terrier

▲ Australian Terrier

▲ Border Terrier

▲ Dandie Dinmont Terrier

► Manchester Terrier

▲ Glen of Imaal Terrier

► Bedlington Terrier

► Bull Terrier (Standard)

▲ Black Russian Terrier

◄ Bull Terrier (Miniature)

▲ American Staffordshire Terrier

▲ Staffordshire Bull Terrier

Toy Group

As civilization advanced and became more stable, people had more opportunity for leisure because less time was required for manual labor. Dogs belonging to the hound, sporting, and terrier groups were bred down in size to produce a whole range of cute, sweet, gentle breeds that are unique both in appearance and character. These aptly named toy dogs were developed as indoor house pets or as status dogs.

Ranging from extremely small, cuddly dogs to lap dogs, they all need human protection and lots of care, even the short-haired ones. As shown on these pages, there are extremely small breeds like Chihuahuas, as well as those with long, elegant coats such as Yorkshire terriers, Malteses, Pekingeses, Australian silky terriers, Pomeranians, Papillons, and Cavalier King Charles spaniels. There are also short-haired Japanese and toy Manchester terriers, and miniature pinschers, plus striking hairless wonders such as Chinese crested dogs and the Mexican hairless.

With a variety of abilities, these living treasures are all alert watch dogs, remaining faithful to their owner until death.

◄ Yorkshire Terrier

► Australian Silky Terrier

► Maltese

▼ Lowchen

▲ Bichon Frise

◄ Papillon

▼ Pomeranian

► Shih Tzu

▲ Chihuahua (Smooth)

◄ Chihuahua (Long)

▼ Pekingese

▲ Papillon (Phalene)

► Pug

▼ King Charles Spaniel

▲ Coton de Tulear

◄ Brussels Griffon (Smooth)

◄ Japanese Chin

◄ Brussels Griffon (Rough)

◄ Affenpinscher

▲ Miniature Pinscher

◄ Toy Manchester Terrier

► Italian Greyhound

▲ Cavalier King Charles Spaniel

▲ Japanese Terrier

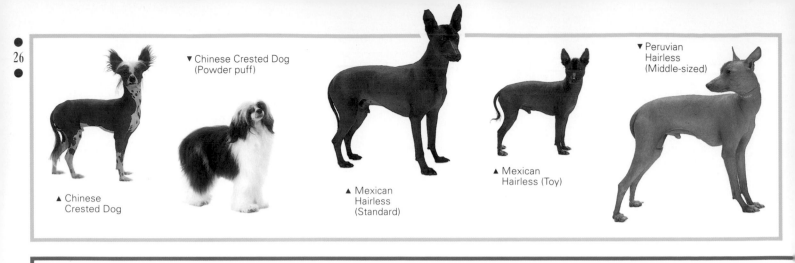

▲ Chinese Crested Dog

▼ Chinese Crested Dog (Powder puff)

▲ Mexican Hairless (Standard)

▲ Mexican Hairless (Toy)

▼ Peruvian Hairless (Middle-sized)

Non-Sporting Group

The breeds in this group are not included within the others due to their unique appearance, historical roots, or characteristics. Some are excellent circus performers; others are better ratters than terriers, or have guard skills superior to those of the working breeds.

Poodles, loved the world over, have beautiful coats that can be uniquely sculpted and a high level of sweetness that equals that of the toy breeds. They are so intelligent and quick-learning that they have found a cherished place in circus and theater performances. Schnauzers have been bred into giant, standard, and miniature sizes—the miniature being a top-performing rodent hunter and the giant being an ever-alert, excellent guard dog (likewise for the smaller Japanese spitz). For sweetness, the French bulldog, Tibetan and Boston terriers, and Lhasa apso rate at the top of the list. Dalmatians are known internationally as dedicated firedogs, and the minimally barking chow chow is a noble guard dog that few would challenge. The small schipperke makes an excellent sheepdog, while the Canaan dog is a military defense dog par excellence. Bulldogs were originally bred to fight bulls.

► Poodle (Miniature)

◄ Poodle (Toy)

► Schnauzer (Standard)

▲ Poodle (Standard)

► Schnauzer (Miniature)

▲ Schnauzer (Giant)

▲ Bulldog

► French Bulldog

▲ Boston Terrier

▲ Shar Pei

◄ Dalmatian   ► Schipperke

► Canaan Dog

◄ Kromfohrlander
(Wire short)

▲ Chow Chow

► Kromfohrlander
(Wire)

▼ Eurasier

▲ Kromfohrlander
(Long)

◄ Japanese Spitz

▲ Keeshond   ▲ Finnish Spitz   ► German Spitz

◄ Tibetan Terrier

◄ Italian Volpino

► Tibetan Spaniel   ► Lhasa Apso

The Body

Carnivores, which are generally believed to have appeared along with other mammals during the Tertiary period approximately seventy million years ago, may be broadly divided into two groups, the plantigrades and the digitigrades. Those in the former group, such as raccoons, bears, and weasels, walk on their heels, while those in the latter, such as dogs, cats, and hyenas, walk on their toes. Comparatively, digitigrades are usually faster and capable of running longer distances. Dogs have five toes on the front and four on the rear limbs, sometimes with dewclaws, but unlike cats, they cannot retract their nails.

As to traits and senses, those of the dog have been passed down from its wild ancestor, in which most of these abilities were necessary for survival. The nose, for example, with its big nostrils, has a complex wrinkled lining that allows for a vast number of extremely sensitive olfactory cells to be exposed to the air within a relatively small area. Of all land animals, dogs are said to have the sharpest sense of smell, approximately twelve million times more acute than that of humans.

Dogs are also equipped with a keen sense of hearing, capable of recognizing noises at levels a few times lower than that of humans and up to forty thousand cycles higher. Thus they can sense other animals not only by sight, but at quite far distances by scent and sound as well. Yet they are generally shortsighted, so probably to compensate for this, they react quickly to moving objects.

Dogs have the stamina to track and race down prey, and the patience to keep prey at bay until the last minute of the attack, at which time their extremely strong jaws and sharp teeth are used to kill and rip it apart.

Dogs can be classified by such criteria as size, hair length, and body conformation. The some 250 breeds seen on the following pages vary greatly, from mini-sized (less than two pounds) Chihuahuas to massive St. Bernards (reaching nearly 220 pounds). To dog-lovers, the body type of a breed is a precious treasure passed down from those who made dedicated efforts to develop it.

Body Part Nomenclature Just like cats, dogs are digitigrades that walk on their toes and can run long distances. Their bodies are full of stamina, and their strong jaws and sharp teeth are powerful weapons.

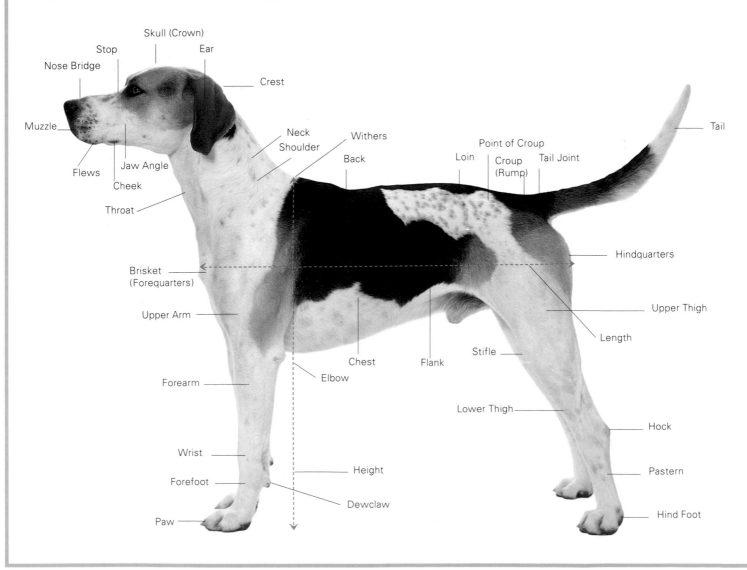

Head & Face The dog's body shape can be divided into three types, and the face into a few more, depending on the balance of nose, mouth, eyes, lips, and cheeks, but the size and shape of the head are extremely variable.

Apple Head

Blocky Head

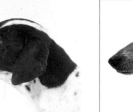

Dome Head

Broken-up Face

Down Face

Dish Face

Snippy Face

Eyes Categorized based on the shape of the ridge, eyes are usually oval, but some other ones are shown here. They come in many colors.

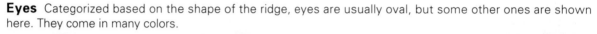
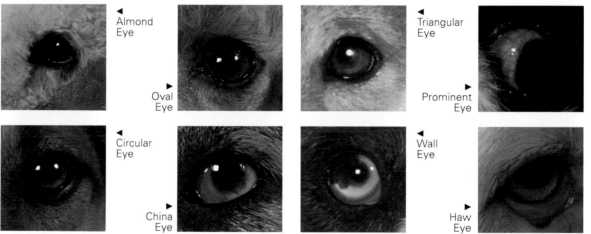

◄ Almond Eye

Oval ► Eye

◄ Triangular Eye

Prominent ► Eye

◄ Circular Eye

China ► Eye

◄ Wall Eye

Haw ► Eye

Ears Other than the three basic forms of prick, semi-prick, or button, further division of ear types, as shown here, can be made when shape, size, thickness, placement, and cropping are also considered.

Prick Ear

Prick Ear (Cropped)

Semi-prick Ear

Tulip Ear

Candle Flame Ear

Bat Ear

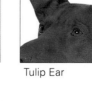

Butterfly Ear

Button Ear

Drop Ear

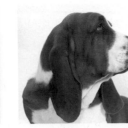

Pendant Ear

Rose Ear

Lobe-shaped Ear

Tails The coccygeal (tail) bones are generally either high-set (level with the back), such as in the Doberman, or low-set (resting, sloping downwards on the buttocks), as in the cocker spaniel.

Gay Tail

Cut Tail

Flagpole Tail

Stern Tail

Docked Tail

Otter Tail

Saber Tail

Brush Tail

Rat Tail

Plume Tail

Hook Tail

Bob Tail

Whip Tail

Flag Tail

Pothook Tail

Sickle Tail

Sickle Tail

Squirrel Tail

Ring Tail

Curled Tail

Double Curled Tail

Screw Tail

Crank Tail

Kink Tail

Colors & Patterns While colors range from pure white to jet black, there is both great variation and subtle mixtures of color in between. Also, this coloration can form many patterns, a few of which are shown here.

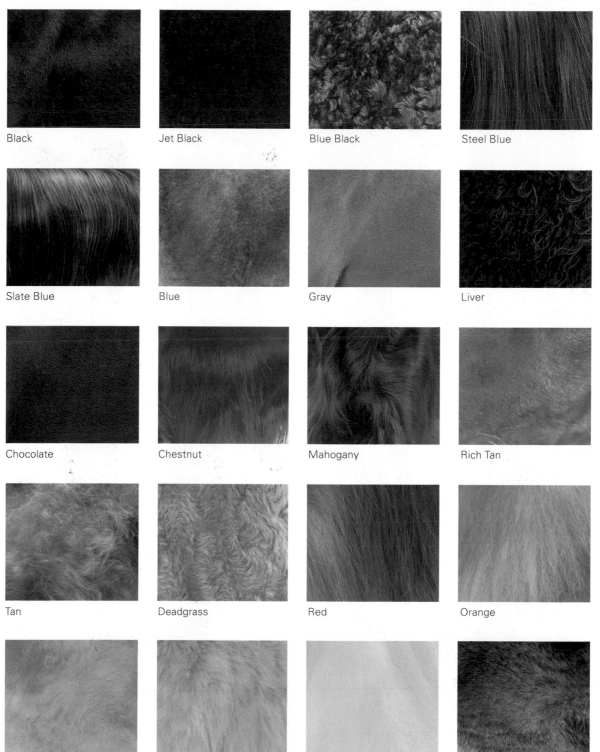

Black

Jet Black

Blue Black

Steel Blue

Slate Blue

Blue

Gray

Liver

Chocolate

Chestnut

Mahogany

Rich Tan

Tan

Deadgrass

Red

Orange

Apricot

Wheaten

White

Wolf Gray

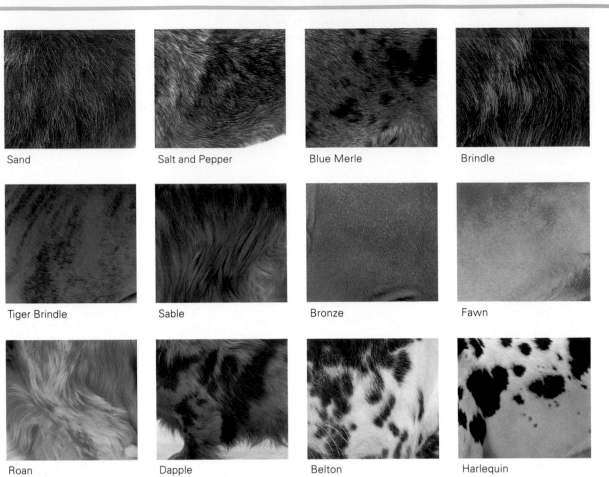

Sand

Salt and Pepper

Blue Merle

Brindle

Tiger Brindle

Sable

Bronze

Fawn

Roan

Dapple

Belton

Harlequin

Trace

Pencil Mark

Blaze

Badger Color

Black Mask

Boston Color

Parti-color

Tricolor

Hound Color

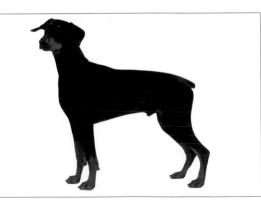

Black and Tan

Australian Stumpy Tail Cattle Dog

Herding Group

Note: In the following text, "M" stands for male and "F" stands for female. The average height and weight of the breed is given in the yellow oval.

Anatolian Sheepdog

Anatolian sheepdogs have lived with humans since ancient times in Turkey and neighboring countries, serving as guard dogs. Today they are found all over the world, including the United States, where they are also used as hunting, military, and sheepdogs.

M 2 years

Background Notes

Known for their large, strong frame and their courage, these dogs were once used to hunt wolves. In 1968, they were exported to the United States where they became widely known. Tireless, they stand up well to bad weather, which makes them excellent guard and sheepdogs.

Key Characteristics

Although the Anatolian sheepdog looks very much like the Great Pyrenees, a large, strong sheepdog said to be of ancient French origin, this breed has a tighter frame and is much more agile. The body coat is short, straight, hard, and thick, colored either white or chamois, with a blackish muzzle and ears.

Intelligent, reliable, and always patient with children, these dogs are loving to their owners but suspicious and wary of strangers. Thus this breed must be kept in a secure yard that has a high enough fence to keep them from jumping over it.

M 2 years

Care and Exercise

Weekly hard brushing is sufficient, but this breed must be exercised thoroughly daily, either on a leash or freely within a large run.

Puppies and Training

There are five to ten puppies per litter. These pups are strong and easy to bring up but, like the adults, are very wary of strangers. For this reason, they should be trained very early.

M 5 years

Male: 28–30 in.
99–150 lbs.
....
Female: 26–28 in.
90–130 lbs.

M 3 years

Australian Cattle Dog

Seemingly tireless even after a long day's work out on the range, this powerful breed had an important role as a cattle driver during Australia's early history. It retains a touch of wilderness today.

M 5 years

Background Notes

Recognized by the American Kennel Club in 1979, this breed dates back to the 1840s. Once called a heeler (the early Australian name for a cattle dog), it carried the name of the place where it was bred (for example, Queensland heeler). This dog was required to chase, herd, and have the courage to challenge cattle when necessary. It instinctively knew to get out of the way and lie down when the herd was on the move, so as not to spook them.

Key Characteristics

The Australian cattle dog is medium sized, tight framed, well muscled, and squarely built. Its head is wide, with a deep, strong muzzle; its ears, set apart and upright, are erect when the dog is alerted; its eyes are medium sized and dark; and it has a sturdy neck. A thick, broad chest is supported by muscular

F 3 years

Male: 18–20 in.
40–45 lbs.
....
Female: 17–19 in.
40–45 lbs.

limbs that thicken at the thighs. Usually the tail hangs down, but when the dog is active, it stands up. Having both a rough, straight outercoat, and a fairly dense double undercoat, the coloring is either blue splashed with blackish blue, or spotted red with dark red markings on the head.

This excellent guard dog, known to challenge other dogs as well as strangers, is loyal and obedient to its owner and family; however, it is not a good breed for young children, as it has been known to attack them when pestered.

Care and Exercise

Very energetic, as it has been bred for extended hard labor, the Australian cattle dog needs a long, vigorous walk at least twice a day. Brushing for about fifteen minutes once a week is adequate.

Puppies and Training

A litter of four to eight all-white (harking back to Dalmatian blood in their heritage) puppies is usual, the coat coloration appearing a few weeks after birth. Early, thorough training of the very aggressive puppies is necessary to get them to adjust to life around people.

Stumpy Tail, F 1 year

Australian Kelpie

One of the best-performing medium-sized sheepdogs, the Australian kelpie, with its well-balanced appearance and beautiful foxy looks, has become a very popular urban pet. They are strong, patient, and speedy.

Background Notes

Thought to have originated from sheepdogs (that accompanied Scottish immigrants) crossed with Border collies and wild dingoes, Australian kelpies became known as a breed in the 1870s. Considered by many to be the best sheepdog, its skill and top performance have made it a favorite of sheep farmers throughout the world. "Kelpie" comes

M 9 months

from the name for water nymphs in Scottish mythology.

Key Characteristics

Extremely agile and light footed, capable of a lightning start and a quick dead stop, this beautiful foxlike breed with a strong, scissorslike bite has incredible stamina and speed, and can go quite a few hours without water. The ideal kelpie has a wide, domed head with a prominent stop, and a muzzle that becomes narrower towards the nose. Its dark almond-shaped eyes (which may be lighter, depending on coat color) have a penetrating stare said to be capable of mesmerizing sheep. Brush tailed, this breed has a water-resistant combination of a short, straight rough-textured overcoat and a short dense undercoat. The hair color varies from black, blackish red, dark chestnut, chestnut, reddish chestnut, and tan to bluish gray.

Guiding sheep with unsurpassable skill by running around the flock or jump-

Male: 18–20 in.
24–31 lbs.
Female: 17–19 in.
20–24 lbs.

F 6 months

M 1 year

ing from back to back of the sheep at incredible speed, this dog reacts quickly to its master's signals even from very far distances. Its keen senses, enthusiasm, and mild aggressiveness towards strangers also make it an excellent guard dog.

Care and Exercise

This very strong breed requires extensive exercise and especially enjoys a free run in wide-open areas. The coat needs very little care, only an occasional brushing or massaging with a towel.

Puppies and Training

Usually a brood of four to seven puppies is delivered easily, the mother caring well for them and not requiring help. Wonderfully intelligent, the puppies are calm, obedient, and learn well.

Bearded Collie

Arched eyebrows and wide-apart eyes give the bearded collie a humorous expression. An ideal companion, family pet, or indoor guard dog, it is sociable and charming, making a maximum effort to entertain the people around it, yet is also quite active and loves to go outdoors.

Male: 21–22 in.
48 lbs.
....
Female: 20–21 in.
48 lbs.

Background Notes

Although little is known of its genealogy, it is certain that this breed is the original form of the Scottish highland sheepdogs, and that by the nineteenth century it was well established there as a guard dog capable of working in all kinds of weather. It was recognized by the American Kennel Club in 1976.

Key Characteristics

Closely resembling the Old English sheepdog, the bearded collie is smaller and thinner, with a body length greater than its height. The back is straight and strong, while the wide, flat head has medium-sized drop ears and a big angular nose (black, unless the coat is brown or fawn). Its limbs are thick and well muscled, the brush tail low set and curled at the end. It has a double coat. The outer coat is long and rough; the undercoat, dense and soft.

M 2 years

M 4 years

M 2 years

Puppies and Training

Beginning life as black, blue, brown, or fawn, the average litter of four to eight puppies gradually develops adult coloration. Early training makes it easier for them to adjust to domestication later on.

Care and Exercise

Sufficient daily exercise is necessary, and this dog loves repetitive indoor games such as catching and retrieving a ball. The coat, being very thick, needs brushing for at least half an hour twice a week to keep the hair from getting tangled and dusty. Professional grooming is not necessary, as a natural look is ideal.

M 4 years

Belgian Shepherd

Belgian shepherds, divided into four breeds in their native Belgium on the basis of coat color, texture, and length (Groenendael, Laekenois, Malinois, Tervuren), have worked for centuries as guard dogs for sheep and cows. They love small children, and become like a brother or sister if raised with them.

Groenendael, F 4 years

Tervuren, M 5 years

Care and Exercise

Except for the short-haired Malinois, which needs fifteen-minute brushing sessions, these breeds need to be brushed once a week for about half an hour. However, during the spring and autumn shedding periods, brushing must be done quite carefully. They all require vigorous daily exercise on a lead, plus time in a wide-open fenced run.

Puppies and Training

The litters usually consist of six to ten puppies. Very friendly toward their family, but wary of strangers, these puppies develop a sharp temper as they grow, so early training is a must.

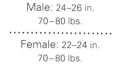

Male: 24–26 in.
70–80 lbs.
....
Female: 22–24 in.
70–80 lbs.

Laekenois, M 2 years

Malinois, F 4 years

Background Notes

As they were originally developed to guard sheep and cows, Belgian shepherds were popular breeders for their strength and diligence. Only later, in the twentieth century, were selections also made by coat. While the American Kennel Club recognizes all four of these breeds as distinct, European countries and the Japanese Kennel Club recognize them as varieties of Belgian shepherd dogs.

Key Characteristics

All four breeds have an elegant, square, muscular body with a deep chest and a long, furry tail. The big, long, flat-topped V-shaped head has a long jaw, a moderately pointed muzzle, and upright ears.

Serious, hardworking, and with a strong sense of responsibility, especially when guarding the family, these breeds are great with children but wary of strangers, yet they won't attack without cause.

A Groenendael should have brown or black eyes and a comparatively long, slightly rough all-black straight coat, although some white is permitted. The Tervuren has a long, fairly rough, straight, dark fawn or reddish mahogany black-tipped outercoat lying flat along the length of the body, and a dense undercoat. It should also have a black mask, as well as brown to dark brown eyes. Especially short on the head, ears, and lower limbs, the Malinois's short, straight coat varies from dark fawn to mahogany, with black tips. Additionally, it should have a black mask, black ears, and brown eyes. The rarest of these breeds, the fawn-colored Laekenois, has thick, rough, wiry hair of about the same length over the entire body though somewhat longish around the mask and eyes, but never brushlike.

Bergamasco Sheepdog

Named after Bergamo, Italy, where it originated, this very intelligent breed with an excellent memory is considered to be one of the best sheepdogs and also is well suited for guarding big, open areas.

Background Notes

More than two thousand years ago, Phoenician merchants brought a few long-haired sheepdogs into Europe where they were selectively bred in Tuscany to develop the Maremma sheepdog. Some of these were taken to northern Italy and became the rootstock of the Bergamasco sheepdog, which was later brought by the Phoenicians to France and Spain where it was used to develop many other sheepdogs. For centuries, this breed has been working with farmers and shepherds, surpassing other breeds at herding and guarding livestock and fighting intruders with amazing courage.

M 5 years

Key Characteristics

With a large head some two-fifths of its height, this breed has a long muzzle about equal to the length of the head; big black nostrils, strong jaws, and teeth with a scissor bite; and triangular drop ears. The limbs are well built, the paws ovoid and firm, and the tail is thick, narrowing toward the end, low set, and hanging down. A double coat consisting of a heavy, hard, rough, and slightly wavy long outercoat and thick, naturally oily undercoat stands up to any weather, and also serves as protection from the jaws of enemies. Long facial hair practically covers the eyes. The coat color, on which the eye color (usually chestnut) is dependent, is gray, gray marked with orange, or black. An excellent guard dog for the house or even large factories, the Bergamasco

M 5 years

M 5 years

Male: 23 in.
70–84 lbs.
....
Female: 22–23 in.
66 lbs.

sheepdog is hardworking, vigilant, and courageous. Especially loving to its master and family, this breed's gentle nature makes it popular as a household pet.

Care and Exercise

Requiring a lot of care, the moplike coat has to be hand divided into fringes of equal thickness, each not too thick or thin. The facial hair, however, needs combing. As the Bergamasco sheepdog is very strong and tireless, ample exercise is necessary.

Puppies and Training

The four to eight puppies in each litter are relatively strong and easy to raise; they require early obedience training.

F 3 years

Bouvier des Flandres

Having worked for centuries as cattle herders in the Flanders region on the border between France and Belgium, this breed remains primarily a working dog, serving excellently in seeing-eye, military, and police roles.

Background Notes

Dating back to the sixteenth century, the bouvier des Flandres is said to have originated from dogs brought to Flanders, Belgium, and northern France by Spanish Crusaders. At first these dogs were used to herd cattle, then later to pull milk carts. *Bouvier* means cow-keeper or cow-chaser in French. British author Ouida's (Marie Louise de la Ramée, 1839–1908) book *A Dog of Flanders* was based on the bouvier and helped to popularize the breed. Due to the local ravages of World War I, it almost became extinct; however, Belgian vets saved a few remaining bouviers and began breeding them. It was only in the 1930s that this breed was introduced to the United States, supposedly by a film producer.

M 4 years

M 4 years

coat along with its prominent whiskers, beard, and longer hair between the toes, allow the bouvier to withstand severely inclement weather. Although the coat usually ranges from fawn to black, including gray, salt and pepper, and brindle, small white star markings on the chest are permitted. Dogs that are white, chocolate, or parti-color, however, are strongly penalized at dog shows.

The bouvier des Flandres appears quite calm and collected; it pays careful attention to, yet is most gentle with, children and family. It is an excellent guard dog and a brave protector, watching out for strangers and other dogs.

Care and Exercise

A thorough half-hour brushing daily will suffice, but this breed requires a good walk twice a day. Because of its size and energy, it does best when kept outdoors where it can run freely in a big enclosed area.

Puppies and Training

A slow-maturing (about 2½ years) breed, a bouvier des Flandres usually has five to ten puppies in a litter. If a puppy's ears are cropped, this should be done at eight to twelve weeks after birth. As the breed has an excellent memory, the puppies are very easy to train and discipline.

Male: 24–27 in.
75–95 lbs.
....
Female: 23–26 in.
75–95 lbs.

Key Characteristics

Compact, square built, well muscled with strong limbs, yet short and wide, the rugged bouvier des Flandres has a big head with a flat skull, a large nose with flared nostrils, high-set ears that are often cropped, and dark brown eyes covered with long eyebrows that give this dog a very melancholic look. The tail is high set and is usually docked at maturity to about four inches. Its harsh, dry, medium-length (2½ inches) outercoat and soft, thick, fine under-

F 4 years

Briard

Known for a long time throughout Europe as the "dog of the grass-lands," the briard has a charming nature, expression, and high intelligence. Its long, rough, shaggy coat has made it one of the most popular household pets.

F 2 years

Background Notes

Popular today as sheepdogs and guard dogs, the breed originally guarded against wolves and poachers and served as military carrier dogs. Like many short-haired breeds, however, it did not have a popular or formal name for a long time. The name briard came to be used in 1989 when people started calling it the *chien berger de Brie* (shepherd dog of Brie).

Key Characteristics

The briard is a large dog with a strong, well-boned frame; flexible muscles; a long head with whiskers and a beard; high-set drop ears that are often cropped; an angular nose with a straight bridge; and large, wide-apart black or brown eyes. Yellow or marked eyes are disqualified. A slightly wavy, rough double coat, about four to six inches long, can be of any uniform color, including

Male: 23–27 in.
75–90 lbs.
....
Female: 22–25 in.
75–90 lbs.

F 10 months

shades of black, gray, or tawny, but not white, although white on the chest or white markings of less than one-inch diameter are permitted.

Although a quick learner, this dog is strongly independent, and wary of both strangers and other dogs.

Care and Exercise

Because the coat gets dirty easily, this breed needs to be groomed for two hours, at least twice weekly. Unlike other herding breeds, the Briard doesn't need much exercise; however, a daily walk will give it a chance to stretch fully. A big house with a garden is the ideal environment for this dog.

Puppies and Training

The eight to ten puppies in each litter are often different colors from the parents. If their ears are to be cropped, this should be done within a few weeks of birth. Training should preferably begin early to get them used to people.

M 4 years

Border Collie

This breed has ancient origins, and although not as graceful as a rough collie, it is nevertheless a highly intelligent, much-loved, hard-working dog that responds quickly and eagerly to training and serves as a faithful companion dog.

Background Notes

Reindeer herders brought into Scotland by the Vikings from the last half of the eighth century to the eleventh century and crossed with local valley sheepdogs are believed to be the ancestors of today's Border collies. This breed was officially recognized, first by the FCI, in 1987. It took a long time before they were recognized as a purebred because they were not as graceful-looking as rough collies, their close relatives. The name comes from the fact that the breed was long used in the border counties of England and Scotland.

Key Characteristics

Very agile, the breed has a well-balanced body; a moderately wide skull with a definite stop; a muzzle that narrows toward the nose to form a slightly obtuse angle; high-set erect or half-erect ears; and ovoid eyes set wide apart.

Two types of coat, straight, hard, thick, moderately long (3 inches) and smooth and short (1 inch) exist. The coat comes in black, gray, or blue merle with white; or black, white, and tan.

Some say that the Border collie is unsurpassed as a sheepdog in terms of patience, agility, and stamina. It is also very well suited as a household pet.

Care and Exercise

To help prevent skin diseases, daily brushing to remove dead hair is a definite requirement, especially when the dog is shedding. Extensive and speedy exercise is preferred, such as having the dog run on a long leash alongside a bicycle.

M 3 years

Puppies and Training

A litter of six to eight puppies is delivered comparatively easily. The puppies are very friendly and extremely intelligent, and they learn quickly.

Male: 20–21 in.
40–51 lbs.
....
Female: 19–21 in.
35–44 lbs.

M 4 years

M 2 years

Catalonian Sheepdog

Said to have originated from the Pyrenean sheepdogs that were brought into Europe by cow farmers and were then selectively bred to better withstand the harsh weather of the mountains and moors, this breed has an excellent learning ability, which has led to its use not only as a herder but also as a police and guard dog.

Background Notes

Hardened by selective breeding, the Catalonian sheepdog was trained to be a farmer's companion, herding cattle, sheep, and horses and to keep strangers away from the farm.

Key Characteristics

Medium sized and muscular, this dog has a truncated conical muzzle; a dark nose; high-set, pointed drop ears; expressive dark amber eyes; extremely strong teeth; and a long, thick tail that is sometimes docked. The longish, hard, wavy coat is usually gray or black, lightening to cream at the tips.

M 3 years

Male: 18–20 in.
40 lbs.
....
Female: 17–19 in.
35 lbs.

Patient, yet active, the Catalonian sheepdog enthusiastically and tirelessly herds livestock. A wonderful playmate for children, it has a gentle nature, intelligence, obedience, and friendliness with people it knows that has made it a popular household pet.

Care and Exercise

Bred to be an outdoor dog, the Catalonian sheepdog's coat needs only the minimal care of combing followed by strong brushing about once every ten days. However, it needs a good amount of daily exercise to maintain its calm disposition.

Puppies and Training

The training of puppies, usually four to eight in a litter, should begin early for their best adjustment to people.

M 3 years (left), F 3 years (right)

Collie

Among the most popular of breeds, the magnificent collie is loved for its noble appearance, high intelligence, and gentility.

Rough, M 2 years

Rough, F 4 years

Background Notes

Originally called the Scotch collie for the country where it was used for centuries to herd sheep, it is believed to have been brought to the New World originally by early settlers, including the Pilgrims. Today's U.S. type, however, can be traced to late-nineteenth-century imports from England. Recognized in 1886 by the American Kennel Club (AKC) as the collie, the United Kennel Club (UKC) recognized it in 1920 as the Scotch collie. Lassie, the rough collie of film and television fame, helped to popularize the breed throughout the world.

Key Characteristics

Considered one of the most beautiful breeds because of its elegant appearance, featuring a distinctively long, tapered muzzle, the collie has a tight muscular body with a deep chest and a long, smooth, well-shaped tail. The narrow flat-topped head has ears that bend naturally at the tip, about three-fourth the distance from the base; dark almond-shaped eyes; and a prominent black nose. UKC standards call for a slightly lower and lighter dog than do those of the AKC. The overcoat of the rough collie is long and harsh, the undercoat, dense and soft; the smooth collie has a short, flat coat. The neck is covered with beautiful feathering, giving the collie a proud look. Officially

Rough, F 7 months

Smooth, M 1 year

recognized colors are sable and white, tricolor, merle, or white.

Proud, but often shy and slightly nervous, this agile, extremely intelligent breed is very friendly, soon becoming familiar with strangers. Quite obedient to even extended-family members, it makes a wonderful companion for children. Some people say this dog has almost telepathic abilities. A collie should not be treated as a guard dog, as it tends to become friends with strangers, rather than attacking them.

Care and Exercise

Frequent shedding, especially during spring and autumn, makes regular brushing of half an hour twice a week for a rough collie, once a week for about fifteen minutes for a smooth collie, a definite requirement. Regular walks with a long lead, or free exercise in a large outdoor yard, is necessary to keep this breed healthy and happy.

Puppies and Training

Litters average six to ten puppies whose coat color brightens and darkens as they age. Although best suited for a large outdoor living space, this breed can be easily trained to live indoors. Some dogs have a tendency to howl, but they can soon be broken of this habit.

Male: 23–26 in.
59–75 lbs.
....
Female: 22–24 in.
51–66 lbs.

Smooth, F 3 years

Dutch Shepherd Dog

Hardly known outside the Netherlands, this loyal, hardworking breed has become an indispensable herder, especially on local dairy and sheep farms. In appearance, it is very similar to the Belgian sheepdogs, from which it is believed to have been developed.

Background Notes

Because it was not as popular as the German shepherd or the beautifully coated Belgian shepherd, this dog remained virtually unknown elsewhere in Europe and in the United States.

Key Characteristics

A relatively large breed, this dog has a muscular and well balanced body. Its blackish eyes are slightly tilted, the ears are erect, and the long muzzle has strong teeth with a scissorslike bite.

The tail curls slightly and hangs down. Most frequently seen is the short- and straight-haired (smooth) variety. Second in popularity is the hard rough-coated type. Quite rare and facing extinction is the long-haired form. The coat color varies from a yellowish red mixture to a brown tinted with gold, or a silverish brindle.

The Dutch shepherd dog, besides being physically strong and able to work in all kinds of inclement weather, has a high sense of responsibility, remaining

Smooth, M 8 years

Male: 23–25 in.
66 lbs.
....
Female: 21–22 in.
66 lbs.

Rough, M 5 years

ever-vigilant over its territory. It is a hard-working manager of sheep, cows, and horses, skillfully serving as a trustworthy assistant. An excellent guard as well as an ideal herding dog, it is very obedient to its owner, quickly responding to commands. With appropriate training, this breed has also proven its usefulness as police and seeing-eye dogs.

Care and Exercise

Brushing once a week, or every other week if the dog is short-haired, is all the care necessary. Daily exercise is also essential, along with an occasional opportunity to run freely.

Puppies and Training

A litter of five to ten puppies is usual, and because this breed is rather alert, the puppies require plenty of training to become used to people.

Rough, M 5 years (left), F 3 years (right)

Komondor

A large sheepdog with a very unusual and distinctive long white corded coat, this breed has served humans as a guard dog in the mountains of Hungary for over one thousand years.

M 4.5 years

M 4.5 years

Background Notes

The Komondor (plural, Komondorok) is believed to have been developed by the Magyars more than a millennium ago from the Aftscharka, an ancient long-legged dog of the southern Russian Steppes, and the Tibetan mastiff. A formidable guard dog, it has proven to be a reliable protector of livestock from such predators as wolves, foxes, and even bears. Excellently protected from the elements by its thick coat, the breed thrives outdoors in cold climates.

Key Characteristics

Extremely large, strong, and big-boned, with well-developed muscles, this breed must have drop ears, dark almond-shaped eyes, and a black nose. It has a double coat, the outer long and coarse, the undercoat softer, with felt-like cords hanging down and in many cases reaching the ground. Only a white coat is acceptable.

Intelligent, powerful, hardworking, brave, loyal, and obedient to family members, this dog is suspicious of strangers. A very reliable guard dog, this breed is best kept in a large outdoor yard in the suburbs, rather than in the city.

Care and Exercise

Never to be brushed or combed, the coat requires special care, preferably by a professional groomer. Intensive exercise, such as pulling and long-distance running is required.

Puppies and Training

The three to ten puppies per litter are white and fluffy when born, the corded coat forming at around three to four months. They should be handled often and early and trained thoroughly.

Male: 26–31 in.
110–130 lbs.
Female: 21–27 in.
79–110 lbs.

M 4.5 years

Kuvasz

A strong, reliable guard dog, this breed played a noted part in history as a constant companion to many royals throughout medieval Europe.

Background Notes

The ancestral stock of the Kuvasz (Kuvaszok in the plural) is thought to have come from Tibet to Hungary many centuries ago. It was bred and raised to serve as a royal guard dog and hunter during the Middle Ages. King Matthias I, who ruled from 1458 to 1490, further protected and developed the breed, ownership in Hungary being limited to the nobility. Later, herders found it to be an excellent guard dog for sheep and cattle.

Key Characteristics

This dog is quite big, sturdy, very well built and muscled, with rear limbs that are particularly thick and strongly developed and a lengthy tail. It has a rather

Male: 28–30 in.
110–130 lbs.
....
Female: 26–28 in.
84–110 lbs.

M 3 years

M 3 years

long head with dark almond-shaped eyes and V-shaped ears that bend slightly forward. The short, slightly wavy double coat should be white with no markings.

Very much a one-family dog, the Kuvasz is extremely loyal, obedient, active, and strong, but is definitely wary of strangers.

Care and Exercise

This large, active breed requires extended daily brushing and needs a rather expansive, securely fenced-in yard for exercise and to keep it from escaping. Decisive training, especially on a leash, is a must to keep it in check.

Puppies and Training

Each litter averages about eight puppies. To nurture a happy character and a love of playing with people, the puppies need to be handled and thoroughly taught at an early age.

Maremma Sheepdog

One of the oldest of the sheepdogs, the Maremma sheepdog is an obedient, loyal, and diligent guard dog with a plentiful beautiful white coat that draws much attention.

Background Notes

This breed is considered to be one of the rootstocks of the sheepdog. It has worked for centuries guarding flocks, especially in central Italy and neighboring European countries.

Key Characteristics

Big and powerful, the Maremma sheepdog has a bearlike head with strong jaws and teeth; a scissor bite; relatively small eyes compared to the size of the face; a straight nose bridge; big dark-colored nostrils; and small triangular drop ears. The medium-length coat is usually dense and solid white.

A fearless and brave guardian, this dog has also proven to be a friendly companion to family members.

M 1 year

M 9 months

F 10 months

Male: 25–29 in.
77–99 lbs.
....
Female: 23–27 in.
66–88 lbs.

Care and Exercise

The coat has to be brushed rather hard, and the shed long hair removed with a comb. As this dog is strong and often independent, care and determination must be taken when walking it.

Puppies and Training

The litter of five to ten puppies needs to be carefully watched, as the heavy mother has a tendency to inadvertently crush the young that crawl under her. Quite defensive when young, the puppies need to get used to people from very early on.

Mudi

Not yet well known or recognized outside its native Hungary, where it is treasured, this medium-sized sheepdog is quite brave, aggressively guarding livestock against even much larger enemies and over large, open areas.

tail either hangs down or is docked. At the loin, the coat, which can be entirely white, black, or an equal salt and pepper mix, is two inches in length; on the muzzle the coat is shorter, and towards the ears it is longer and more plentiful. The mudi is gentle and makes a good domestic companion dog, yet it never hesitates to respond to a threat, no matter how violent the enemy may be.

Care and Exercise

A mudi has to be groomed thoroughly once a week, with special attention given to places where the coat is long, such as the ears and tail. Sufficient daily exercise must consist of pulling exercises, a free run in a wide open area, or retrieving a ball.

Puppies and Training

The four to eight puppies per litter develop very well and easily get used to people. Highly intelligent, they are quick, obedient learners.

F 3 years

Background Notes

The mudi originated in Hungary around the turn of this century, and has proven to be a very versatile guarder and herder of sheep and cattle, as well as a catcher of wild mice and other small animals like weasels. It is equally at ease guarding a large field, farm, or backyard.

Key Characteristics

Medium-sized and deep chested, this breed has a short straight back; a slightly narrow long head with a prominent stop; V-shaped erect ears; dark brown oval eyes; and a strong, well-muscled jaw with a scissor bite. The

F 3 years

Male: 14–18 in.
18–29 lbs.
....
Female: 14–18 in.
18–29 lbs.

Old English Sheepdog

Among the earliest of sheepdogs from England, this breed is loved the world over as a companion dog, especially by children who are attracted by its fluffy, cuddly looks.

Background Notes

This breed was developed originally in western England for driving livestock, flushing and retrieving game, and bringing lost sheep back to the fold. At the time, owners of herding dogs were taxed, and the dog's tail was docked as evidence of payment, hence the breed's other name, bob-tail. About 150 years ago, the breed became what it is today. At one point, its hair was used in England for making cloth, but this practice was soon discontinued. Although it may look like a cuddly stuffed animal, it is a hard worker.

Key Characteristics

This dog has a sturdy, tight body with an extremely short back, but the shaggy coat makes it look bigger than it really is. The loin is set higher than the shoulders, the limbs are short and thick, and the chest is heavy and wide. Its big and somewhat angular head has medium-sized drop ears, a big black nose, and usually dark eyes whose color is dependent on coat color. Generally, the tail is docked at the joint. A long, profuse coat covers the entire dog, especially on the head and around the nose, often covering the eyes. The coat coloration varies from shades of gray or grizzle to

F 6 months

Male: 23–24 in.
65–90 lbs.

Female: 21–23 in.
65–90 lbs.

M 6 months (left), F 6 months (right)

blue or blue merle, either with or without white markings.

Care and Exercise

For show dogs, a long coat is preferred,
but for house pets, trimming the coat
helps facilitate care. Because the soft
undercoat gathers a lot of dust, a weekly
half hour of combing, and shampooing
when the coat gets dirty, are necessary
to keep the dog neat. Brushing should
be done from the tail towards the head.
Long periods of exercise, at least twice
daily, are also required.

Puppies and Training

Tail docking on the litter of five to eight
puppies is done two to three days after
birth. Even though this breed takes
about two years to mature, obedience
training must begin at a very early age.

F 3 years

Polish Lowland Sheepdog

Found today throughout Europe as an ideal family pet and guard dog, this sheepdog has ancestral stock that was brought into Poland by the Phoenicians. The profuse hair flowing down its forehead gives it a rather humorous appearance.

Background Notes

This breed belongs to the Bergamasco sheepdog group, which has a common early heritage. An excellent sheepdog, the Polish lowland sheepdog's gentle nature also makes it a favorite companion dog.

Key Characteristics

The head is relatively wide and slightly domed, the nose is big and black, the wide drop ears are heart-shaped, and the muzzle is strong. This dog should have a thick, slightly wavy coat (a curly coat is not permissible) completely covering its body, especially around the forehead, cheeks, and jaws. Any color is acceptable.

Intelligent with a good memory, agile and diligent, and especially calm and gentle, this dog loves playing with children. As its reputation spreads, the number of Polish lowland sheepdogs increases.

Care and Exercise

To prevent matting, the coat should be brushed frequently, at least once every two to three days. Quite self-controlled, the dog readily adapts to any exercise routine. Lack of exercise will cause obesity.

M 3 years

Male: 17–21 in.
66 lbs.

Female: 16–18 in.
55 lbs.

M 3 years

Puppies and Training

If any of the litter of four to eight relatively strong puppies is born with a tail, it should be completely docked early. A sufficiently nutritious diet should be given to promote growth once the puppies begin feeding. Grooming should be started early to get them used to brushes and combs. This dog's excellent memory facilitates easy training.

F 3.5 years

Puli

As its name, which means "leader" in Hungarian, implies, the puli, with its distinctive corded coat, is a very brave sheepdog.

Background Notes

The puli traces its ancestry to the sheepdogs that the Magyars brought with them when they invaded Hungary over a millennium ago.

Key Characteristics

A medium-sized dog, the puli has a domed skull, V-shaped drop ears, a nose with a straight bridge, and large dark brown eyes. The tail usually curls upward at the end. The long corded weather-resistant double coat unique to this breed usually touches the ground. The coat is usually a rusty black.

Despite its short legs, the puli moves very fast, is extremely agile, and has endless stamina. It has a good sense of judgment and is playful.

M 9 years

Care and Exercise

The long coat requires about forty-five minutes of grooming weekly to prevent matting and felting, preferably by a professional. Extremely energetic, this breed needs lots of extended, vigorous daily exercise.

Puppies and Training

Puli puppies, four to seven to a litter, have a tufted coat at birth; as it grows, the undercoat becomes intertwined with the outercoat as in the adult form. Maturity is reached in about fifteen to eighteen months. Highly intelligent, the puppies are quick to learn.

Male: 17 in.
29–33 lbs.
....
Female: 16 in.
27–31 lbs.

M 9 years

M 6 years

Pumi

Still relatively unknown outside its native Hungary, where it has done duty as a cattle herder and guard dog, this breed has curly hair and semi-prick ears that give it a deceptively sweet look, as it is rather aggressive and wary of strangers.

Background Notes

Believed to have originated from a puli and German shepherd dog cross during the 1700s, pumis worked mainly as herders for Hungarian dairy farmers. Some say they also have terrier blood as they are excellent hunters, very good at spotting and flushing foxes and rabbits from their lairs.

Male: 13 in.
18–29 lbs.
....
Female: 13 in.
18–29 lbs.

M 5 years

Key Characteristics

A square-chested and square-loined, medium-sized breed, the pumi has a well-balanced head with a high set muzzle; half-erect ears bending at the tip; coffee-colored eyes; and a black pointed nose. The tail must be docked to two-thirds its original length from the joint. Its thick, tough, medium-length coat may be slate, silver, dark gray, white, or reddish brown, and it should be curly, not tending to felting.

This breed is ever alert, strong, and agile and readily fawns on its master and family, which makes it a good family pet or companion. A restrained barker, it is adaptable, but not very friendly with strangers. With its keen sense of hearing it makes an ideal farm, home, or factory watch dog.

Care and Exercise

The pumi's dense undercoat requires strong, regular brushing. This very active dog loves plenty of vigorous exercise.

Puppies and Training

Some three to six puppies are born per litter. The extremely loving mother takes excellent care of the puppies. Because these dogs have inherited the high intelligence of the puli, training is quite easy.

M 5 years

Pyrenean Sheepdog

Lesser known than the massive Great Pyrenees and Pyrenean mastiff, this sheepdog is a fixture on farms in the Pyrenees. Even though it has a cheerful personality and charming looks, it is extremely robust and hardworking.

Background Notes

One of two breeds of sheepdogs from the Pyrenees, the Pyrenean sheepdog serves as a herder rather than as a protector of livestock. Believed to have descended from French sheepdogs, it played a major role in locating injured soldiers during European wars.

Key Characteristics

Medium-sized, with sturdy limbs and well-developed thigh muscles, this breed has a black nose and chestnut eyes surrounded by black rims. The long, heavy, and coarse woolly coat is slightly wavy on the back. Its color is basically gray, often tipped with grayish silver, white, or yellow. Quite fearless and healthy, the Pyrenean sheepdog is well known for its ability to withstand fierce weather conditions and adversity.

Care and Exercise

Brushing is necessary once every two to three days. Regular daily exercise is also required.

Puppies and Training

The three to six puppies born in each litter are easily whelped and very strong. They are easy to train, as they are highly intelligent.

Male: 16–20 in.
44 lbs.
....
Female: 16–20 in.
44 lbs.

F 4 years

F 4 years (left), F 1 year (right)

Saarloos Wolfhond

A recently developed breed definitely not for the inexperienced handler, the Saarloos wolfhond, named for both its creator and lineage, is an excellent guard dog when well trained. Although loving toward its owner, it is very suspicious of other people and dogs.

Male: 28–29 in.
79–90 lbs.
....
Female: 27–29 in.
79–90 lbs.

F 5 years

M 9 years

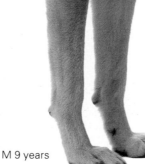

F 5 years

Background Notes

Geneticist Leendert Saarloos of the Netherlands bred this dog by backcrossing the German shepherd dog to the wolf.

Key Characteristics

This breed's back is straight; the chest, deep and well developed; the head, medium sized with a muzzle narrowing toward the nose and a prominent stop; the eyes, almond shaped; and the triangular ears, high set and erect. The short, dense coat on the tail, chest, and lower abdomen is slightly longer than on the rest of the body, and has wolflike brownish, grayish, cream, or white coloration.

This dog is especially wary and aggressive toward other dogs and animals, and has strong pack instincts. Because it is strong willed, its owner must be decisive in handling it.

Care and Exercise

The coat needs brushing only once a week. This breed requires a lot of exercise, ideally away from other people and dogs.

Puppies and Training

A litter usually numbers four to eight puppies that require intensive early training to get them used to people and domestication.

Sarplaninac

Although suspicious of and defensive toward strangers, this sheepherder shows its owner and family overflowing love and obedience on command.

M 2 years

Background Notes

Although its origins are unknown, this breed is indigenous to Sar Planina, the portion of Bosnia and Herzegovina, Montenegro, and Albania bordering the Adriatic Sea. The Sarplaninac was first exported to the United States in 1975. Until 1970 it was against the law in Yugoslavia to take this breed out of the country.

Key Characteristics

Heavily boned and fully coated, this medium-sized breed appears bigger and sturdier than it really is. It has V-shaped drop ears, strong teeth with a scissor bite, and a moderately long high-set tail, usually hanging down but kept level with the back when the dog is on the move. The eyes and nose should be dark; light-colored eyes being faulted for shows. Both the overcoat and undercoat are dense, the former being more than four inches long. Ideally, the coat should be a single shade of gray; a white, light yellow, or brown coat is disqualified for shows, as are white markings on the chest or paws.

Care and Exercise

Requiring frequent brushing, this breed's long hair also needs combing, especially while shedding. The Sarplaninac needs to be taken on daily walks by someone with strength, as it tends to pull very hard.

Puppies and Training

The four to eight puppies per litter should be trained very early.

F 1 year

Male: 27 in.
121 lbs.
....
Female: 27 in.
121 lbs.

M 2 years

Schapendoes

Also known as the Dutch sheepdog, this guardian and herder of livestock has been bred in limited numbers, only recently gaining popularity as a household pet.

M 4 years

Background Notes

Although its origin is unknown, this breed was recently discovered in the less-populated outer regions of the Netherlands by a local canine scholar working on a book about indigenous dogs. Representative Schapendoes from throughout the country were then selectively bred to produce a pedigreed dog that could be registered. It was finally recognized by the Dutch Kennel Club in 1968.

Key Characteristics

Similar in appearance to the bearded collie, briard, and Bergamasco sheepdog, with hair from the top of the head covering the eyes, this medium-sized breed has a biggish head and a long narrow muzzle with a strong scissor bite. Its dense, long, slightly wavy coat can be any color; however, blue-gray and black are favored.

Very alert, hardworking, and able to withstand inclement weather, the Schapendoes constantly keeps moving around while watching its territory. It is especially loyal to its owner.

Care and Exercise

Prone to felting, the soft coat needs regular combing. Because this dog is a real athlete and full of stamina, it requires a good amount of exercise.

Puppies and Training

The four to eight puppies per litter are strong and adaptable to their surroundings, but need thorough training to learn obedience to humans.

M 4 years

Male: 17–20 in.
31 lbs.
....
Female: 17–20 in.
31 lbs.

M 4 years

Shetland Sheepdog

Affectionately known as the "Sheltie," this smaller version of the collie is beloved by all and has a wide popularity throughout the world.

Background Notes

Internationally one of the most popular breeds, this dog originated in the Shetland Islands, where the scarcity of food favors small animals. It was introduced into England at the end of the nineteenth century.

Key Characteristics

The body of a Shetland sheepdog resembles that of a rough-coated collie. The frame is tight and covered with hard hair; the back is short and straight. The head is long and V-shaped. The eyes are medium-sized, almond shaped, the color dark, with blue or silver eyes acceptable if the coat is blue merle. The bridge of the nose is long and straight, and the color of the nose is black. The high-set small button ears bend forward at three-fourths of their length from the head. The tail is long. A Shetland

F 10 months

sheepdog is double coated, with a straight rough overcoat and a dense undercoat. The color is black, blue merle, tricolor, or sable, with markings in colors of white and tan, white, or tan.

Despite its smallness, the Shetland is a wonderful sheepdog; it always works keenly and enthusiastically. It bites at the heels of sheep and can chase a flock for a long time. A Shetland sheepdog is agile and gentle; though not friendly to strangers, it is to other dogs. Kind to its owner and active, it makes a good playmate for children.

Care and Exercise

Twice-weekly brushing for about fifteen minutes each time is needed, with special attention being paid during the spring shedding period. Walking and playing in a large, open area are also important.

Puppies and Training

The puppies, born in litters of four to six, are easy to rear, and take about fifteen to eighteen months to mature. Some are extremely shy, and these should be taken out in public frequently from the time they are small, so that they become sociable and used to people and noise. Thorough training is necessary to help discourage unnecessary howling.

F 2 years (left)
F 1 year (right)

Male: 13–16 in.
20 lbs.
....
Female: 13–16 in.
20 lbs.

M 3 years

Welsh Corgi Cardigan

In Welsh, *corgi* means tiny dog. This one came from central Europe with the Celts when they migrated into Wales around 1200 B.C.

Male: 10–12 in.
30–40 lbs.
....
Female: 10–12 in.
24–34 lbs.

M 2 years

M 2 years

Background Notes

The corgi is believed to have a common ancestor with the dachshund, and both have an elongated body, short legs, and a fluffy tail. The Welsh corgi Cardigan can be traced back more than three thousand years to when the ancestral stock was brought to the Welsh highlands, then called Cardiganshire. The corgi proved invaluable to the Celts for guarding children; flushing out game and small animals such as weasels, foxes, and mice; and chasing stray cattle. Principally a drover, the Cardigan remained relatively unknown outside Wales, where stories of its agility and courage were legion. Corgis became known to the general public in 1933, when the then Duke of York, later King George VI, kept the breed in his palace, triggering its popularity in the United Kingdom.

Key Characteristics

A small-sized dog, short both in height and loin, this breed differs from the Welsh corgi Pembroke in being somewhat shorter in height, having slightly larger erect ears set wider apart, more rounded paws, and possessing a long, fluffy tail. It has dark eyes and a medium-length dense flat-lying coat that feels

M 2 years

Puppies and Training

The litters of five to seven puppies take twelve to fifteen months to mature, and should be played with from quite early on. These puppies are good listeners, and are very affectionate, which makes their training and upbringing easy.

rough. The coat color can be brindle, blue merle, black and tan, sable, or black, with or without blue brindle points. Usually a Cardigan is white around the neck, on the chest, limbs, face, abdomen, and the tip of the tail.

Active, agile, and fearless, acting as if it were much larger, it is rather wary of strangers and is well suited as a guard dog. On the other hand, it is quite fond of playing, doting on and giving its master's family lots of love. If a male and female are kept together, they play and get along very well with each other.

Care and Exercise

A five- to ten-minute brushing twice a week is sufficient, but plenty of exercise at least twice a day is preferable. This dog does best when given lots of room to run around freely, but it easily adapts to any surroundings.

M 2 years

Welsh Corgi Pembroke

Originally a hardworking Welsh cattle drover, this household pet is now known worldwide as the favorite of Queen Elizabeth II.

Background Notes

This corgi breed has a lineage traceable back to the twelfth century. Further development of the breed occurred in Pembrokeshire, Wales, hence its name. Although stemming from different ancestral stocks, the two corgi breeds have been popular with the British royal family for generations, but this one took the edge in 1936 when King George VI gave a Pembroke to his daughter, now the reigning Queen.

Key Characteristics

Short in height and limbs, the Welsh corgi Pembroke has a foxy, oval-shaped head; a straight bridge running to its black nose; medium-sized erect ears; dark eyes; and a very short tail. Its medium-length, straight, hard, rough coat ranges in color from fawn, tan, red, and sable to black. Some white markings are permitted, but a predominantly white dog, known as a "whitelie," is disqualified for show purposes.

Extremely active, this breed is very good-natured and friendly. Ideally a brace, male and female, should be kept together.

M 3 years

F 7 months

Care and Exercise

The coat needs brushing only twice a week for about ten minutes. Twice daily exercise is preferable.

Puppies and Training

Usually five to eight puppies are born per litter, and they take twelve to fifteen months to mature. It is important to get them used to people very early.

Male: 10–12 in.
24–30 lbs.
....
Female: 10–12 in.
22–28 lbs.

Alaskan Malamute

Working Group

Akita

A large dog, originally developed in northeastern Japan for bear hunting by the nobility, this breed is now widely renowned for its fierce love, loyalty, and obedience to its owner.

Background Notes

In the 1630s, a feudal lord in Akita encouraged his samurai to develop a larger form of the medium-sized hunting dogs indigenous to that region. The dog they produced was an excellent fighter and guardian and was named for this prefecture during the Taisho era (1912–26). In 1931, the Ministry of Education designated the Akita a national monument, the first breed to be protected by law. The most famous of the breed is Hachiko, whose story is commemorated by a statue and wall sculpture next to Shibuya station in Tokyo. Hachiko met her master, Professor Eisaburo Ueno, at the station daily in the late afternoon, but one day in May 1925, the professor died while at work at Tokyo University. Not knowing this, Hachiko faithfully continued returning to the station each afternoon, waiting for him to come home.

Key Characteristics

Graceful movement, power, a thick frame, and a dignified facial expression all combine to make this largest of all

M 6 months

Japanese breeds arguably the most beautiful one. The body height to length ratio is ten to eleven; the back, straight; the tail, high set and curling up tightly over the back; the front limbs, straight, thick boned, and tight at the elbows; and the rear limbs, well developed and set at a moderate angle. The head has a prominent stop; moderately developed cheeks; a large nose with a straight bridge; strong jaws with a scissor bite; and dark eyes that are comparatively small and triangular, the corner pointing upward in the unique shape found in Japanese breeds. An Akita's double coat is composed of a soft, dense undercoat and a rough, straight outercoat, with the hair on the rump being slightly longer than the rest of the body and longest on the tail. The color varies from red, tiger brindle, brindle to white; even in the nonwhite areas, the skin surface,

Male: 26 in.
106 lbs.
....
Female: 24 in.
88 lbs.

M 6 months

especially on the abdomen and under the jaws, should preferably be white.

An excellent guard dog, this breed is also a superb companion.

Care and Exercise

The Akita requires daily brushing. It also must be exercised for at least one hour per day, and care should be taken to prevent it from becoming overweight.

Puppies and Training

Bottle feeding the litters of five to seven puppies may be necessary. Care must be taken to prevent the mother from inadvertently crushing the puppies. The Akita is easy to train.

M 9 months

Alaskan Malamute

Among the oldest of the Arctic dogs, this native breed from Alaska has well served humans as a good companion for thousands of years, pulling sleds and carts loaded with goods and human cargo, even in very harsh weather.

Background Notes

Said to be indigenous to northeastern Alaska, the true origin of the Alaskan malamute is unknown. Early Russian explorers reported that these dogs were used by the Mahlemuts, the native Inuit tribe for which the breed is named, to pull big sleds across the snow and ice. The breed was officially recognized by the American Kennel Club in 1935.

Key Characteristics

Bred for its strength and endurance, this dog has moderately short loins, a well-muscled back and chest, and a thick curled tail. The wide pointed head with erect V-shaped ears and long, prominent muzzle gives the malamute a distinct wolflike countenance. Its weather-resistant double coat is composed of a relatively short, dense guard (outer) coat and a soft, woolly, oily, one- to two-inch undercoat. The coat color varies from a light to wolf gray, black with white markings (chest, mask, feet, and so on), or in some cases, pure white, the only solid coloring acceptable.

Loyal and friendly, this breed makes an excellent companion.

Care and Exercise

In order to keep the Alaskan malamute's coat in top condition and parasite free, it needs to be well brushed daily, especially during the shedding season from spring to summer. Because this is a heavy breed, to prevent damage to the

M 2 years

Male: 25 in.
86 lbs.
....
Female: 23 in.
75 lbs.

M 4 months

M 2 years

M 3 years

dog's nails they need to be kept cut from the time it is quite young. This breed needs daily vigorous exercise and plenty of attention, with a good-sized yard to run around in; it should not be kept in a hot, humid environment. Diet should also be strictly controlled. An inadequately exercised dog will become overweight.

Puppies and Training

The litters of four to ten puppies need to be born into a very clean environment that must be maintained after delivery, and the puppies must not be overly handled, especially by many different people. Thorough training should be started early, especially if the dog is to be used to pull a sled or cart, and also to keep the dog from barking unnecessarily or getting into trouble with other pets.

Appenzeller Mountain Dog

This compact, spritely breed exhibits superb versatility and plenty of stamina as it speedily chases and herds sheep, or pulls carts of cargo.

Background Notes

Some say that this Swiss sheepdog is indigenous, dating back as far as the Bronze Age. Others, however, believe the ancestral stock was introduced by the Roman legions when they invaded Switzerland.

Key Characteristics

The Appenzeller mountain dog has a muscular body with strong, straight limbs, a wide, flat skull, a narrow muzzle, V-shaped drop ears, and smallish dark eyes. Its coat is short, thick, dense, and tricolored. This black, yellow, or tan and white pattern should be symmetrical, and should have a thin white blaze as well as a small tan spot above each

M 3 years

eye. Unlike other Swiss sheepdogs, this breed has a tail that curls up over the back.

Sociable, active, cheerful, charming, and loving, the Appenzeller mountain dog is highly adaptable: it makes an excellent sheepdog, a diligent and loyal guard dog, or an uncomplaining cart puller. Ever vigilant in looking after the house or farm, and filled with surprising stamina, this dog never seems to rest, even when it doesn't have any work to do.

Care and Exercise

Easily cared for, this breed's coat needs brushing just once every two weeks; however, sufficient daily exercise is necessary. Ideally, the dog should be kept outdoors and allowed to run freely in a large, open yard.

Puppies and Training

The litter of four to eight puppies per litter are strong and easy to raise, but they should be kept free from excessive cold.

M 3 years

Male: 19–23 in.
48–55 lbs.
....
Female: 19–23 in.
48–55 lbs.

M 3 years

Austrian Shorthair Pinscher

Brave and sturdy despite its small size, this ever-alert breed has a terrier-like character and is an excellent guard dog and hunter.

Background Notes

Although it has terrier blood, this breed is quite different from the German hunting terrier and the Zwerg (miniature) pinscher.

Male: 14–20 in.
26–40 lbs.
....
Female: 14–20 in.
26–40 lbs.

F 3 years

Key Characteristics

The medium-sized Austrian shorthair pinscher has well-developed muscles; strong limbs; a pear-shaped head with a wide skull; a biggish dark-colored nose; ears that range widely from bat to button, semi-prick, or drop; and a tail that curls upwards. The tail can either be docked or left as it is. The coat is short and straight, with coloring ranging from light yellow and fawn to red and tiger, plus white markings.

Quite powerful for its size, the Austrian shorthair pinscher will bravely guard its territory and is very loyal to its owner.

Care and Exercise

The coat needs almost no care, simply an occasional body wipe down with a towel. This breed, however, does like a long daily walk and a large outdoor area to run around in.

F 3 years

F 3 years

Puppies and Training

The four to seven puppies per litter are usually born without complications, and the litter requires minimal attention afterward, as the pups grow.

Bernese Mountain Dog

The most popular of the four types of Swiss mountain dogs, and the only one with a long coat, the Bernese mountain dog is now gaining a solid following as a gentle household pet.

M 2 years

Background Notes

This sheepdog takes its name from the canton of Bern in the central farmlands of Switzerland, where for over two millennia it has served as a drover and guard dog.

Key Characteristics

The Bernese mountain dog has a full body that is slightly longer than it is tall, with a deep chest, the loin being somewhat short; sturdy, straight limbs with a relatively short pastern; a flat, slightly furrowed head; a strong, rather long muzzle with a scissor bite; V-shaped

M 3 years

Male: 26–27 in.
79–107 lbs.
....
Female: 25–26 in.
75–90 lbs.

M 2 years

drop ears that are held slightly forward, and hazel or brown almond-shaped eyes. The long, thick tail hangs down, and complements the slightly wavy, moderately long tricolored coat. The color is basically black, with either dark tan or tan edging on the limbs and sides of the muzzle, and small spots above the eyes; the feet should be white, and there should be a prominent long white blaze and an inverted-cross chest mark.

Originally a working dog, it has also proved to be a cheerful, intelligent family pet and makes a wonderful companion dog.

Care and Exercise

Daily brushing and occasional bathing are required as well as cleaning out the inside of the ears with baby oil, keeping the nails cut short, and brushing the teeth well to prevent heavy tartar formation. The Bernese mountain dog needs long, daily exercise if kept as a household pet.

Puppies and Training

The mother has keen maternal instincts and more than adequately cares for the litters of four to ten puppies. It is recommended, however, that the puppies become accustomed to humans early.

M 2 months

Boxer

Originally a hunting dog, this breed has a smart appearance, agility, and intelligence that has quickly made it highly treasured and popular not only as a companion and show dog, but also as a police and military dog.

Background Notes

The boxer is the direct result of mid-nineteenth-century crossings of the Bullenbeisser (mastiff) and bulldog. Its beautiful well-balanced frame and its courage soon made it one of the world's most popular dog breeds. Earlier used for hunting boar, bear, and deer, it later became a widely praised guard, police, military, fighting, and companion dog. It first entered a dog show in 1850, and now is a popular show dog breed.

Key Characteristics

Squarely built and medium-sized, this breed has a short, straight, muscular back; a deep, thick, well-developed chest; wrinkles on the forehead; pronounced flews on the muzzle but no dewlaps on the back of the head; drop ears that naturally incline forward and are usually cropped to stand erect in show dogs; dark brown eyes with a vertical flap over them; an undershot bite with the lower jaw protruding and arching slightly above the upper jaw; a docked tail that is held high; and rather short, angled lower hind limbs. Its gait tends to be bouncy, but powerful. The fawn or slightly brindled mahogany coat is short and glossy, lying smoothly along the body, usually with white markings on the head, muzzle, throat, chest, and lower limbs, plus a black mask.

Despite the boxer's rather pugnacious countenance, it is very gentle and makes a good playmate for children.

Care and Exercise

Coat care is easy, requiring just a light brushing, but the nails must always be kept short and the diet carefully balanced to prevent the breed's tendency to be overweight. The boxer is very energetic and needs lots of exercise. It should be taken for walks on a leash, but is happiest when allowed to run free in a big fenced area. A boxer adapts to any environment, either in the city or in the suburbs, as long as care is taken when temperatures change. Obedience, however, requires thorough training.

M 3 years

M 1.5 years

M 3 years

F 3 years

Male: 22–25 in.
70 lbs.
Female: 21–23 in.
60 lbs.

Puppies and Training

The mother cares well for her litters of five to ten puppies, watching over them as they grow. Puppies that are entirely white or white with a slight brindle are not favored, and will not make it to the show bench.

F 3 years

Bullmastiff

This large, sturdy, and energetic dog was bred by crossing the bulldog and mastiff. As the name implies, it was originally used to guard hunting areas from poachers.

Background Notes

In early nineteenth-century England, poaching on large estates and game preserves became a major problem, and heavy penalties were imposed on these intruders. Thus gamekeepers would often be attacked or shot if they came across such violators, especially under the cover of darkness. This breed was created to combine the power, speed, and keen sense of smell of the mastiff with the bulldog's courage and aggressive nature. Bullmastiffs made the rounds with gamekeepers. They were trained to attack and, if commanded, pin the poacher down without unduly hurting him. This large, rather energetic breed proved to be a perfect guard dog, and has since also been used for police and military work.

F 5 years

M 2 years

Male: 25–27 in.
110–132 lbs.
....
Female: 24–26 in.
99–119 lbs.

Key Characteristics

Bred for large size, great strength, and endurance, not looks, this breed has a short, straight back; a wide, deep chest; wide, muscular loins with thick, straight front limbs and well-boned and -muscled rear thighs and limbs; big yet tight well-arched (almost catlike) rounded toes; a large head with short muzzle; an undershot bite; good-sized flews; a wrinkled forehead; dark brown, medium-sized eyes set wide apart; a short nose; dark, round-tipped, V-shaped, relatively small drop ears; and a long, high-set hanging tail. The double coat consists of a dense,

M 2 years

F 5 years

short undercoat and a slightly rough overcoat. Coat coloration ranges from red and brindle to fawn, with a small white upper-chest spot and a black mask. An ideal bullmastiff would have a jet black nose, muzzle, and ears, and black markings around the eyes.

Although rather standoffish with strangers and fearless in the face of enemies, this dog is loving toward its owner and is normally very gentle, cheerful, and calm. It makes a good household pet.

Care and Exercise

The short coat requires only simple care: use a cloth or very soft brush to massage the body daily for about 10 minutes. This breed's nails should always be kept short. Diet and daily exercise must be carefully balanced to ensure that this large dog doesn't become obese, an often difficult task for the inexperienced, and something to seriously consider before deciding to keep this breed. Obedience training should be begun as early as possible.

Puppies and Training

An average litter numbers five to eight puppies, which must very early be given the opportunity to become accustomed to people and other animals.

Bordeaux Mastiff

Rather rare in its native country of France, this breed was originally developed to aggressively hunt large animals such as boar and bear, or to fight bulls in circuses.

M 5 years

Background Notes

Some say that this breed originated from the Greek mastiffs, which were used in wars and arenas by the Romans, while others claim that they stem from the mastiffs used by the Celts to hunt wild animals. Today it is well known as a police dog and also a domestic guard dog, but it is decreasing in number.

Key Characteristics

An extremely large guard dog, the Bordeaux mastiff has a deep, wide, well-developed chest; a big wrinkled head with a square muzzle; egg-shaped eyes set wide apart; and round-tipped drop ears. The coat, which is fine, short, and soft, ranges in color from mahogany to fawn and gold.

Careful breeding has modified the originally aggressive character of this dog, so that today it has a calm, generous, loving, obedient, and loyal nature.

Care and Exercise

While a moderately hard brush should be used over most of the body, the tail and thighs, where the hair is somewhat long, should be combed. Daily exercise should include at least half an hour of walking on a leash. Ideally, this dog should be kept in a large yard where it can exercise freely.

Puppies and Training

Five to nine puppies are born per litter, and they need to be watched as they often are inadvertently crushed by their massive mother. It is recommended that obedience training be started early.

M 5 years

Male: 24–27 in.
110 lbs.
....
Female: 21–24 in.
99 lbs.

M 5 years

Dogo Argentino

Popular today as a playmate for children, the dogo argentino was originally a fighting dog created at the beginning of the twentieth century by crossing some hunting breeds.

Background Notes

Ancestors of this breed were brought from Europe to South America by Spaniards in the early 1900s and were bred to produce a fast-running, aggressive fighter capable of hunting wildcats and boar in rugged mountain terrain. Later, crosses with Great Danes, bull terriers, and pointers, among others, curbed some of the aggressive nature of the breed.

Key Characteristics

A superb runner, the dogo argentino has a powerful, well-boned and -muscled body; a big head with a slightly angular skull; erect, usually cropped ears; a jet

F 7 years

Male: 24–27 in.
79–99 lbs.
....
Female: 24–27 in.
79–99 lbs.

F 7 years

black nose; and a tail that is either parallel to the backbone or pointing slightly upwards. Its solid white coat (dark markings on the head are permitted), is short, thick, and straight.

The dogo is a loyal, brave, and courageous companion dog that truly loves children and makes an excellent household pet.

Care and Exercise

This breed needs strong brushing every two to three days. It requires plenty of exercise, including some retrieval routines.

Puppies and Training

The litters of six to twelve puppies are relatively strong, easy to raise, and grow fast. If large broods outnumber the mother's teats, care must be taken to make sure each puppy has enough to eat, and nutrient- and calcium-rich supplements should be provided. Vigorous obedience training is recommended to bond the dog to its owner.

Doberman

Universally known as a police dog and for its devotion to duty on the German front during World War I, this breed with its strong streamlined body has remained a perennial favorite among dog lovers throughout the world.

Background Notes

Created from crosses of an old indigenous German breed and the Rottweiler, German pinscher, and English black and tan terrier, this dog with its aristocratic bearing takes its name from Louis Dobermann of Apolda, Thueringen, who, around 1890, was instrumental in its development.

Key Characteristics

Medium sized, yet very powerful, muscular and well boned, the Doberman has a compact squared body; a short, almost horizontal back; a chest with well-developed ribs; a long V-shaped head; drop ears that naturally bend

M 2 years

Male: 26–28 in.
70–75 lbs.
....
Female: 24–26 in.
59–64 lbs.

M 2.5 years

forward or are cropped to make them stand erect; dark almond-shaped eyes; and a short docked tail. The coat is short, glossy, and tough, lying flat on the body, and is usually bicolored black or blue with dark red, fawn, or rust-tan markings above the eyes, on the muzzle, throat, upper chest, limbs, feet, and underside of tail.

Agile, energetic, and ever alert, the doberman is a loyal, fearless guard and watch dog.

Care and Exercise

Coat care is easy, as it only needs to be massaged with a soft cloth or brush. If the dog is to be shown, the whiskers should be removed. Moderately hard dried food is preferable to help prevent tartar formation. This very active breed requires extensive daily exercise in-cluding a lot of running, such as galloping alongside a bicycle, motorcycle, or jogger, and ball retrieval games within a securely fenced area.

Puppies and Training

The ears of the three to eight puppies per litter should be cropped eight to twelve weeks after birth. As this breed can be quite aggressive, thorough obedience training from a very early age as well as handling by a number of people are strongly recommended.

German Shepherd

This globally popular breed rates top honors as an all-round police, guard, search, rescue, seeing-eye, and companion dog.

Background Notes

Dating back several centuries to early Europe, this breed's rootstock was the mountain sheepdog of Germany. Around 1880 the German army modified this breed for work as a military dog to carry medicine and ammunition. A German parent club for the breed was formed in 1899. Later, the military further modified the breed to act as a guard dog for hostages during the two

Male: 24–26 in.
66–90 lbs.
....
Female: 22–24 in.
57–77 lbs.

F 2 years

world wars. As it truly loves to work with people, its popularity in the United States rose greatly after World War I, when many soldiers brought dogs back from Germany. Today it is one of the most popular herding dogs registered with the American Kennel Club.

Key Characteristics

The German shepherd is both strong and agile, with a sturdy, well-muscled body that is slightly longer than high; a straight back; a deep chest; a slightly pointed, rather lean head with a well-muscled neck; a strong, long, V-shaped muzzle; high-set erect ears; and a slightly curved bushy tail. Its outer coat is short, straight, and harsh, lying flat on the body, and can be almost any color—black, tan, gray, a black saddle on tan—however, a white one is disqualified.

Extremely intelligent, this breed can be trained to handle multiple responsibilities. Although a bit wary of strangers, and uneasy around strange dogs, especially small ones, this shepherd completely trusts, and is devoted to, its master and family, including children. Care is necessary, however, to avoid provoking its aggressive behavior or disturbing its territorial sense.

Care and Exercise

As this breed tends to shed constantly, brushing for ten minutes three times a week is needed. Long, daily walks on a lead are essential, and if possible, the dog should be kept in large, open yard, never in a small, confined space. If not

kept busy or properly cared for, this breed tends to become excessively nervous, cowardly, mischievous, noisy, and generally uncontrollable and possibly dangerous to handle.

Puppies and Training

A litter numbers five to ten puppies, and early handling as well as thorough obedience training are best. Maturity, however, is not reached until they are 1½ to two years old.

F 5 years

M 5 years

Great Dane

A superb companion and guard dog, this elegant breed of great size is strongly identified with Germany and was once renowned throughout Europe for its prowess as a wild boar hunter.

Background Notes

Traceable back some four hundred years as a distinct breed, it is known in its native Germany as the *Deutsche dogge*. Probably a mixture of ancient breeds, its suggested lineage has included the Tibetan mastiff, Old English mastiff, and greyhound. Although originally a savage boar hound, today it is a

F 2 years

M 5 years

M 2 years

other hand, this powerful breed tends to be a bit distrustful of other dogs. When properly trained this breed makes a better companion and guard dog than almost any other.

Care and Exercise

Only brief daily brushing is needed to maintain its glossy short coat, and its nails need not be cut if worn down naturally by exercise. Adult dogs require considerably fast, strenuous daily exercise, such as galloping alongside a bicycle or motorcycle. Puppies under ten months old should never be given long or strenuous exercise, as their bones are still forming, and overexercise could cause abnormalities to develop. Rather, a puppy should be given plenty of space to freely exercise on its own. As this dog is a ravenous eater, food and exercise must be very carefully balanced.

Puppies and Training

Usually, there are five to twelve puppies in a litter. If the ears are to be cropped, this should be done at about eight weeks of age. Very early obedience training is a must, although it instinctively has a strong sense of responsibility.

lovable gentle giant, very popular internationally because of its great size, strong looks, noble, dignified appearance, and reputation as an affectionate companion and loyal guard dog.

Key Characteristics

Well boned and muscled, the Great Dane is among the tallest of dog breeds. It has a rather square body when viewed from the side; a deep chest; a big, long, deep head with a clearly defined stop; round black eyes that are as piercing as those of an eagle; drop ears that naturally bend forward, but more often are cropped erect; and a very long, uniformly tapering tail, hanging down. The coat is short, thick, smooth, and shiny, and colors range from fawn and a yellow-gold brindle, both with a black mask, to a pure steel blue, entirely black, or even harlequin.

This is definitely a dog for the suburbs, not city living, and one that requires special handling by people who know dogs very well. Even though this breed is massive, it loves children and proves to be a very gentle playmate and loyal guardian for them. On the

Male: 30–31 in.
119–143 lbs.
. . . .
Female: 28–30 in.
99–121 lbs.

M 2 years

Great Pyrenees

Common to much of Europe, this truly pleasant, gentle breed of enormous size has served as a brave sheepdog in the mountains between France and Spain for over three millennia.

M 2 years

Background Notes

A truly ancient breed whose fossil remains have been found in Bronze Age (1800 to 1000 B.C.) deposits, the Great Pyrenees is depicted in Babylonian paintings. Able to withstand severe, snowy winter weather due to its thick, long coat, this dog can still be seen working as a sheepdog in Europe. In the United States it has gained popularity as a household pet and companion dog.

Key Characteristics

Big boned and sturdy, the Great Pyrenees is usually just a bit longer than high. It has a big V-shaped head with relatively small drop ears and almond-shaped eyes; big and distinctive double dewclaws on the hind limbs that must not be removed; and a long, hanging saber tail. This breed's thick double coat lying close to its body must be all white to show, but light gray and tan markings on the head (a full mask), ears, and tail base are permitted.

Extremely intelligent, gentle, and loyal to its family, and an excellent playmate for children, it still makes a good guard dog as the great is quite wary of strangers.

Care and Exercise

The double coat requires thorough daily brushing and combing, especially during the shedding season from spring to summer. If kept in an amply large yard, the dog will get plenty of free, regular exercise, especially if it is taught and

M 2 years

Male: 27–32 in.
110–132 lbs.
....
Female: 25–29 in.
99–121 lbs.

sometimes used to pull a cart. Even so, its diet needs to be carefully controlled.

Puppies and Training

The mother's delivery and care of the six to ten puppies per litter requires little assistance. The puppies, which take a few years to mature, should be handled early to keep them from becoming exceedingly shy or nervous around people.

M 2 years

Hokkaido

Also known as the Ainu dog, the Hokkaido is considered to be the oldest of the Japanese breeds. It is locally renowned for its bravery in fighting the brown bear and for withstanding the severe winter environment of Hokkaido.

Male: 19–20 in.
44 lbs.
....
Female: 18–19 in.
33 lbs.

M 5 years

M 5 years

Background Notes

It is claimed that this breed stems from the ancient hunting dog (Matagi Inu) that accompanied the Yamato tribe as it migrated and populated Japan, including the northern main island of Hokkaido.

Key Characteristics

A medium-sized Japanese breed, the Hokkaido is considered to be the wildest and most foxlike in appearance of this group. It has a dense bone structure; well-developed muscles; strong loins; high withers; a straight back; a deep chest; a tight abdomen; a strong neck; a well-developed skull with a shallow forehead but with a clearly defined stop; small triangular dark eyes with edges slightly pointing upwards; ears that are small, triangular, erect, and slightly bending forward; tight lips; and a scissor bite. It is double coated. The outer coat is hard and straight; the under soft and fluffy, making the dog well suited for withstanding cold, inclement weather. The coat color can be red, white, black, sesame, tiger, or fawn.

The Hokkaido is renowned for being a fearless hunter, and is extremely loyal and devoted to its master.

Care and Exercise

Daily brushing and walks of about thirty to fifty minutes on a lead are required.

Puppies and Training

The three to seven puppies in a litter are susceptible to the cold and need to be watched carefully if born in winter.

Hovawart

A popular breed in Germany today where it is recognized as an outstanding guard dog, the Hovawart was well known in Europe during the late Middle Ages and Renaissance, but slipped into oblivion until it was resurrected some sixty years ago.

Background Notes

Well known in medieval Germany as a guard dog for large estates (from which it got its name), the breed was barely surviving in the early part of this century when its preservation was undertaken by a group of breeders from the Harz Mountains.

Key Characteristics

The sturdy, well-balanced, large-bodied Hovawart has a big, firm head with a convex forehead; triangular drop ears; a scissor bite; and a long bushy tail reaching down below the hock. Its long, thick, wavy coat is colored black, dark blonde, or black with light tan markings. Dark eyes, nose, and nails are desired.

M 9 months

This intelligent, loving, obedient breed makes an excellent watchdog, especially for big, open spaces.

Care and Exercise

Thorough, overall brushing every couple of days is necessary. This breed should be given sufficient daily exercise.

Puppies and Training

The delivery of the four to ten strong puppies per litter is relatively easy. Grooming should be started early to get them used to coat care.

M 1 year

Male: 23–27 in.
66–88 lbs.
Female: 21–25 in.
55–77 lbs.

M 8 years

Iceland Sheepdog

This spitz-related breed once faced extinction, but was bred back to life by enthusiastic breeders and is now popular as a sheepdog and household pet.

Background Notes

It is claimed that this breed was introduced to Iceland along with the settlers who colonized the island. At one point, distemper devastated its numbers, but the dog was bred back by dedicated homeland and British breeders. Today, it is used as a sheepdog, watchdog, and companion.

Key Characteristics

The Iceland sheepdog has well-muscled limbs; a long tapering muzzle; a black nose; and a tail that curls over its back.

M 1 year

Its medium-length overcoat and profuse undercoat lying flat on the body are colored chestnut, fawn, gray, black mixed with some white, or all white. Intelligent, loving, and active, it is a ravenous eater, favoring fish. An excellent sheepdog, guard dog, and companion, this breed gets along with all animals.

Care and Exercise

While the dense undercoat needs strong brushing, the long overcoat should be combed. Brief daily exercise is sufficient.

Puppies and Training

Delivery of the litters of three to six puppies is easy, and the strong puppies are calm, gentle, and no problem to raise. Their ears stand up at around six to eight weeks after birth. It is claimed, however, that this breed's character takes about 1½ years to form, something to consider in order to avoid creating a nervous adult.

Male: 13–16 in.
24–31 lbs.
....
Female: 12–15 in.
20–24 lbs.

M 1 year

Jamthund

Also known as the Swedish elkhound, this breed is of considerable antiquity and is known throughout Scandinavia as an excellent sleigh dog hunter, yet is a gentle and energetic watchdog for the home.

F 2 years

and a tail that slightly curls down over the back. Its profuse, dense and woolly undercoat is covered with a long, hard outer coat that is colored light or dark gray.

This breed is gentle and loyal to its owner, and is a keen worker and an alert, brave defender against enemies and other animals, making it an excellent domestic watchdog.

Care and Exercise
Strong, thorough brushing is needed once a week, especially to remove shed hair. This breed really loves exercise.

Puppies and Training
The four to eight puppies per litter should begin obedience training early.

Male: 23–25 in.
66 lbs.
....
Female: 23–25 in.
66 lbs.

Background Notes
Believed to descend from Stone Age stock, this dog was first used to hunt elk and bear, then later, marten and snow grouse. A brave military dog, it is especially well suited for cold, snowy weather.

Key Characteristics
A large, foxy-looking hunting dog, the jamthund has straight, agile limbs; a longish, narrow head with a straight muzzle; a big, broad nose; small, dark eyes; large, pointed, erect ears that are quite sensitive to the smallest noise;

F 2 years

Kai

The Kai, or "Kai-tora" as it is sometimes called for its brindle- or tiger-patterned coat, comes from the southern Japan Alps where it has served as a tireless, all-weather hunting breed.

Background Notes

The Kai bears the ancient name of the region in Japan from which it comes.

Key Characteristics

A medium-sized hunting breed, the Kai is unusual in that it exhibits a degree of sexual dimorphism. It has a well-balanced, tight-muscled body with no excess fat; a short, straight back; well-developed loins; a wide forehead with a shallow groove; a clearly defined stop; well-developed cheeks; tight lips; a scissor bite; erect triangular ears that are somewhat larger than those of other Japanese breeds and that bend slightly forward; and either a fully curled or sickle-shaped tail set high over the back. Its double coat, a soft, close-lying

M 2.5 years

Male: 20–22 in.
24–51 lbs.
....
Female: 18–20 in.
24–51 lbs.

undercoat and a hard, straight overcoat, can be either black or red brindle, with a limited amount of white on the chest and lower limbs permissible.

Retaining a touch of wildness, this mountain breed always remains obedient to its master.

Care and Exercise

Daily care requires only brief brushing, and walks on a leash of about thirty to forty minutes.

Puppies and Training

As the three to seven puppies per litter are susceptible to the cold, they and the mother should be given a warm, secluded area for delivery during the winter, and one with plenty of ventilation during hot months. Puppies are born solid-colored; the brindle pattern appearing as they mature.

M 4 years

Karelian Bear Dog

A brave hunter of large animals, this breed, named for one of the provinces of Finland, has distinctive coloring and is well suited for the snowy mountains and desolate fields of Scandinavia.

Male: 21–23 in.
44–48 lbs.
....
Female: 21–23 in.
44–48 lbs.

F 4 years

the undercoat is soft and dense, the outercoat is straight and hard. White markings—a long narrow blaze extending from the forehead to the nose, a neck band, throat, chest, and paws—distinctively divide the solidly jet black areas.

Although definitely a fearless, ever-ready fighter, this dog is always obedient to its master.

Care and Exercise

This breed requires only occasional grooming with a slightly hard brush. A very strong dog, care should be taken during ample daily exercise to avoid other dogs and animals, because the Karelian loves to fight.

Puppies and Training

Early obedience training is definitely necessary for the four to eight puppies per litter.

F 4 years

Background Notes

It is generally believed that this breed descends from hunting dogs brought into Finland by the Russians a few centuries ago. Still in the process of being bred to better hunt bears in Finland and Scandinavia, it first catches the scent, devotedly runs in pursuit, then attacks the bear while barking fiercely.

Key Characteristics

A powerful, medium-sized breed, the Karelian bear dog has well-developed bones and muscles, especially in the shoulders; a deep, broad chest; a wedge-shaped head with a moderately big black nose; small, rather charming eyes; medium-sized erect ears that are angled slightly outward; and a curled tail, tipped in white, that arches down below the top line of the back. While

F 4 years

Kishu

Originally a deer and boar hunter, this medium-sized ancient breed is a very intelligent, devoted family dog that has become highly popular in Japan as a household pet.

Background Notes

Hailing from the Japanese mountains, especially in the Wakayama and Mie prefectures, this breed extends back to before recorded history. Although it was first a boar hunter, today it mainly serves as a domestic pet.

Key Characteristics

The Kishu is well balanced in bone structure and muscles. It has considerable stamina and a rhythmical gait; rather plain, yet noble, looks; and a straight back and wide, strong loins; a wide forehead combined with a slightly thick, wedge-shaped muzzle separated by a clearly defined stop; relatively well-

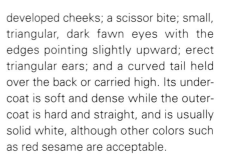

M 6 years

developed cheeks; a scissor bite; small, triangular, dark fawn eyes with the edges pointing slightly upward; erect triangular ears; and a curved tail held over the back or carried high. Its undercoat is soft and dense while the outercoat is hard and straight, and is usually solid white, although other colors such as red sesame are acceptable.

Care and Exercise

Usually light daily brushing is sufficient, but during the shedding season careful combing to remove dead hair is necessary. Daily exercise of thirty to forty minutes on a lead is needed.

Puppies and Training

The three to seven puppies per litter are susceptible to the cold, and as the mother is skittish around strangers, she should be given a warm, secluded area for delivery during the winter.

F 2 months

Male: 20–22 in.
24–51 lbs.
....
Female: 18–20 in.
24–51 lbs.

M 3 years

Laika

There are three forms of the Laika—an agile, energetic, and aggressive hunting dog indigenous to Russia—all capable of working in a wide range of environments.

M 4 years

Care and Exercise

This breed requires only monthly grooming with a hard brush. Thorough daily exercise is required.

Puppies and Training

As with many other hunting breeds, the three to six puppies born per litter are strong, but susceptible to the cold. To instill full obedience, training should be initiated early.

Background Notes

This native Russian breed was developed for hunting in the snowy Ural Mountains, as well as in forests and swamps. All three variants, the European and the West and East Siberian Laika, are similar, but the West Siberian Laika is rated first in number, popularity, and hunting ability.

Key Characteristics

All three varieties of the Laika are medium sized and sturdy. They have a wide, well-developed skull and deep-set almond-shaped eyes; triangular pointed ears; and a tail that curls over the back. The double coat is composed of a soft, dense, thick undercoat and a hard, smooth outercoat that can be white with black or red markings, black, or gray, among other colors.

Very alert and loyal, this breed makes a superb hunting companion.

Male: 21–25 in.
40–51 lbs.
....
Female: 21–25 in.
40–51 lbs.

M 4 years

Landseer

A large, very gentle, highly friendly companion dog for children, this rescue dog really loves the water.

Background Notes

Considered by many to be a color variant of the Newfoundland (see page 110), this breed is named for Sir Edwin Landseer (1802–73), who depicted it in many of his famous animal paintings. By 1920, this breed was virtually extinct, but German breeders re-created it by crossing the St. Bernard with the Great Pyrenees.

Puppies and Training

If the puppies, usually four to ten per litter, outnumber the mother's teats, supplemental formula feeding will be necessary. Born with an instinctive love of the water, the puppies will grow into powerful swimmers.

M 5 years

Male: 30–31 in.
132–154 lbs.
....
Female: 27–28 in.
119–139 lbs.

M 5 years

Key Characteristics

Large sized, massive, strong, and heavily boned, the Landseer has slightly longer limbs and head than the Newfoundland; a quite massive head; large, rounded drop ears; and a long, bushy, hanging tail. It has a soft, close-lying undercoat, and a long, thick, slightly curly outercoat. The coat color is white, but with an entirely black head and markings on the chest and back.

Instinctively brave, intelligent, and mild, this dog makes a great, friendly companion, especially for children.

Care and Exercise

Frequent brushing is needed, especially when it is shedding, and dead hair should be carefully removed. Ample exercise should center around a pulling routine.

M 5 years

Leonberger

This large German water dog, a born swimmer, is famed throughout Europe as an excellent lifesaver dog, and is also favored as a gentle companion for children.

Background Notes

The Leonberger was created in 1846 by Mayor Heinrich Essig of Leonberg, Germany, who crossed the Newfoundland with the St. Bernard to produce a dog that matched the one on the town crest, hence the breed's name. Probably the Great Pyrenees also figured in the breed's ancestry.

Key Characteristics

Strong and fairly massive, with well-developed muscles, the Leonberger has a wide, medium-sized head with dark chestnut medium-sized eyes; a big black nose; a tight mouth; wide-set, feathered, round-tipped pendant ears; and a quite bushy and slightly curled hanging tail. Its weatherproof coat is long, forming a mane on the throat and feet. A black mask and muzzle should be present, but body color varies greatly from light or golden yellow to reddish brown, sand, and silverish gray.

A superb, fearless lifesaver with an instinctive love of the water, this breed has rounded, tightly webbed paws and a water-resistant coat to enhance its swimming ability. The Leonberger moves with great agility, yet is never hurried, and has a gentle, loving nature.

Care and Exercise

This breed needs extensive daily brushing, especially during the shedding season. Exercise periods should include a pulling routine.

M 2 years

Puppies and Training

Usually five to ten puppies are born in a litter, and as the mother is quite massive, extra care will be needed to keep her from inadvertently crushing one or more of her puppies.

Male: 30–31 in.
88 lbs.
....
Female: 30–31 in.
88 lbs.

M 2 years

Mastiff

Truly a breed of great antiquity, depicted in drawings dating back some five thousand years, the mastiff has served on estates and the battle-field as a faithful guard dog and, in the nineteenth century, as a popular British fighting dog.

Background Notes

The mastiff is believed to have origi-nated in Asia. The earliest extant draw-ings of the ancestral form of this breed were found in an Egyptian tomb of about 3000 B.C., and it was noted in a Chinese document of 1121 B.C. In the early nineteenth century, it gained popularity as a fighting dog. After dog-fighting was banned in England, its popularity rose as a faithful working guard dog.

Key Characteristics

A massive, powerful, symmetrically well-boned and muscled giant, the mas-tiff has a deep chest; a broad, squarish head; ideally a scissor bite, although a slightly undershot one is permissible; dark brown eyes; pendant ears; and a moderately high, slightly curved taper-ing tail hanging down to around the hocks. Its short, thick, flat undercoat and short, hard outercoat can be fawn, apricot, or brindle colored, but it must have a very dark or black mask, muzzle, and ears.

Intelligent, but not excitable nor overly agile, the mastiff is a very reli-able guard dog, and retains its ancient fighting spirit against other dogs.

M 2 years

Male: 29 in.
180 lbs.
....
Female: 27 in.
169 lbs.

Care and Exercise

Daily brushing and a carefully balanced diet are essentials. Obedience training must begin early. Once the limbs are fully developed, regular exercise is a must.

Puppies and Training

As this breed craves attention and praise, the puppies (two to five per litter) need human contact early on.

M 4 years

Neapolitan Mastiff

One of the world's oldest breeds and a popular watchdog worldwide, this massive dog's history as an aggressive fighting dog belies its gentle, intelligent nature.

Background Notes

This breed's heritage can be traced to the Roman molossus (*Canis molossus*) dogs that Alexander the Great brought into Rome around 300 B.C. All existing mastiffs in Europe are of great antiquity, possibly tracing their ancestry to the Tibetan mastiff.

Male: 25–29 in.
154 lbs.

Female: 23–27 in.
154 lbs.

M 3 years

Key Characteristics

The powerful, extremely large Neapolitan mastiff has a big, broad head; very loose skin forming innumerable dewlaps; thick, pendulous lips; deep-set round eyes; and ears that are usually cropped to a triangular shape to stand erect. Its short, thick, shiny coat can be black, lead, gray, tiger, or fawn, with white markings permitted only as a tiny chest star or paw spots.

Reliable and loving, this dog fearlessly attacks only on command.

Care and Exercise

Simple grooming consists of an occasional whole body massage with a towel and brushing every few days. The mouth should be periodically wiped clean with a towel. Vigorous daily outdoor exercise should include a pulling routine.

Puppies and Training

Although the mother cares well for her litter of five to eight puppies, if she cannot furnish sufficient breast milk, supplemental formula feedings may be necessary. Also, extra care will be needed to keep the mother from inadvertently crushing her puppies. Early handling of the puppies as well as firm obedience training makes for a better watchdog and companion.

M 3 years

Newfoundland

Equipped with a thick, oily coat, this gentle giant is perfectly designed to navigate the icy waters of its native southeastern Canadian waters as a lifesaver and fisherman's companion.

M 4 years

Background Notes

Hailing from Newfoundland Island, which gives the breed its name, this breed's ancestors arrived with the first British and French fisherman to reach these North Atlantic shores. Its ancestral stock probably included the Great

F 4 years

Pyrenees, but today's stock mainly descends from those brought back and bred in England, possibly with some retriever blood. This breed's love of water and strong swimming ability made it popular in ports, where it helped fishermen pulling in fishnets and rescued people in distress from the surrounding waters. It was also used to pull carts and as a hunter. Today it is a popular household pet throughout Europe and North America.

Key Characteristics

Big bodied and sturdy, the Newfoundland has a broad, straight back; well-developed and -muscled limbs, the front ones being quite straight; a deep chest; a big broad head with a straight bridge and short muzzle; small dark brown eyes set well apart; small drop ears; and a long bushy tail that hangs with the tip pointing slightly upwards. Its profuse, thick double coat is rough, oily, and waterproof, but doesn't form a mane on the ears and is quite short on the muzzle. The coat color should be a solid black, brown, or gray, with some small white markings on the chest, chin, paws, and tip of the tail permissible. For the Landseer (black and white) variant, see page 106. A traditional children's playmate and protector, this breed is gentle and kind.

Care and Exercise

Thorough brushing twice a week, and an occasional swim in fresh water help maintain its coat, but sea water should be avoided, as it may sting the skin. After a swim, dry and clean out the inside of the ears. A balanced diet should be fed in two to three equal portions daily. Until it is about one year old, this dog should be allowed to exercise freely in a large outdoor fenced yard, but after it gets older, exercising on a lead alongside a bike or a motorbike will give it a good workout.

Puppies and Training

The eight to ten puppies born per litter may be skittish, but if given careful handling by a number of people they will mature into friendly and gentle adults.

Male: 28 in.
130–150 lbs.
....
Female: 26 in.
99–119 lbs.

F 4 years

Pinscher

A smaller, less muscled version of the Doberman, this breed of considerable history was recognized in Germany by the end of the nineteenth century and is ideally suited as a guard dog for city living.

F 2 years

Background Notes

Known also as the German or standard pinscher, this breed is intermediate in size between the larger Doberman and much smaller miniature. Resembling the schnauzer in body structure and character, it is distrustful of strangers, and thus makes a reliable watchdog for guarding property, livestock, and cars.

Key Characteristics

Medium sized and streamlined, the pinscher has a smart-appearing body; a long, lean head with a narrow, pointed muzzle without a pronounced stop; a strong, complete scissor bite; dark egg-shaped eyes; V-shaped drop ears that are usually cropped erect; a long, moderately narrow, arched neck; and a tail docked very short to be level with the top line of the back. Its short, hard, shiny coat lies flat on the body and can be colored a solid brown, from fawn to stag red, or black, with chestnut, stag red, blue gray, or salt and pepper markings. Despite the fact its name means "biter" in German, the pinscher is not aggressive; rather it is intelligent, agile,

F 2 years

high-spirited, loving, obedient, and absolutely devoted to its master.

Care and Exercise

Easy to care for, the smooth coat only needs occasional massaging with a towel. Thorough daily exercise on a lead is necessary, but the collar must be selected carefully as the head could easily slip out during exercise.

Puppies and Training

As the mother is often nervous after delivery of the three to six puppies, strangers are best kept away. The tail should be docked within one week of birth.

Male: 18–19 in.
18–22 lbs.
Female: 18–19 in.
18–22 lbs.

F 2 years

Podengo Portugues

An excellent small-game hunter, similar to the greyhound in body shape, this breed is also a devoted guard dog for its master.

Standard, M 3 years

Background Notes

The ancestry of this breed is unknown. There are three size variants of the podengo Portugues, the *grande* (large), *medio* (standard), and *pequeño* (small), all either with a smooth- or wire-haired form. They have been used as small-game hunters in northern Portugal, capturing hares alone, or working in a pack to capture larger animals.

Key Characteristics

All six varieties of the podengo Portugues have a long, slender body; a pyramid-shaped head with a straight muzzle; large, pointed erect ears that tend to twitch nervously; a powerful, muscular neck; and a long tail held horizontally when the dog is still, slightly higher when on the move. Its coarse coat can be either straight and short or wiry and long. Coat color ranges from yellow and tan to dark gray and white with markings.

Extremely active and very agile yet patient, this breed is perfectly suited for city living, serving as an obedient, reliable, and ever-alert guard dog, barking fiercely should strangers or unknown dogs approach.

Care and Exercise

Its coat is easily maintained by brushing once every two weeks. For exercise, it enjoys pulling activities and running freely in open spaces.

Puppies and Training

The puppies, three to eight per litter, are easily delivered and are strong and easy to raise.

Standard, M 3 years

Male: 15–21 in.
35–44 lbs.
. . . .
Female: 15–21 in.
35–44 lbs.

Male: 8–12 in.
11–13 lbs.
. . . .
Female: 8–12 in.
11–13 lbs.

Miniature, F 2 years

Rottweiler

Originally a drover and guard dog for butchers' cattle, and later a police dog in its native Germany, this extremely powerful and muscular breed has become one of the most popular dogs in the United States.

Background Notes

This breed was known at one time as the Rottweiler Metzgerhund, named after the town that produced it and its task as a butcher's dog. It is believed by many that it stems from mastiff stock that crossed the Alps while herding cattle used to feed the Roman soldiers who invaded central Europe. Active, agile, and full of stamina, this dog was later bred to manage livestock. Its outstanding strength also made larger Rottweilers ideal for pulling carts to market. In the twentieth century, cattle driving and the use of dogs as cart pullers was outlawed, and the breed almost became extinct. In later years, it regained favor as a police dog, household pet, and guard dog.

Key Characteristics

The Rottweiler has a sturdy, firm body with a well-developed, -muscled, and -boned chest and legs, especially the hindquarters; a wide head in harmony with a muzzle of medium length; a powerful, long, and thickset neck; medium-size almond-shaped dark brown eyes; high-set pendant triangular ears; and a short, single-joint tail, which is docked at the first joint to be level with the top line of the back. Its double coat of a

F 3 years

M 4 years

M 5.5 years

Male: 24–27 in.
114 lbs.
....
Female: 22–25 in.
99 lbs.

short, hard, dense outercoat lying flat on the body, and soft undercoat on the neck and thighs, is predominantly black with tan markings above the eyes and on the cheeks, muzzle, chest, and limbs.

This intelligent breed has natural guarding instincts, but is not vicious. Furthermore, it loves hard work.

Care and Exercise

Even though the coat is short it still should be wiped and massaged with a damp towel, then rubbed dry. A bath is needed if the dog gets dirty. Care is also needed in maintaining a healthy balance of diet, exercise, and play, with food being divided in half and given twice a day, rather than all at once. After the dog is one to 1½ years old, vigorous exercise should include running on a lead alongside a bicycle or motorbike.

Puppies and Training

The four to ten puppies per litter should begin obedience training early, and have as much contact with people as possible to accustom them to activity around them in the house. Be aware that even as puppies this breed needs a lot of free exercise.

Russian Sheepdog

Three distinct breeds fall under this name, and all are large muscular dogs that are instinctively aggressive and tend to attack strangers if threatened or placed on the defensive.

Male: 25 in.
88–99 lbs.
....
Female: 23 in.
84–95 lbs.

South Russian, M 1 year

Male: 25 in.
77–88 lbs.
....
Female: 23 in.
66–84 lbs.

Central Asian, F 2 years

Background Notes

The Central Asian sheepdog, of which there are a number of local variants, comes from the region east of the Caspian Sea encompassing Kirgizia, Kazakhstan, Uzbekistan, and Turkmenistan. It was developed by nomads to guard them and their livestock from wolves as well as to withstand the extreme heat and dryness of the region.

At the end of the eighteenth century, the ancestors of the South Russian sheepdog came from Spain along with the Merino sheep they were to manage

Male: 25 in.
99–110 lbs.
....
Female: 23 in.
88–99 lbs.

breed, variants include lightweight, heavyweight, short-haired, and long-haired types, and their combinations.

Key Characteristics

All forms have a muscular body and legs; dark almond-shaped eyes; V-shaped high-set ears, usually pendant; and a bushy, well-feathered tail. The coats are generally of medium length, profuse, and close lying. The coat color for the Central Asian sheepdog can be gray, white, light cream, light fawn, red, black, brindle, or spotted; for the South Russian, white, white and lemon, light red, or smoke; and for the Cauca-sus, reddish blonde, white with brown markings, or gray. Training takes time, patience, and firm handling, as this breed is both insistent and assertive.

Care and Exercise

Only occasional brushing is necessary; however, white coats might require more care. Thorough daily exercise, combined with speed routines, is most definitely needed or otherwise the dog becomes irritable and excessively aggressive.

Puppies and Training

The four to eight relatively strong puppies in each litter should have their ears cropped and tail docked short. These puppies need to begin thorough obedience training early on.

and guard, but their small frame was no match for the indigenous wolves. To bring it up to today's size and power, it was probably crossed with the Tibetan mastiff. Because the breed is now strong, aggressive, and assertive, often attacking without warning, it is also called the "bear dog."

The blood of the Tibetan mastiff definitely flows through the veins of the Caucasus sheepdog, which has worked for centuries fiercely guarding sheep from wolves in the Caucasus Mountains and around Astrakhan. Of this

Caucasian, M 3 years

St. Bernard

Certainly among the most massive of all dog breeds, this famous rescue dog has an unmatched appearance and a very gentle nature.

Background Notes

Probably no other dog conjures up such a distinctive image to so many: a somewhat sad-looking, massive rescue dog trudging through snowy mountains with a small keg of brandy hanging from its neck in search of people in distress. This day-and-night patrolling for people lost in the Swiss Alps has gone on in association with the monks of the Hospice of St. Bernard since its founding in A.D. 1050, but the breed probably descends from the Roman molossus dog introduced to the Alps some two thousand years ago.

Key Characteristics

Strong, muscular, and thick boned throughout, the St. Bernard has a wide, straight back; a well-developed chest; a thick, strongly muscular neck; a big, wide head with a short, squarish muzzle; dark, relatively small eyes with the tips pointing downwards, often showing haws; medium-sized ears dropping forward; and a long, thick tail, carried low. Never solid white or without white, the coat coloring is usually red and

Rough, M 3 years

Smooth, F 2 years

Male: 27 in.
165 lbs.
....
Female: 25 in.
145 lbs.

Rough, M 5 years

white, or brindle with white, all preferably with white markings on the chest,
neck band, nose band, feet, and tip of
the tail, and dark colors on the muzzle
and the edges of the ears.

Despite its massive size, the St. Bernard is intelligent, obedient, and makes
an excellent guard dog for family, children, and other animals.

Care and Exercise

Frequent brushing is a must, as is regular swabbing of the inside of the dog's
ears with baby oil and keeping its nails
cut short and the eyes free of tear resi-
due secreted from the lachrymal glands,
especially during spring. Extensive daily
exercise in big open spaces is required.

Puppies and Training

The six to eight puppies per litter
should have as much early contact with
people as possible to keep them from
becoming shy and nervous adults. Also,
intensive obedience training should begin early during puppyhood.

Samoyed

An Arctic dog with a unique "Samoyed smile" extending from ear to ear, this breed has a beautiful, pure white, very heavy, weather-resistant coat that makes it ideal both as a reindeer herder and as a quite friendly household pet.

M 9 months

M 2 years

Background Notes

Named for and developed by the no-madic Samoyed peoples of northeast-ern Asia, this breed remained separate from others for centuries as it hunted and herded reindeer, fished, and pulled sleds in the wilds of Mongolia. The coat color once varied from dark sable to black and white, until about one hun-dred years ago when the dog was introduced into England by Arctic ex-plorers and color was limited to a solid pure or near white. Although this breed still works as a sled dog in the Arctic, its noble appearance, gentle tempera-ment, and rapport with humans have made it popular worldwide as watch-dog and house pet.

Male: 21–23 in.
55–70 lbs.

Female: 19–21 in.
40–55 lbs.

from the body, and producing a distinct ruff around the neck. Coat coloration should be pure white, cream, biscuit, silver white, or silver biscuit.

The Samoyed is active, intelligent, gentle, especially good with children, obedient in its own way, and definitely vocal.

Care and Exercise

This breed needs extensive combing and brushing at least once a week, especially during the spring and summer shedding season. Nails must always be kept cut short, while the teeth and ears require constant care. Daily free exercise in a big open space combined with exercising on a lead is ideal.

Puppies and Training

The newborn puppies, numbering five to nine per litter, look very sweet, almost like teddy bear cubs. They do best with early contact with a number of human strangers, and obedience training should begin very early.

M 9 months

Key Characteristics

The Samoyed has an extremely sturdy, well-balanced body; a straight top line; wide, strong, well-muscled loins and chest; long legs in harmony with the body; a straight, extended, powerful neck; a slightly triangular, V-shaped head with a medium-length, slightly tapering muzzle; firm lips that give it a characteristic smile and a thousand expressions; dark almond-shaped eyes; erect, slightly round-tipped ears; a black nose; and a long, thick, bushy curled tail that is carried well over the back. Its thick, profuse double coat is composed of a soft, dense, short, almost woolly close undercoat interspersed with a slightly hard, curl-free outercoat sticking straight out

Shiba Inu

Japan's most popular indigenous breed, the Shiba Inu has a more than three-thousand-year history. This strong, muscular, uniquely determined looking dog is renowned for its alertness and intelligence.

Background Notes

Discovery of bones of this breed from Jomon period (c. 3000–400 B.C.) has reinforced the theory that its ancestral stock migrated from the south of Japan.

F 1 year

Male: 15–16 in.
20 lbs.
....
Female: 14–15 in.
17 lbs.

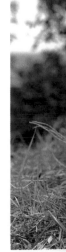

M 1 year

Indigenous to Honshu, the main island of Japan, and the mountains of Shikoku Island, in ancient times it was used for flushing and hunting small game and sometimes wild boar, and received the name shiba, meaning either small one or brushwood. In 1937, the Japanese Ministry of Education, recognizing the need to protect this native dog by law, officially designated it a national monument and began providing annuities for the maintenance of breed champion lines. This breed is also gaining worldwide popularity as a household pet.

Key Characteristics

Small, somewhat petite, but very well balanced with a light, agile movement, the shiba has a strong back; broad loins; strong, straight forelegs and powerful hind legs bending slightly at the stifle; bulbous paws with firm, springy pads; a thick, muscular neck; a broad forehead with a clearly defined stop; well-developed cheeks; small, deep-set, almond-shaped dark brown eyes with their tips pointing upwards; small, triangular erect ears inclining slightly forward; a black nose and firm lips; a scissor bite; and a thick tail firmly curled over the back or sickle-shaped. Its double coat is composed of a soft, dense undercoat and a straight, hard overcoat, somewhat longer on the tail, and usually colored red. Other acceptable colors are sesame, red sesame, black sesame, black and tan, white, and light red. The white markings on the muzzle are a characteristic of this breed.

F 1 year

This dog is a survivor, possessing acute senses, and able to jump quite high. Ever vigilant and extremely patient, the breed makes a good guard dog. It is also fiercely loyal and obedient to its master.

Care and Exercise

Daily care should include a brief brushing and exercising on a lead for about half an hour.

Puppies and Training

A warm, hygienic birthplace should be provided for the litters of two to five puppies, especially during the winter as they are susceptible to the cold. The puppies normally double in weight ten days after birth. The mother is quite protective and usually reluctant to leave the puppies during their first week, even to go outdoors. She will be happiest left alone, but should be given a small amount of exercise in the morning and evening.

Siberian Husky

One of the world's most popular dogs, this breed is capable of easily handling severe Siberian winters. Gentle in character and with determined looks, the Siberian husky truly loves working, especially pulling sleds.

Background Notes

The Siberian husky was developed by the nomads of northeastern Asia specifically to haul heavy loads over long distances, even during incredibly inclement winter. One authority states that this breed's ancestry dates back to the time when Siberia and Alaska were still attached, and that Russian adventurers brought the husky to Siberia to help them when surveying the coastline. It is said that the name derives from the husky nature of the breed's howl. Although somewhat smaller and lighter than most other sled dogs, it outshines all in sheer speed, especially when working in a team. In fact, husky teams have always scored high in Alaskan sled competitions. The breed was recognized by the American Kennel Club in 1930.

Key Characteristics

Medium-sized, yet incredibly powerful, the Siberian husky has a sturdy, agile body; a strong back; a well-developed chest; especially muscular hind legs; a V-shaped head with a pointed muzzle and prominent stop; erect medium-sized triangular ears; almond-shaped eyes with tips pointing slightly upwards and set slightly apart, their color being brown or blue, sometimes parti-colored, or even the right and left being differ-

M 11 years

Male: 21–23 in.
44–59 lbs.
....
Female: 20–22 in.
35–51 lbs.

parent M 3 years, young 1 month

ently colored; and a well-feathered, foxy tail carried up, sicklelike, when the dog is active. Its medium-length double coat consists of a soft, close-lying undercoat, usually absent during the shedding season, and a slightly hard, straight outercoat lying flat on the body. The coat color combinations range widely, but usually include white. The face markings are quite striking.

A working dog par excellence, the husky is obedient to its master, loves people and makes a superb, if sometimes overly affectionate, playmate.

Care and Exercise

The Siberian husky needs to be thoroughly brushed at least once a week, and special attention must be given to the skin and coat during the shedding season (spring to early summer). Also, the teeth and insides of the ears require careful cleaning, and the nails should be clipped if not worn down during exercise. A good one to two hours of exercising daily on a lead is recommended, because lack of exercise tends to make the dog nervous and shy. It even enjoys pulling a sled or cart. Strict obedience training is also a must.

Puppies and Training

When born, the six to eight puppies per litter look like small bear cubs. Early human contact with a number of strangers is desirable.

M 11 years

M 3 years

Shikoku

Although this ancient breed indigenous to Japan is medium-sized, and now a vigilant, devoted, and loving household pet, its tight, muscular body and outstanding stamina once made it a superb boar hunter.

M 2 years

Background Notes

Originally, this breed was developed for hunting wild boar. Today, it is popular as a very loyal household pet.

Key Characteristics

This breed has a straight back top line; broad, strong loins; a deep chest; well-spanned ribs; a tight abdomen; a thick, muscular neck; a broad forehead with a clearly defined stop; well-developed cheeks; dark fawn almond-shaped eyes; erect triangular ears slightly inclining forward; and a somewhat bushy, well-curled or sickle tail held over the back when the dog is active or down to the hocks when in repose. The nose must always be black. The undercoat is soft and close-lying, the outercoat, hard and straight. The coat color is sesame, black sesame, red sesame, black brindle, or red brindle.

The Shikoku is an excellent household pet.

Care and Exercise

Only light brushing and regular exercise, including pulling on a lead, are required.

Puppies and Training

The three to seven puppies in a litter need to be kept warm if born during the winter. Adults, however, are well suited for the cold. Obedience training is quite easy.

Male: 19–21 in.
40–53 lbs.
....
Female: 17–19 in.
33–44 lbs.

F 3 years

Spanish Mastiff

Once a military dog and fighter, this breed has proven to be a devoted companion and household dog.

M 1.5 years

M 1.5 years

Background Notes

As its name implies, this breed is indigenous to the hills of Spain where it has long been beloved for its vigorous fighting ability. Today, its enormous stamina is well shown in a variety of tasks, including guarding big factories, farms, and fields, hunting boars and other large animals, and pulling heavy carts.

Key Characteristics

This sturdy, heavily boned, muscular breed has a relatively long muzzle; well-developed lips and powerful jaws; dewlaps on the neck; small eyes; triangular drop ears; and a long, bushy tail. Its coat is usually reddish, but can be wolf, fawn, brindle, or black, gold, gray with white. It is loving, loyal, reliable, and obedient.

Care and Exercise

Although brushing once a month is sufficient, daily exercise for at least half an hour is necessary, and is best done by someone able to handle this dog's powerful pulling tendencies.

Puppies and Training

The five to ten puppies per litter should have early contact with strangers, to later take obedience training easily.

Male: 25–27 in.
132–154 lbs.

Female: 23–25 in.
121–143 lbs.

M 1.5 years

Swedish Vallhund

Recognized in 1948 by the Swedish Kennel Club, the native dog of that country is an energetic, tireless herder, and an excellent companion and watchdog.

Background Notes

Indigenous to Sweden, this breed bears a strong resemblance to the Welsh corgi and may be related to it. It has been bred by countless generations of farmers to serve as a watchdog for their cows, sheep, and farms, to keep away unexpected visitors, and to herd stock and work as a ratter.

Key Characteristics

Small, low, muscular, yet powerful and energetic, the Swedish vallhund has a long, straight body; short, wide loins; a broad rear gently sloping downward;

M 1 year

M 1 year

Male: 13–14 in.
20–33 lbs.
....
Female: 13–14 in.
20–33 lbs.

a long, deep chest; a wedge-shaped head; very dark brown oval eyes; pointed prick ears; and a tail that, if present, is docked very short. An abundant, soft woolly undercoat is covered by a medium-length, hard, close-fitting outercoat that is gray in color, and usually darker on the back and withers.

Extremely brave, vigorous, and an enthusiastic worker despite its size, this dog is loyal and obedient to its master, doting on praise but definitely wary of strangers.

Care and Exercise

Only occasional brushing is needed when appropriate, but as it loves exercise and constantly keeps moving, a large yard to run free in would be best.

Puppies and Training

The mother well cares for her four to eight puppies per litter, and they are comfortable around people and easy to raise.

F 3 years

Tibetan Mastiff

A breed of considerable antiquity, the Tibetan mastiff has worked for thousands of years in the Himalayan foothills guarding livestock from predatory animals.

Background Notes

This breed was developed in Tibet and neighboring countries to serve as a flock, farm, and home guardian against unwanted intruders, whether human or animal, and as a hunter. In fact, Marco Polo described this dog as "as great in size as a donkey, his voice somewhat like that of a lion's, dramatic and full of strength."

Key Characteristics

A giant, well-boned, but not massive breed, the Tibetan mastiff has a broad, strong head with a fairly broad, squarish muzzle that is narrower than that of the English mastiff; a thick, well-muscled, powerful neck with very little dewlap; medium-sized expressive brown eyes; heart-shaped drop ears; and a well-feathered tail usually slightly curled over the back. Its long, plentiful, coat should be close lying, and can be colored black, tan, gold, or bicolored.

Care and Exercise

The extremely dense undercoat needs thorough grooming with a hard brush, especially during the shedding season. Long hours of exercising on a lead are desirable.

Puppies and Training

Each litter numbers from four to eight extremely strong puppies. Thorough obedience training should be started quite early. Females may come into heat only once a year.

F 3 years

Male: 25–27 in.
143 lbs.
....
Female: 23–26 in.
132 lbs.

M 2 years

Tosa

This "Japanese mastiff," full of fighting spirit, is a true meeting of East and West. It is famous for the sumo wrestler garb that was created especially for this breed.

M 2 years

Male: 23 in.
148 lbs.
....
Female: 21 in.
132 lbs.

M 4 years

this dog also makes a friendly, loyal companion.

Care and Exercise

Daily care includes brushing the coat and working the dog on a lead for as long as possible.

Puppies and Training

Care must be taken in raising the five to ten strong puppies per litter as they tend to fight fiercely with each other as they mature.

Background Notes

During the Ansei era (1854–60), a dog lover in Tosa, Shikoku Island, crossed the indigenous dog, now known as the Shikoku, with a large aggressive dog he had brought back from Nagasaki. From a successive series of carefully planned breedings, the original form of the Tosa resulted. This was further crossed during the early Showa era (1926–89) with such large foreign breeds as bulldogs and mastiffs, resulting in the breed we know today. For show, a grand champion (*yokozuna*) is decked out in a ritual outfit, shown here, known as a *kesho-mawashi*.

Key Characteristics

Quite dignified, the large, powerful Tosa has a wide skull with a steep, moderately long muzzle; well-developed cheek muscles; dewlaps on the throat and neck; a big black nose; relatively small, thinly fleshed drop ears hanging onto the cheeks; and a tapered hanging tail. The short, hard, close-lying coat is colored red, brown, or black, with a few small white markings permissible. Patient, yet fearless and willing to fight,

Golden Retriever

Sporting Group

American Cocker Spaniel

An excellent bird and small-game hunter, this breed is famed as one of the world's most popular household pets.

Background Notes

This breed was created by crossing setters and spaniels. During the seventeenth century, it was divided into water and land spaniels, the latter group being further divided into big and small spaniels. Further selection from the smaller ones created cockers and toy dogs. The cocker spaniel is considered the smallest of the sporting breeds; its name comes from its superb ability to ferret out woodcocks. Introduced from England to the United States between 1870 and 1880, the American form slowly evolved into a distinct breed that is extremely good at flushing and retrieving small game birds, especially quail. A perennial international favorite, ranked number one in American Kennel Club registrations of 1984, this breed was featured in Disney's classic cartoon film *Lady and the Tramp* and became world famous. England developed a different line of the cocker spaniel recognized as the English cocker spaniel.

Key Characteristics

The sweetest in temperament and the smallest of the gundogs, the American cocker spaniel has a short, firm body with a deep chest; shoulders that slope slightly from withers to loin; a wide, distinctly domed head with a clearly defined stop; an angular muzzle; long, low-set pendant ears; round, full dark brown eyes; and a tail that is customarily docked. Its straight or slightly wavy silky coat is fairly short on the head, but quite full on the ears, chest, abdomen, and limbs. Coloring includes solid jet black, other solid colors, and parti-color. The nose should be black, except that a liver nose is allowed for dogs with a solid brown or liver coat, and a red nose for dogs with a parti-color coat.

Free in spirit, extremely cheerful, speedy, an untiring hunter, and a companion always eager to please its master, this breed is also charmingly delicate, loving, and gentle with children.

Care and Exercise

Careful grooming for about forty-five minutes twice a week is definitely necessary. The hair on the head, chin, and shoulders should be kept cut neatly. Although readily adaptable to city dwelling, this dog needs sufficient exercise to keep it from becoming overweight.

F 3 years

Male: 15 in.
29 lbs.
....
Female: 14 in.
26 lbs.

M 2 years

M 7 years

Puppies and Training

Puppies are born in litters of four to six. Solid-colored dogs are born as solid-colored puppies, but parti-colored ones are almost completely white for two weeks after birth. Cockers are alert and easy to train. Daily lessons are best, but be careful not to give the puppies excessive attention as it tends to make them selfish and noisy.

F 2 years

Brittany Spaniel

A true all-around dog, capable of hunting, pointing, and retrieving, yet fully content as an urban household pet, this breed is smaller than a setter but leggier than a spaniel.

F 11 months

M 2 years

Male: 19–20 in.
33 lbs.
....
Female: 18–19 in.
29 lbs.

M 4 years

Background Notes

Said to have originated in the French province of Brittany, from which it gets its name, this breed is depicted in seventeenth-century French and Dutch paintings.

Key Characteristics

The Brittany has a deep chest; a rounded, slightly V-shaped head with a well-defined stop; dark-colored eyes; drop ears; and a tail that is naturally short or is docked to about four inches. Its parti-colored coat is white with orange, liver, or roan. The dark nose color should be in harmony with that of the coat. The Brittany is a gentle, friendly companion and is good with children.

Care and Exercise

Grooming consists of a five-minute brushing twice a week. Exercise is important, as lack of exercise will tend to make this dog nervous, and keeping it penned in will cause it to bark excessively.

Puppies and Training

There are six to ten puppies per litter. If necessary, the tail of a puppy should be docked within its first week. Training must begin early to get the puppies used to people.

Chesapeake Bay Retriever

One of the few American breeds created from English stock, this wavy-coated dog makes an active, water-loving duck hunter, as well as a friendly, gentle guide dog.

Background Notes

The ancestry of this breed is claimed to be two Newfoundlands, rescued in 1807 from an English brig shipwrecked off Maryland, which were bred to flat- and curly-coated retrievers.

Key Characteristics

Inexhaustible, strong, and energetic, the Chesapeake Bay retriever has a well-developed muscular body; a deep chest; a broad, rounded head with a medium-length muzzle; and yellow or amber eyes set wide apart. Its dense woolly undercoat is covered with an oily, short, dense, partly wavy outercoat (except on the face and legs, where the hair is straight) that ranges from dark brown to tan. White markings on the chest, abdomen, and paws are permissible for show dogs.

Gentle, friendly, and deeply loving with people, this breed adjusts to urban living as long as it gets adequate exercise. It is an avid bird hunter.

Male: 23–25 in.
65–71 lbs.
....
Female: 21–24 in.
55–65 lbs.

M 5 years

Care and Exercise

This breed needs plenty of exercise away from other dogs, as it tends to attack them.

Puppies and Training

The litter of seven to eight puppies will develop adult coloration within four months.

M 7 months

M 7 months

Clumber Spaniel

Rather stubby looking, yet quite reserved and intelligent, this heavy, very distinctive lemon-tipped white spaniel has a stealthy manner and a style all its own.

Background Notes

Unlike other spaniels that are named for their hunting habit or prey, this breed is named for Clumber Park, home of the kennels of the Duke of Newcastle in Nottinghamshire, England, and a traditional hunting ground for the British aristocracy. Legend has it that the Duc de Noailles, who had been keeping this breed for generations, sent some of his dogs to England around the mid-eighteenth century. Yet some say that the Clumber was indigenous to Nottinghamshire. This breed's stubby looks and heavy body are said to have come from basset hound and early Alpine spaniel blood.

Key Characteristics

In addition to its very distinctive short legs and heavy, squarish muzzle with strongly developed flews, the Clumber spaniel has a low, heavy body; muscular shoulders; a deep chest; a long, broad back; a massive, flat-topped, squarish head with a sharply defined stop; dark amber eyes partly covered by heavy brows; a long, heavily furrowed double neck; an upper lip hanging down over the lower one; low-set, broad, triangular-shaped drop ears; and a well-feathered tail that is customarily docked. Its silky, straight, and plentiful coat is long on the limbs and abdomen, and should be plain white with a few lemon or orange markings mainly on the head and limbs.

Calm, gentle, and extremely loving, this breed, unlike other spaniels, rarely shows its emotions. Slow but deliberate in its movements, it can sneak right up to its game bird quarry, which it loves to retrieve. This breed's combination of keen sense of smell, dignified appearance, and pleasant demeanor has attracted a number of dog-lovers, who have found it to be a comical and gentle companion for children, as well as a loyal watchdog.

M 1 year

Male: 18 in.
75 lbs.
....
Female: 16 in.
65 lbs.

M 2 years

Care and Exercise

The coat needs to be cared for frequently, and should be trimmed at least twice a month, especially if the dog is kept indoors. A good deal of walking is required to prevent this dog from becoming overweight.

Puppies and Training

Generally, delivery of the two to eight puppies per litter is normal, but occasionally a cesarean is necessary. Obedience training, beginning with easy commands, should begin as early as possible, usually about four months after birth, and as the Clumber learns slowly, patience and repetition are required.

M 2 years (left), F 2 years (right)

Curly-coated Retriever

Capable of working long hours in all types of weather and in the water, this powerful, agile dog of ancient heritage, with a distinctively tight-curled coat, remains a popular gundog, retriever, and guard, as well as a faithful companion.

Background Notes

The lineage of this breed is believed to extend back to the English water spaniel and the retrieving setter, as well as some Irish water spaniel, the St. John's Newfoundland, and poodle blood. It was first shown in 1860 at a Birmingham, England, exhibit. Later, it was introduced to New Zealand, and around the same time to Australia, where in both places it proved popular as an unsurpassed duck and quail retriever. The curly-coated retriever reached the United States in 1907.

Key Characteristics

Quite intelligent, and with abundant endurance, this dog has a strong, well-balanced, rather slim body; a deep chest; muscular hindquarters; a long, well-proportioned head with a gradual, almost imperceptible stop; big black or brown eyes; low-set triangular-shaped drop ears; and a tapered, moderately short tail that is held out. Its thick water-proof coat should be tightly curled over the whole body, including the tail, but should be smooth on the face. The coloring must be solid black or liver, with only a little white permissible.

A hard, all-weather worker, never hesitating to jump into icy-cold water, this breed is a loyal and calm household pet, but it does tend to be a bit wary of strangers, making it more suitable as a watchdog than other sporting breeds.

M 3 years

139

Male: 23–25 in.
64–77 lbs.
....
Female: 22–24 in.
55–70 lbs.

M 3 years

M 4 years

Care and Exercise

Despite its profuse curly coat, only regular brushing is needed. Full of stamina, this breed requires a lot of vigorous outdoor exercise, including extensive retrieval games and, if possible, time in the water. Dogs that get insufficient exercise and are kept cooped up tend to become moody and noisy.

Puppies and Training

Usually litters number eight puppies, which are colored at birth like their parents. Handled early on by a number of people, the puppies quickly become accustomed to human contact. Likewise, obedience training should begin very early.

English Cocker Spaniel

With its elegant body and most gentle demeanor, this medium-sized hunting breed, one of the oldest of the land spaniels, remains highly popular both as an ideal household pet and a show dog.

Background Notes

The spaniel is first described in an early eighth-century Welsh statute. In seventeenth-century Wales, the spaniel was used in woodcock hunting, from which his name "cocker" derives. In 1983 this name was recognized by the Kennel Club and was later fixed internationally. Despite the theory that it is the immediate ancestor of the American cocker spaniel, the English cocker was recognized as an independent breed in England in 1892. In the United States, these two breeds have developed independently since 1935, when crossing them was prohibited. They were recognized by America in 1946 as two independent breeds.

Key Characteristics

Compact but bigger than the American cocker, the English cocker spaniel has

F 3 years

M 3 years

F 2 years

a deep, well-developed chest; a firm abdomen; a straight back, whose top line gently slopes downwards from shoulders to loin; a slightly flat crown with a clearly defined stop; long, low-set ears; medium-sized dark or hazel eyes that are set apart; a straight, long nose bridge; a big nose; an angular muzzle; powerful, muscular jaws; strong, straight front legs; wide, muscular hind thighs; and a tail, customarily docked, set on the flowing line of the back.

Its silky coat of medium length is either straight or slightly wavy, soft, and dense, though short on the head and quite full on the ears, chest, abdomen, and legs. The coloring includes buff, black, and black and tan. Belton variations are in blue, liver, red, and lemon.

This breed is obedient, good mannered, cheerful, loving, gentle, and good with children. A speedy bird retriever full of stamina, the English cocker is a fine field dog, but will adapt to all environments, even to apartment living, if required. Like the American cocker, it usually keeps well fit, is easy to look after, and makes an ideal house pet.

Care and Exercise

This dog needs to be brushed only once a week if not a show dog. After a walk, however, careful grooming is needed. Sufficient exercise is required, as this is a very active dog.

Puppies and Training

I itters number three to eight puppies. Parti-colored puppies will grow darker, and blue roan ones also change color gradually. The tail should be cropped within a week of birth. Training should begin at an early age.

Male: 15–16 in.
24–33 lbs.
....
Female: 15 in.
24–33 lbs.

M 3.5 years

English Pointer

The English pointer is a hard-working hunter who displays its hunting instinct even as a puppy. The breed's name is derived from its ability to point to its quarry. This dog is an outstandingly able and one of the oldest bird retrievers.

M 2 years

Background Notes

Little is certain as to its origin, but the English pointer is thought to have the blood of the foxhound, greyhound, and bloodhound. This breed was popular in medieval France, Belgium, Germany, Spain, and Portugal. The oldest record states that it was in England in 1650. In the early eighteenth-century, this dog was admired for its outstanding bravery and concentration, and came to be used exclusively as a bird dog who lowers its body, raises a front leg, and points at its prey.

Key Characteristics

The English pointer has a firm, muscular body; a straight, strong back; a well-muscled loin; a rounded rump; shoulders that slope gently downwards; a deep chest; a long, moderately wide head; big, round, dark eyes; drop ears set level with the eyes; and a wide muzzle of the same length as the head. The short, thick, straight coat should be liver, lemon, black, orange, or white, with patches of the colors mentioned.

An ideal field dog with a strong sense of independence, the English pointer understands the basic purposes of its tasks and is willing to work; its stamina and devotion are outstanding among bird dogs. As it is also somewhat short-tempered, stubborn, and excitable, obedience training is very useful. Given thorough care and training from puppyhood, the English pointer becomes easy to handle and makes a good pet, one that is appropriate even for a person who has never had a dog. This breed is most suited to living

Male: 25–27 in.
50–55 lbs.
....
Female: 24–26 in.
44–50 lbs.

M 2 years

in a kennel outdoors, however, and living in an apartment or small space is not advisable.

Care and Exercise

This breed needs a light massage with a cloth for two to three minutes a few times a week. The pointer works extremely hard and is full of stamina, requiring occasional intense exercise.

Puppies and Training

The five to eight puppies per litter are lighter in color than their parents, but will grow darker as they mature. Some will show hunting instincts as early as two months old. If handled early and frequently, they will become accustomed to people. Thorough obedience training is necessary.

F 3 years

English Setter

The English setter has been a treasured English bird retriever for the last four hundred years. A hunter by nature, it has a graceful appearance, good agility, thoughtful-looking eyes, and a noble gait.

F 1 year

Background Notes

This breed is thought to have come from the Spanish pointer, water spaniel, and Spanish spaniel. Today's English setter hails from the dog created by Lord Edward Laverack, who devoted himself to the creation of a gentle setter breed.

Male: 25–27 in.
70 lbs.
Female: 24–25 in.
63 lbs.

F 1 year

M 2 years

affectionate with its master, friendly with other people and animals, it makes a loving house dog.

Care and Exercise

Daily brushing is necessary for a rich-looking and healthy coat. Occasional professional grooming is desirable. Thorough coat care is recommended after a walk, as the coat easily catches the seeds and leaves of plants. Originally an active hunter, this breed grows bad-tempered if retained in a kennel or kept indoors unnecessarily long. Consistent training and strenuous exercise is necessary for a good-natured dog.

Puppies and Training

The six to eight puppies in each litter are delivered without assistance and are easy to raise. Newborns are white for the first week; after this time, their coat colors will begin to change.

M 4 years

Key Characteristics

The English setter has a lean head with a clearly defined stop, an angular muzzle, and low-set drop ears covered with silky hair. A medium-length coat lies flat on the body. The legs, abdomen, and tail have a good amount of moderate-length hair. Coloring includes black, white and brown (tan), black and white, blue belton, orange and white, orange belton, liver and white, and white. Spots spread all over the body are preferred to big patches. The eyes are dark brown.

In a field, this dog lowers itself and waits until the hunter has fired, and starts to search for the quarry on the master's command. Gentle, good-mannered, merrier than any other sporting breed, the English setter is often called an aristocrat among dogs, for it keeps its distance from other dogs and cautiously approaches them with a prudent attitude. Quiet, loyal to and

F 2 years

English Springer Spaniel

The English springer spaniel has been an English hunting breed since the beginning of the eighteenth century. One of the larger spaniels, this breed has a well-balanced, springy body that makes it very attractive. Its charming facial expression makes it a popular domestic dog.

Background Notes

This bird dog was recognized as an independent breed in early eighteenth-century England. The name seems to have been derived from the dog's speedy dash for its quarry.

Key Characteristics

Merry and gentle, the English springer spaniel has a compact, well-balanced body; a wide, long head; dark eyes; and a tail that is customarily docked. Its coat is long and slightly wavy, and bushy on the ears, chest, abdomen, and legs. The coat colors are in liver and black with white markings; white and tan with black or liver markings; and liver, black, or white with tan, blue, or liver roan.

Gentle, cheerful, playful, calm, and affectionate, this breed is a good guard dog. Loyal to its master, it is also a fine gundog with good concentration. The English springer also adapts to city life.

M 3 years

M 1 year

Care and Exercise

Once-a-week grooming will keep the coat shiny and beautiful; professional trimming is required a few times a year. This dog needs plenty of exercise in a large space.

Puppies and Training

The average litter numbers seven puppies. Provided with early training, they quickly become accustomed to people and are easy to care for.

Male: 20 in.
48 lbs.
Female: 19 in.
48 lbs.

M 2 years

M 2 years

Field Spaniel

Small in number and little known, field spaniels are diligent workers, friendly, and make good companions. This well-balanced and extremely handsome spaniel deserves to become more popular.

Male: 18 in.
44 lbs.
....
Female: 17 in.
35 lbs.

F 11 months

Background Notes

Much of the origin of this breed remains unknown, though a long-bodied gundog that was popular in the late nineteenth century is thought to be its ancestor. It is a close relative to the cocker spaniel and springer spaniel.

Key Characteristics

Extremely agile and equipped with an astonishing sense of smell, the field spaniel has a muscular back and loin; a long head; a lean muzzle; drop ears that are longer and set lower than those of other spaniels; hazel or brown eyes; and a low-set tail carried lower than the top line of the back even when docked. It is shorter than the springer spaniel and taller than the cocker spaniel. Its rich, straight, silky coat is very shiny and slightly wavy. Coloring includes black, liver, golden liver, mahogany red, or either of these colors with tan.

A willing worker, the field spaniel is most fit for hunting in a big area. Gentle, calm, loving, and obedient, this versatile, useful breed is a good domestic dog and also a good watchdog.

Care and Exercise

The field spaniel needs to be brushed for five minutes twice a week. Trimming is necessary only a few times a year. As this is an active breed, it is important to let it run freely sometimes, if it lives indoors.

Puppies and Training

A litter of seven puppies is average. As with other breeds, the earlier the training, the better.

M 7 years

M 1 year

Flat-coated Retriever

This sturdy and powerful breed has Labrador retriever and Newfoundland blood. The beautiful mane makes it look very noble. Intelligent and cheerful, it adapts to any environment and gets on well with people and other animals.

Male: 23–24 in.
55–77 lbs.
....
Female: 22–23 in.
48–70 lbs.

M 2 years

M 3 years

Background Notes

By breeding a few other breeds with a cross between the Labrador retriever and the Newfoundland, this dog was perfected in England and made its first public appearance in a dog show in 1860. It became widely popular in the early twentieth century.

Key Characteristics

The flat-coated retriever has an angular body; a short back; a deep chest; a wide, flat head; dark brown or hazel eyes; and small drop ears. A feathery coat covers the chest, back of the legs, and the abdomen. If the coat is black, the nose should be black as well; a dog with a liver coat should have a brown nose.

This excellent water-bird dog is cheerful, noble, intelligent, and highly trainable. It is good with children and makes a fine companion.

Care and Exercise

Minimum coat care is sufficient; brushing will keep it beautiful. This breed loves to retrieve and swim, and needs to run outdoors freely and regularly.

Puppies and Training

Litters number from six to nine puppies, colored like their parents. Trained early, the puppies quickly become obedient and accustomed to people.

M 2 years

German Spaniel

This German gundog was created by crossing several small- to medium-sized long-haired breeds. Although small, it is an excellent hunter, strong willed, full of stamina, and willing to hunt in any environment.

M 6 months

Background Notes

The German spaniel was created in the early twentieth century by a German breeder, Frederick Roberth.

Key Characteristics

Resembling the German pointer, the German spaniel has a big nose; big, wide drop ears; a strong, wide muzzle with a scissor or level bite; strong teeth; thin lips; and a tail, customarily docked at the tip, that points upwards or is held level with the back. The coat is hard, thick, longish, and slightly wavy. Coloring includes black with tan or gray, stag red, yellow-red with light color markings, and white with red tones. The muzzle is chestnut. This dog shows outstanding hunting instincts, even on snowy, muddy, or marshy terrain. Endowed with endless stamina, it can easily hunt and chase quarry all day. The German spaniel indomitably attacks its prey, but is obedient and loving to its master.

Care and Exercise

Thorough weekly brushing is needed. During the hot season, the German spaniel loves to take showers. Sufficient exercise must be given, including occasional swimming.

Puppies and Training

Litters number four to seven puppies. Within a week after birth, the tails are docked at approximately one-third the length from the tip.

M 6 months

Male: 16–20 in.
48 lbs.
....
Female: 16–20 in.
44 lbs.

M 6 months

German Pointer

An all-around gundog, this pointer hunts prey from birds to small animals. An excellent watchdog, this energetic breed needs a considerable amount of exercise, but is easy to care for because of its sturdiness and short coat.

Background Notes

This breed comes in two varieties: short-haired and wire-haired. The short-haired is thought to have been bred by crossing the German bird dog and the Spanish pointer. A sophisticated pointer suited to all purposes, it is an excellent chaser and retriever, used to hunt pheasants, quails, raccoons, foxes, and even deer. The wire-haired German pointer is said to have been created in Germany around 1870, a cross between the short-haired German pointer and numerous other breeds.

Key Characteristics

The short-haired German pointer has a deep chest; a straight back; shoulder bones that slope gently downwards; a lean head; wide drop ears set level with the dark brown eyes; a big, well-developed muzzle; a dark brown nose; a docked tail; and web toes. Its short coat feels rough and hard. The coloring includes liver, liver and white, and black and white.

The wire-haired is similar to the short-haired, except that it is slightly

Short-haired, M 6 years

Male: 23–25 in.
44–55 lbs.
....
Female: 21–23 in.
40–48 lbs.

Wire-haired, F 1 year

longer than it is tall, with a short back sloping sharply downwards from the withers to the buttocks. It is also double coated, with a hard and wiry outercoat, and an undercoat that is thick in winter and thin in summer. Its thick eyebrows protect the eyes from thorns in bushes, and its whiskers and moustache are also thick. The coat color is liver or liver with small white markings, except for the head, which is liver and white, or brown.

Although slightly short-tempered, this dog can be a friendly companion and an excellent watchdog. An active breed that barks the most among all sporting dogs, lack of sufficient exercise will make him even noisier.

Care and Exercise

About twice a week, the short-haired needs to be rubbed with a rough cloth. Brushing is sufficient for the wire-haired, but careful combing is needed during the spring shedding period. Both the short-haired and the wire-haired need a considerable amount of exercise and should be controlled and trained thoroughly, as they tend to be mischievous with livestock.

Puppies and Training

The short-haired has an average of eight puppies per litter. They are born white and grow into adult coloration. The wire-haired has a litter of six to ten puppies. They are born liver or liver and white, and acquire adult coloration after five months. Both types need early training, beginning in the sixth week after birth. Obedience training should be finished by the time the puppies are six months old.

Short-haired, M 3 years

Wire-haired, F 1 year

Golden Retriever

This popular domestic dog has a soft, shiny, golden coat. Originally a gundog, it responds well to its master's requests, and also works as a guide dog. Its gentle, tender character is the charm of this breed.

Background Notes

In the early nineteenth century, hunting was a popular sport in England and Scotland. This created the demand for a bird dog who could move speedily both on land and in water. The setter, the water spaniel, and the curly-coated retriever were then crossed to create the golden retriever. An excellent gundog, the golden retriever boasts superb abilities in outdoor retrieving trials and in obedience training alike. The three champion dogs at the first obedience training contest held by the American Kennel Club in 1977 were all golden retrievers.

Key Characteristics

The golden retriever has a strong, well-balanced body; a short, straight back; a flat, wide skull; a wide, deep muzzle of the same length as the skull; dark brown eyes with a black outline; medium-sized drop ears set slightly toward the rear of the head; and a natural long tail. The thick water-repellent coat is soft, not quite "silky," but not rough, either, with feathering on the chest, front legs, thighs, abdomen, and underside of the tail. The coat color is beautiful, shiny gold, with the feathering slightly lighter than the rest of the body.

A gentle, loving dog, with a tender, intelligent facial expression, the golden retriever is good with children and

M 1.5 years

Male: 22–24 in.
64–75 lbs.

Female: 21–22 in.
55–63 lbs.

M 4 years

other animals, and friendly and loyal to its master. Well behaved and extremely intelligent, this breed works widely as a rescue dog and guide dog.

Care and Exercise

The double coat should be kept clean by weekly brushing and shampooing. It needs to be thoroughly dried, or skin disease may result. At least two hours of exercise a day is necessary, including occasional swims.

Puppies and Training

Litters number from six to ten puppies. Newborns are shaded gold, growing into the adult's dark gold in ten to fourteen months. The coat color may darken further between the age of fourteen months and five years. Puppies learn well if obedience training is started about eight weeks after birth. Make sure that they do not overeat and give them as big a kennel as possible, to allow for exercise.

Gordon Setter

A large breed created by the Duke of Gordon of Scotland in the late eighteenth century, the Gordon setter is the biggest of the setter family, with a beautiful, shiny coat and a sturdy, well-balanced body. Although it was originally an excellent gundog, this breed also makes a good house companion because of its loving nature.

Background Notes

Because of its beauty and abilities, this breed gradually gained popularity among dog-lovers after the nineteenth century, when the American politician Daniel Webster first imported it to America. It has since been modified every year to improve its hunting abilities.

Male: 23–26 in.
55–80 lbs.
....
Female: 22–25 in.
45–70 lbs.

F 6 years

M 2.5 years

Care and Exercise

Proper care must be given to maintain the coat's beauty and noble appearance. Lack of exercise will make this dog nervous and difficult to handle. Obedience training must be thorough, especially in the city, and it is necessary to walk or run the dog a distance of at least one mile a day. Because this dog has the setter's habit of pacing it does not adjust to living indoors.

Puppies and Training

The litters average eight very healthy and strong puppies. Easy to care for, they soon grow accustomed to a new environment and people.

F 2 years

Key Characteristics

The Gordon setter has a well-balanced, well-boned body; a strong, shortish back; a sculpturesque, sharp head; dark brown eyes; and a relatively short tail. The soft, shiny coat is either straight or slightly wavy, with feathering on the ears, abdomen, legs, and tail. The color is black, or chestnut, with reddish mahogany markings above the eyes, and on the muzzle, throat, chest, toes, inside of the hind legs, and underside of the tail. Black should not be mixed in with these markings, but white markings on the chest and black penciling on the toes is permissible.

Loving, cheerful, curious, agile, active, fearless, and brave, the Gordon setter is very gentle with children, and is ideal as a domestic dog. This breed is very quiet, understands its master well, and is highly obedient. Alert to strangers and sometimes aggressive toward other dogs, it also is suspicious in nature and makes a good guard dog.

M 3 years

Irish Setter

This oldest of setters dates back to the fifteenth century and has seen service as a gundog, a pet, and a guard dog. This breed is friendly and amusing, with an expressive face; its graceful wavy red coat gives the Irish setter an aristocratic look.

Background Notes

The Irish setter was developed as a bird dog, and was well accepted because of its peculiar habit of indicating the location of quarry by lying down. The breed seems to be a cross between spaniels, setters, and pointers. Its coat was red and white until the nineteenth century, when a chestnut red coat was developed. Today, red is the only color recognized by American standards.

Key Characteristics

Racy, noble in appearance, and well boned, the Irish setter has a straight back that slopes gently downwards toward the tail; sturdy, muscular loins; shoulders that slope moderately downwards; a long, lean head; low-set, moderately large drop ears with a neat fold at the top, hanging right behind the cheeks; brown almond eyes set wide apart; a deep muzzle with an angular tip; a long, straight nose bridge; big nostrils; strong, straight, well-boned front legs; slightly arched pasterns; firm, arched paws; thick, rubbery pads; long muscular hind thighs; and long lower thighs. Dark nails are preferred. The medium-length coat is soft and flat, not wavy nor curly, and is short on the head, the tips of the ears, and the feet, and long and silky on the back of the front legs, paws, hind legs, abdomen, chest, and tail. The coloring includes mahogany red and dark chestnut red with no trace of black. Small markings on the chest, throat, and feet are permissible.

M 4 years

Male: 25 in.
55 lbs.
....
Female: 23 in.
51 lbs.

M 7 years

Care and Exercise

Daily care is necessary to keep the coat and appearance beautiful. Although the Irish setter can live in the city, it has to be taken outdoors for regular, vigorous exercises. Lack of exercise can make this dog restless and difficult to train. It has a habit of pacing, but properly trained, it can walk without a lead.

Puppies and Training

Litters averaging eight lightly colored puppies are usual. Adult coloration appears as they grow. Too much exercise is not desirable while puppies are small. Constant contact with people will help them become accustomed to people.

Friendly with people, it makes a good pet, gundog, and watchdog. An excitable character is a shortcoming that is largely due to lack of proper training and exercise.

M 4 years

M, F 2 months

Irish Red and White Setter

White-based with beautiful red patches, this breed somewhat resembles the Irish setter in appearance and abilities. Despite its small size, it is an agile and ideal gundog. A loving and gentle nature makes this dog a good house pet and a companion.

Background Notes

This breed has been known since the eighteenth century, but was not shown until 1987 in England, in the Craft Exhibition.

ly shorter and wider body, and a shorter and less profuse coat. Loyal to its master and excellent at work, the Irish red and white setter is cheerful, loving, and especially good with children. It also makes a good hunting dog and gundog.

Care and Exercise

The coat needs to be brushed once or twice a month. This small-sized but energetic dog needs a daily walk.

Puppies and Training

The three to five puppies per litter are strong and easy to raise. The tail should be docked within one week of birth.

M 3 years

M 2 years

Male: 23–25 in.
51–66 lbs.
....
Female: 21–23 in.
44–62 lbs.

Key Characteristics

Heavy in bone, the Irish red and white setter has a muscular body; a deep chest; a firm back and loin; a wide, domed head with a clearly defined stop; slightly prominent, round dark eyes; pendant ears set level with eyes; an angular, sharp muzzle with a scissor bite; and arched and moderately muscled powerful jaws. The tapering tail is thick at the joint, well feathered, and carried level with the back or hanging. The bushy coat is long and shiny, with a sight wave permissible. The color is a clear parti-color on a white base, with red patches of various sizes. Compared with the Irish setter, the red and white has smaller and higher-set ears, a slight-

F 3 years

Irish Water Spaniel

The tallest of the spaniel family, the Irish water spaniel is a breed of great antiquity. With its tight ringlets and mousy tail, this dog looks like no other. It loves to swim.

Background Notes

The Irish water spaniel is said to have existed for six thousand years, although much of its origin remains unknown. A similar dog has been excavated from old Roman remains. Supposedly this breed once worked in Ireland as a water-bird retriever. It was officially recognized in England in 1859 and first appeared in an American dog show in 1877.

Key Characteristics

The Irish water spaniel has a roundish body; a chiseled face; long, low-set pendant ears; a long, mousy tail; dark hazel eyes; and a liver nose. The thick ringleted coat is hard, rough, and invariably liver in color.

Gentle and calm, the Irish water spaniel makes a loyal domestic dog if it has proper training. This breed's long history of hunting has made it a dog with a strong sense of independence, requiring an environment that allows considerable freedom.

M 3 years

M 9 years

Male: 21–23 in.
55–61 lbs.
Female: 20–22 in.
45–58 lbs.

Care and Exercise

This dog needs careful coat care. A minimum of one hour of trimming weekly is necessary to keep its curls tidy. Active and needing a lot of exercise, it is not a city dog. It should be allowed to swim as often as possible.

Puppies and Training

The four to twelve puppies in each litter need to begin living with people at a very young age so that they will grow accustomed to humans.

M 3 years (left), M 2 years (right)

Italian Spinone

A breed from ancient France and Italy, the Italian spinone is an excellent gundog with a good bone structure and strong muscles, and is a capable and willing worker in all weathers and on rough terrains.

Background Notes

The Italian spinone has long been praised by Italian hunters and horse riders for its outstanding ability to hunt in forests and swamps. It is claimed that this breed comes from the French griffon, though some say that it has the blood of the German pointer. The general view, derived from its overall appearance, is that this dog is a cross between a pointer and a foxhound.

Key Characteristics

Medium-sized, the Italian spinone has an angular body contour; that is, its body height and length are approximately the same. Other physical characteristics include a longish head with a wide skull; a slightly arched, long nose bridge; a slightly angular muzzle; strong jaws with a scissor bite; round wide-open eyes; triangular hanging ears touching the cheeks; and a tail carried level with the rump or slightly below. The long, hard coat is dense, thick, and lies flat on the body. Coloring includes white, white and liver or chocolate, and white and orange. Black is not permissible.

This breed is gentle, loving, sociable, and patient, with an intelligent expression.

Care and Exercise

This dog should be brushed hard once a week. Combing is needed around the mouth. Full of stamina, the Italian spinone requires a good deal of exercise, including occasional running.

Puppies and Training

The five to ten puppies per litter are delivered easily. They are relatively strong and easy to raise.

F 5 years

M 1 year

Male: 23–27 in.
70–81 lbs.
....
Female: 23–25 in.
62–70 lbs.

F 2 years

Kooikerhondje

An indigenous Dutch dog, the kooikerhondje has long worked as an able assistant to duck hunters. A glamorous dog depicted in old paintings, it is now popular as a companion.

M 3 years

F 7 years

Male: 14–16 in.
20–24 lbs.
....
Female: 14–16 in.
20–24 lbs.

Background Notes

The kooikerhondje was named for a Dutch duck hunting technique that has been practiced for several centuries. In this method, the kooikerhondje's job was to go to the canal where wild ducks were resting and to chase them into a net at the edge of the canal. This method is no longer in use except for scientific research.

Key Characteristics

Resembling a small-size setter and spaniel, the kooikerhondje has a small head, a lean muzzle, and drop ears set high and forward. A slightly wavy long coat covers the whole body, and the tail is well feathered. The coat color is red and white. This cheerful, intelligent, delicate, and gentle dog is obedient and loyal, and loves to work for and to be with its master.

Care and Exercise

Despite its length, the coat is easy to maintain. The long coat should be combed and the short be brushed once a week. A daily walk is enough exercise.

Puppies and Training

The three to six puppies born in each litter are easily whelped, strong, and easy to raise.

M 3 years

Labrador Retriever

A breed from Newfoundland Island who worked there helping fishermen, the Labrador was imported to England in the early nineteenth century. It served first as a mine detector during the war, then as a guide dog and police dog. Its strong body and gentle, intelligent nature have gained this dog great popularity.

M 6 months

Background Notes

The Labrador was first brought to England on a ship carrying salted codfish. On Newfoundland Island, it worked collecting fish that fell out of the fish nets, and was also excellent at retrieving water birds. This dog has further proved to be an excellent military dog, as its strong sense of smell allows it to detect mines buried deep in the ground.

Key Characteristics

The Labrador retriever has an intrepid appearance, with a short, wide, strongly built body; a wide chest; a short, straight back; well-muscled hind legs; long shoulders that slope moderately downwards; a firm abdomen; a broad skull with a slight stop; rather small drop ears that are wide where they join the head, and that touch the cheeks and are set far back; strong jaws; and eyes that are usually brown but can be hazel or yellow or black. The tail joint is round and thick, gradually taper-

M 4 years

ing toward the tip. The front legs are straight and well boned; the hind legs, strong. The thick, short coat with no wave is black, yellow, or chocolate. Small white stars on the chest are permissible.

Good-natured, loyal, and hardworking, this breed is more patient than the golden retriever. Popular as a show dog, it is also stable, calm, and excellent as a guard dog, gundog, and domestic pet. This breed accepts any given task with a sense of enthusiasm. Although it is well rounded, adaptable, and able to endure long hours of training, it is undesirable to keep the Labrador in a locked space. It is a good companion for children and other dogs, and it loves to work and to socialize. It is never aggressive, but the more training and opportunities this dog has to mingle with people and animals, the more friendly it will be. Frequent excursions will help socialize the Labrador.

Care and Exercise

A minimum amount of light brushing every day will keep the coat shiny. This breed needs daily contact and regular, vigorous exercise, including swimming, as it loves to swim.

Puppies and Training

The seven to eight puppies per litter are born with adult coloration and are easy to train and raise.

Male: 22–24 in.
59–75 lbs.
....
Female: 21–23 in.
55–70 lbs.

F 2 years

Large Munsterlander

A good hunter's helper with much patience, this dog is willing to work in forests, fields, or even in water, and in all weather, including rain and snow. It is a brave retriever, watchdog, and capable guard dog for livestock.

Background Notes

This breed is a cross between the spaniel family and the German long-haired pointer and was first bred in the early nineteenth century in the German city of Münster.

Key Characteristics

Tireless and tough, the large Munsterlander has a lean head; a sharp muzzle; dark eyes slightly covered by the eyelids; not-very-long ears; and a docked tail held level with the rump. The long coat is white with black patches or stars all over. An all-black coat is undesirable. The general appearance resembles that of the German long-haired pointer. This dog is brave, fearless, cheerful, intelligent, and extremely obedient.

Care and Exercise

The coat needs to be brushed twice a week, and the long area should be combed once a week. Daily exercise on a leash is necessary and occasional free exercise in a field is desirable.

M 4 years

Male: 23–25 in.
48 lbs.
....
Female: 23–24 in.
44 lbs.

F 10 months

M 4 years

Puppies and Training

The mother takes loving care of each litter of four to eight puppies, making them easy to raise.

Nova Scotia Duck Tolling Retriever

The smallest of the retriever family, this breed works as a tolling dog, which means a dog that is used to attract game. Strong and reliable, it never hesitates to jump into icy-cold water. It is an excellent hunter and an obedient companion.

F 1 year

Male: 20 in.
51 lbs.
....
Female: 20 in.
51 lbs.

F 1 year

Care and Exercise

This dog needs only occasional brushing except during the shedding season. Daily exercise on a leash and occasional free exercise in a field is required.

Puppies and Training

The four to six puppies in each litter are carefree, obedient, and easy to raise.

Background Notes

This breed is indigenous to Nova Scotia, Canada, where it was bred by crossing the indigenous Indian dog, the cocker spaniel, the setter, and the collie. A hunting contest for Nova Scotia duck tolling retrievers still takes place in Canada today.

Key Characteristics

The smallest of the retriever family, this breed has a flat skull, high-set V-shaped ears that bend forward, and a scissor bite. The smooth coat is of medium length on the body and long on the tail. The coat color is red, with white on the chest and nose permissible. The eyes and nose are light colored. This extremely cheerful breed is easily trained, making it a popular house pet.

M 1 year

Pont-Audemer Spaniel

A small breed from southern France, the Pont-Audemer spaniel surpasses all other spaniels in its ability to hunt in swamps. An all-round hunter who works in fields, mountains, and plains, it is more popular today as a house pet.

Background Notes

This breed was created in Pont-Audemer, France, as a cross between the old French spaniel and the Irish water spaniel. An excellent retriever, it combines speed and stamina. Dog lovers are attracted by this dog's gentle facial expression, but it is still largely unknown outside southern France.

Key Characteristics

Compact and energetic, the Pont-Audemer spaniel has a round skull; small dark amber eyes; a pointed brown nose; pendant ears covered with plenty of hair; and an always cheerfully wagging tail that is docked at one-third the original length. The rich coat forms a long, shiny mane around the neck. The

M 3 years

F 5 years

Male: 20–23 in.
40–53 lbs.
....
Female: 20–22 in.
37–51 lbs.

M 3 years

coat color is grayish chestnut, which reflects light well. This dog is energetic on the hunting field and quiet at home.

Care and Exercise

The curly coat needs frequent brushing. This breed loves exercise. Daily exercise is required, and occasional swimming is important.

Puppies and Training

Each litter numbers four to eight puppies, which are well cared for by the mother. Puppies easily grow accustomed to people.

M 8 years

Portuguese Water Dog

Although this web-footed, excellent swimmer is agile and quick to react to its surroundings, it keeps calm, making it both a popular house pet and a working dog.

M 4 years

M 4 years

Background Notes

This breed is believed to have come from the Algarve, Portugal, where it has worked with fishermen for over a century, retrieving the fish that escape from fishnets.

Key Characteristics

Strong and beautifully built, the Portuguese water dog has a wide head, a slightly lean muzzle, and black or brown eyes. For swimming ease, the thick curly or wavy coat needs to be either lion clipped (face clipped and body clipped from the last rib, leaving a mane on the forequarters) or working-retriever clipped (clipped all over except on the head and limbs), with long hair left on the tip of the tail. Coloring includes black, brown, and grayish white.

Care and Exercise

The ears need to be cleaned every week, especially after swimming, to prevent diseases. Exercise should consist of free exercise in a big space and swimming.

Puppies and Training

The four to eight puppies in each litter are delivered easily.

M 4 years

Male: 20–23 in.
42–59 lbs.
....
Female: 17–21 in.
35–51 lbs.

Sussex Spaniel

The Sussex spaniel has charming big eyes and long eyebrows, and is cheerful and gentle with people. The legs are short and its tail customarily docked; the bushy coat is easy to care for. Not only is this spaniel an excellent gundog, but it also makes a good house pet for children.

Male: 16 in.
40–44 lbs.
....
Female: 15 in.
35–42 lbs.

F 4 years

Care and Exercise

A ten-minute brushing twice a week is enough. The Sussex spaniel loves outdoor exercise and needs a good deal of it.

Puppies and Training

The five to six puppies per litter are born brown, growing into a golden color as they mature. Puppies are of weak constitution until they are six months old, and females have a high death rate. Although this breed is not very quick to learn, it is resolute, and may be trained to be an excellent, attentive guard dog.

Background Notes

This old English breed was first recognized by the Kennel Club. Its coat has distinctive tones of gold and liver. Developed as a gundog and a house dog, it is still uncommon in the United States.

Key Characteristics

Low in height, the Sussex spaniel has a long, muscular, strong body; a well-developed broad chest; a sturdy back; a long, broad head with a pronounced stop; long eyebrows above big hazel eyes; a lightly hanging muzzle; and a low-set docked tail. The dark golden liver coat is straight and slightly oily on the abdomen, with feathering on the ears, legs, buttocks, and tail.

Unlike other spaniels, this breed is calm but stubborn. At the same time, it is cheerful, gentle, and makes a good house pet, especially for children. Although known as a gentle companion, this dog is not widely bred and is difficult to obtain.

F 4 years

F 4 years

Vizsla

The smartly built vizsla, a gundog used to hunt hares and water birds in Hungary, became popular after World War II. Although its appearance is somewhat daunting, this dog is gentle and loving.

Background Notes

A tenth-century lithograph depicting this breed has generated a theory that it once lived with the Magyars of Hungary. In this rural environment, the vizsla worked as a hunter along with pointers. Equipped with a strongly built body and a good sense of smell, this dog caught quails and hares hiding in tall bushes.

The two world wars saw a dramatic decrease in the number of vizslas. During the Russian occupation of Hungary in 1945, most of the vizslas were taken out of the country by fleeing citizens, making this dog almost extinct in its own country. Vizslas were bred in Italy, Austria, and Germany, and were recognized in 1960 by the American Kennel Club.

Key Characteristics

Low in height, the vizsla has a sturdy, broad body resembling the pointer's; a deep chest; a top line that is rounded from loin to the tail joint; a lean, muscular head; a skull that is wide between the ears; thin low-set ears hanging down close to the cheeks and rounded at the tips; medium-sized deep-set eyes with white around the eyeballs, the color of the irises harmonizing with the coat; an angular brown nose; a square, tapering muzzle with a slight stop; and a tail that is docked, leaving two-thirds of the original length. The short, straight coat, lying flat on the body, is thin and silky on the ears. The coat color is russet gold; small white markings on the chest and feet are acceptable.

F 1 year

Male: 22–25 in.
44–66 lbs.
....
Female: 21–23 in.
44–66 lbs.

F 1 year

This is a dog most fitted to live in the country. It cannot adjust to the suburbs, let alone the city, and these environments often make it ill. An excellent gundog, a properly trained vizsla makes a good house pet, as it is calm and loving.

Care and Exercise

The coat needs to be brushed for a couple of minutes a few times a week. The vizsla, a hunter by nature, needs a considerable amount of exercise. Kept indoors, it tends to grow destructive and violent, so it must be taken out every day for a long run.

Puppies and Training

The six to eight puppies per litter are born with adult coloration. The tail should be docked within a week of birth. Basic training should be started when puppies are two months old, general training at six months. Although this breed is extremely intelligent, some dogs find it difficult to be trained as a house pet. Early contact with people prevents puppies from becoming shy.

M 2 years

Weimaraner

Striking in its beautiful, smooth coloration of gray, the weimaraner is a breed long treasured by the aristocrats of Weimar, Germany. Agile and speedy, a hunter for large animals, this dog needs to be trained thoroughly.

M 2 years

M 2 years

Background Notes

This noble German dog, said to have been developed from the bloodhound, has a one-thousand-year history and is kin to the German short-haired pointer. Though its origin remains uncertain, a seventeenth-century Van Dyck painting depicts a light-colored dog very similar to the weimaraner, and in the nineteenth century it was treasured by German nobility. The weimaraner has an excellent sense of smell, and is gentle, brave, and quick. It hunts both large and small animals, which made it popular in Germany.

The bloodline was strictly controlled and the dog was bred under the Weimaraner Club regulations. Two weimaraners were first exported from Germany in 1929 by Howard Knight, American member of the club. The American Kennel Club recognized this breed in 1943.

Key Characteristics

The weimaraner has a straight back; a well-developed chest; sturdy limbs; a clean, angular head; high-set pendant ears; light amber or blue-gray eyes; a gray nose; and a tail that is generally docked six inches from the tail joint. The short, straight, shiny coat may be gray to silver; blue and black are disqualified.

Graceful and gentle, yet assertive, this dog has an aristocratic air. An agile, well-balanced hunter with good stamina, it is friendly, loyal, and obedient to its master.

Care and Exercise

Occasional brushing keeps the coat shiny. Thorough exercise is essential, and a sufficient space and good management for exercise are required. This is not a dog for the city.

Puppies and Training

The five to seven puppies per litter need to start playing with people at the age of seven weeks. Training should start between five to eight months of age. Properly trained, the weimaraner makes a good guard dog. Lack of training and exercise will make it aggressive and difficult. Professional training is ideal in addition to ordinary domestic training.

M 5 years

Male: 24–27 in.
57–77 lbs.
....
Female: 22–25 in.
55–70 lbs.

M 5 years

Welsh Springer Spaniel

The ancestor of this dog is the red and white spaniel depicted in ancient Welsh paintings and prints. Having worked for a long time as a hunter, it is now becoming popular as a pet because of its good nature and adaptability.

Background Notes

The Welsh springer spaniel is claimed to have been bred in Wales for more than four hundred years. Old Welsh paintings show that the red and white spaniel has existed for more than one thousand years, but some say that the Welsh springer, because of its appearance and the shape of the ears, is a cross between the Clumber spaniel and some indigenous Welsh spaniels. Because of its adaptability to all climates, the Welsh springer spaniel was exported to various countries including India and Thailand. It was called the Welsh cocker when it appeared in a dog show in the late nineteenth century, and was given its current name in 1902. Today the Welsh springer is popular both as a gundog and a pet.

Key Characteristics

Compact and well balanced, the Welsh springer spaniel is shorter in length and smaller than the English springer. It has a strong body; long legs; a short, straight back; a domed head of proportionate length with a clearly defined stop; an angular muzzle; relatively small ears hanging close to the cheeks; hazel or dark eyes; long muscular jaws; moderately feathered long front legs of medium length; strong, muscular hind legs; and a tail docked two-thirds the length from the tail joint. Its short, thick coat should be soft and silky with feathery ears, chest, lower abdomen, and limbs. Coloring should be rich red and white only.

Strongly independent, intelligent, calm, brave, and agile, this dog is good with children and other animals because of its cheerful, gentle, friendly, and obedient nature. Equipped with an excellent sense of smell, it can hunt both on land and in water. A tireless, strong gundog, it also makes a good watchdog and a house pet.

M 1.5 years

M 1.5 years

M 1.5 years

Care and Exercise

The coat will remain beautiful if brushed twice a week. Occasional professional trimming is desirable. The Welsh springer spaniel is an active breed, needing a lot of outdoor activity to keep it calm and satisfied.

Puppies and Training

The six to ten puppies in each litter mature to adult size in nine months. It is desirable to keep them as close to people as possible from a very early age. Obedience training and retrieval exercises can be started at six months of age.

Male: 19 in.
37 lbs.
....
Female: 19 in.
37 lbs.

Wetterhoun

For more than sixteen hundred years, this extremely strong breed has been used in otter hunting in Holland. Excellent at working in water, it has great stamina.

Background Notes

For many centuries the wetterhoun was bred as a hunter by the Frisians, who lived and preserved a peculiar culture and language on the Frisian Islands. Its ancestor is certainly the European water dog, but the tail curling up over the back shows that it may be also related to Scandinavian dogs.

Key Characteristics

Medium-sized, the wetterhoun has an angular head; a muzzle that is lean toward the nose but not pointed; firm lips; strong teeth with a scissor bite; medium-sized brown eyes; spatulate ears covered with wavy hair; and a curled tail. A thick, curly coat covers the whole body except the head, which is smooth; oily to the touch the coat repels water. Coloring includes black, liver, black and white, and liver and white.

Active, brave, and fearless, this dog can work for long hours in water. It can be aggressive to other pets.

Care and Exercise

Only light brushing is needed, except during the shedding season, when dead hair must be carefully brushed out. A sufficient amount of exercise should be given daily.

Puppies and Training

The four to six puppies in each litter must have obedience training when young.

F 1 year

F 1 year

F 1 year

Male: 21 in.
33–44 lbs.

Female: 21 in.
33–44 lbs.

Beagle

Hound Group

Afghan Hound

One of the oldest breeds, with a history dating back six thousand years, the Afghan hound is an elegantly built dog with a beautiful long coat. Its aristocratic appearance has made it a more popular show dog than a gundog, which it once was.

M 5 years

Male: 27 in.
59 lbs.
....
Female: 25 in.
51 lbs.

Background Notes

Originally from Afghanistan, this dog once worked protecting sheep and cattle and even hunting leopards and gazelles. Until the early twentieth century, it was called the Eastern greyhound or the Persian greyhound. A Persian hound known as Zardin made an appearance in an English dog show in 1907, and became the base of today's Afghan hound. Once a ruthless hunter, the Afghan hound was later modified into an obedient, gentle dog.

Key Characteristics

Tall and lean, resembling the greyhound, the Afghan hound has prominent hip-bones that make it well adapted to run in fields; a not-too-narrow skull with a prominent occiput; a long face; and teeth with a level bite. It has a long,

M 3 years

silky coat on the flanks, thighs, legs, tail, and feet and a long topknot on the dome of the head; the coat is short on the forehead, shoulders, back, and tip of the tail. Coloring includes fawn, gold, cream, red, blue, white, gray, brindle, and tricolor. White markings on the head are highly undesirable. The Afghan hound has a tendency to be aloof with people it doesn't know, which may make it seem cowardly. Dignified and assertive, though not aggressive, this intelligent and highly trainable breed makes a good guard dog.

Care and Exercise

Fifteen to twenty minutes of daily combing and brushing is necessary, especially where hair is long. The dog should be bathed two to three times a month, and the coat dried with a hair dryer. The inside of the ears must be cleaned carefully.

The Afghan hound loves to run and should run briskly outdoors for one to two hours every morning and evening.

Puppies and Training

Six to eight puppies are born in each litter. Some newborns may have jaw disorders, but most become normal by nine months of age. The Afghan hound is a sensitive breed, and it is desirable to wait until the puppies are eight to twelve weeks old before starting real training.

Basenji

Known as the "barkless hound," the basenji is an old breed that is indigenous to Africa. Despite this dog's small size, its firm body, erect ears, and curled tail show the unpolished beauty of its wildness. Curious and playful, the basenji loves to run in the woods.

Background Notes

Though details remain unclear as to its origins, the basenji is thought to have come from a purebred dog used by the Pygmies for hunting in the Congo. History tells us that the dog was also given to the pharaohs of Egypt by traveling high priests. It was first introduced overseas as the "forest dog" and the "barkless Congo dog." The present name basenji means wild and violent in Swahili, which suggests the once-aggressive nature of this breed. Today's basenji still remains slightly primitive in nature. Brought to America in 1930, this dog was recognized by the American Kennel Club in 1943.

F 6 years

F 6 years

Male: 17 in.
24 lbs.
....
Female: 16 in.
22 lbs.

M 3 years

Puppies and Training

The six puppies per litter are delivered with some difficulty. Mating occurs only once a year during a period of thirty days. Early handling will help the basenji to grow accustomed to people. The absence of such human contact will result in an extremely difficult adult dog.

F 2 years

Key Characteristics

The basenji has a square body, that is, its height and length are equal; an arched neck; a straight back; a head of medium length that tapers slightly toward the muzzle; erect ears; wrinkles on the forehead, giving it a meditative look; a black nose; dark hazel eyes; and a tail tightly curled right over the spine with its tip touching the side. The short, silky coat comes in chestnut, red, black, and black and tan with white on the neck, chest, limbs, and tip of the tail.

The basenji is obedient, cheerful, rather assertive and quite proud. It is suitable as a house pet, as it is quiet and barks little. When this dog barks, it sounds as if it is laughing or yodeling.

Care and Exercise

No special coat care needed. Use a mild shampoo for bathing. Despite the fact that its ancestors lived near the equator, the basenji adapts to northern Canada and Alaska. However, during the cold season, it should have a warm bed with a blanket and should be kept out of drafts. This dog is very curious and has a tendency to walk off aimlessly, so it should be exercised on a lead. It is extremely suitable for scent competitions using lures.

Basset Hound

With the head of a bloodhound and the body of a dachshund, the basset hound is humorous-looking and slow moving, with a mild facial expression. This dog is an excellent hunter, with an outstanding sense of smell and great stamina, and is also popular as a domestic dog as it is good with children and loyal to its master.

F 2.5 years

Background Notes

This old breed is said to have come from the bloodhound. Its extremely long ears, wrinkles above the eyes, and an excellent sense of smell support this theory. The name basset came from the French word *bas* (low), for the dog's short-legged, long-bodied appearance. It still hunts hares, pheasants, and other birds in its native country of France. In the United States and England, however, it is more popular as a house pet because of its appearance and facial expression. The basset was recognized in the United States in 1885.

Key Characteristics

The basset hound has extremely low-set, long, pendant ears, reaching well

M 2 years

beyond the end of muzzle if pulled forward; deep-set eyes with a haw sometimes showing; thick, short, well-boned legs; and big, firm feet. The hard, short coat is smooth and dense. Coloring includes black and tan and white, black and tan, white and tan, or any other hound colors.

This dog has a charming deep, sonorous bark. The basset hound is an excellent gundog, as it possesses an outstanding sense of smell and stamina. Absolutely obedient, devoted to its master, and willing to face any difficulty, this breed makes a good guard dog and house pet.

Care and Exercise

The coat should either be massaged or brushed gently to remove dead hair. The basset should be bathed two to three times a month. The long ears need to be frequently cleaned, especially inside. The basset hound tends to get fat without proper diet and exercise. Lack of exercise will also cause constipation and bloating.

Puppies and Training

Puppies, eight to ten per litter, grow fast. It's important that they are given sufficient calcium in their diet or they will develop bone disorders. Their ears can also become infected due to being bitten while the puppies are playing with each other. The basset is gentle and good with children, but lack of training during puppyhood can make this dog a stubborn adult.

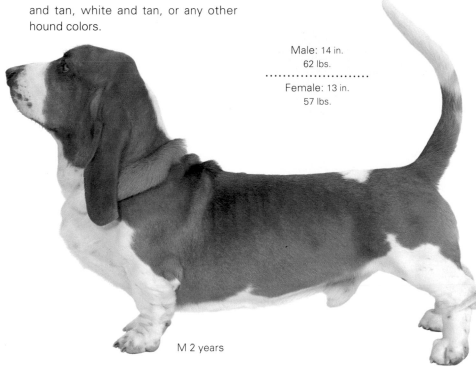

Male: 14 in.
62 lbs.
....
Female: 13 in.
57 lbs.

M 2 years

Beagle

Smallest of all the hounds, the beagle is named from a French word meaning "small." Its barking is subdued for a hound. Loving and calm, this breed is the most popular of all dogs today.

M 2 years

Background Notes

Although the beagle is a first-class family pet, it has a history as a hunter. During the Renaissance, it hunted in Wales and France, and was later acknowledged as the best hare dog among all the small hounds. Today, two to three beagles are used together to hunt hares and quails and are sometimes used in larger packs, as they were in the past. The American Kennel Club classifies the beagle into two groups according to its size, irrespective of its use as a show dog or a hunter.

Key Characteristics

The beagle has a squarish body with firm muscles; sloping shoulders; a moderately long, wide, domed skull that is slightly rounded at the back; high-set pendant ears; gentle-looking brown or hazel eyes set well apart; a straight nose bridge; an angular muzzle; a black nose with big nostrils; and a high-set tail carried gaily with a slight curve, but not curled forwards. The short, dense coat is glossy and smooth. The coat color is white and tan with black; other hound colors are permissible.

Gentle, loving, and responsible, the beagle is also a good guard dog. This dog loves to explore and often wanders off.

Male: 13–15 in.
18–20 lbs.
....
Female: 12–14 in.
13–15 lbs.

M 3 years

Care and Exercise

The beagle needs no special coat care, though it should be massaged from head to tail. A mild shampoo should be used for bathing. Exercise should be taken either on a lead or in a fenced area to prevent this dog from wandering away.

Puppies and Training

Seventeen puppies were recorded in one litter, but the average is five to seven. Puppies grow quickly and without any trouble. Mating beagles of different sizes can make delivery difficult. This dog may bark excessively if left alone. This, however, can be prevented by training. Dogs used as hunters should be trained to bark in a higher tone.

The beagle's habit of wandering away needs to be controlled. A collar with a name tag is a good idea.

M 2 years

F 3 years (left), F 4 years

Basset Fauve de Bretagne

Loving and quiet, the basset Fauve de Bretagne works bravely as a hunter and is a good family dog. Its popularity is growing in its native country of France, but this breed is still uncommon elsewhere.

Background Notes

This breed was created by repetitive crossing of the grand griffon Fauve de Bretagne and the basset hound. A strong sense of smell, inherited from the basset hound, makes this an excellent gundog, while a gentle, friendly nature makes it a popular family dog in France.

Key Characteristics

Brave, active, but quiet and calm, the basset Fauve de Bretagne has a basset-like long body; a slightly lean head; a short, thick, muscular neck; medium-length pendant ears; intelligent eyes; and a hanging sickle tail. The short coat is hard and dense. The coat color is fawn, with shades of other colors; white markings on the chest are permissible. Intelligent, obedient, and good with children, this breed makes a good gundog, house pet, and companion. As a gundog, it is strong and fearless, willing to jump into shrubs or thick woods for its quarry.

Care and Exercise

Coat care is easy, but a great deal of exercise is necessary for this energetic dog. Lack of exercise makes it fat and may cause illness.

Puppies and Training

The eight to ten puppies per litter must be put on a balanced diet, as they grow fast.

M 10 months

Male: 13–14 in.
35–40 lbs.
....
Female: 11–13 in.
31–35 lbs.

M 10 months

M 10 months

Bavarian Mountain Hound

A medium-sized hound, the Bavarian mountain hound is kept as both a house pet and a gundog. Relatively easy to care for, this dog attracts more dog-lovers each year.

Background Notes

Created by crossing the old Bavarian hound and the Tirolean hound, the Bavarian mountain hound was repeatedly modified in Bavaria, in southern Germany, to result in this energetic, agile breed. Because of its excellent sense of smell, it was largely used as a hare and bird dog.

Key Characteristics

Well boned, muscular, and sturdy, the Bavarian mountain hound has a strong, muscular back; a firm, tucked-up abdomen; a broad, slightly arched forehead; big ears hanging close to the cheeks; firm lips; clear chestnut eyes; and a

F 2 years

F 2 years

Male: 20 in.
55–77 lbs.
....
Female: 19 in.
48–73 lbs.

black or brown nose. Its coat is short, thick, and hard, and shiny on the head and ears. The coloring includes dark red and yellowish red with shades of bronze or gray.

This very brave dog is obedient to its master, especially during hunting, and a loving pet who loves to fawn on its family.

Care and Exercise

The coat needs to be massaged daily with a soft brush or a cloth. This energetic breed needs a lot of exercise on a lead; free exercise in a fenced space is desirable as well.

Puppies and Training

The four to eight puppies in each litter have a tendency to be nervous after delivery, so the mother needs to be kept calm and insulated from strangers.

F 2 years

Berner Laufhund

One of numerous Swiss hounds, the Berner laufhund is a descendant of the Nile dog. Extremely brave and active, this breed is excellent at hunting small animals and birds, and is also popular as an intelligent and gentle family dog.

M 2 years

F 1 year

Background Notes

The Berner laufhund is a breed of considerable antiquity. After being introduced into the Mediterranean islands and the Continent by the Phoenicians and Egyptians before the Christian era, the Nile dog became popular from southern Europe to the coast of England, and in Switzerland under Roman occupation. The Berner laufhund is treasured for its sense of smell and ability to chase, and is used worldwide to hunt hares and other small animals. It is also a capable bird dog.

Key Characteristics

Medium sized, the Berner laufhund has a lean body; a sharp, honed-looking muzzle; long cone-shaped pendant ears; dark, gentle eyes; and a tail that is slightly bent and carried horizontally or hanging down. The coat is short and dense. The coat is tricolored white, black, and tan, or varying tones of these colors.

Very intelligent and normally gentle, this dog is brave during hunting and willing to work despite all difficulties. Obedient to its master, it is very trainable, even by an nonprofessional.

Male: 16 in.
33–40 lbs.

Female: 17 in.
33–40 lbs.

Care and Exercise

Coat care is easy; brushing with a natural-bristle brush is sufficient. This energetic breed needs a lot of exercise, both on a lead and free, preferably in steep terrain.

Puppies and Training

The litters of four to seven puppies are easily delivered. The puppies are strong and easy to raise.

F 2 years

Black & Tan Coonhound

A large, fearless dog used to hunt even pumas, the black and tan coonhound has the blood of the English Talbot hound. This dog is gentle and hardly barks; however, the moment it corners its prey up a tree, it barks loudly in triumph.

Background Notes

Developed from the Talbot hound in eleventh-century England, the black and tan coonhound was first shown in America. Its bloodline includes the bloodhound and the American foxhound. Its bone structure and large ears are similar to those of the bloodhound.

Key Characteristics

The black and tan coonhound resembles the bloodhound, but is not as heavily boned. It has long pendant ears and hazel or dark brown eyes. The

F 2.5 years

straight and shiny coat is black and tan. It does not bark during hunting, unless necessary.

Gentle and friendly by nature, good with small children, this breed makes a good family dog.

Care and Exercise

This dog needs grooming two to three times a week. Extremely active, it requires a good deal of space for exercise and will be happiest kept on a farm.

As a gundog, it has to be exercised at least one hour a day. As a house pet, it should be allowed to run outdoors on a lead.

Puppies and Training

The record litter size is thirteen puppies, but seven to eight per litter is average. Delivery is normally easy. Newborns are usually black, with tan markings soon appearing on the legs and muzzle.

F 2.5 years

Male: 25–27 in.
86 lbs.
....
Female: 23–25 in.
79 lbs.

F 2.5 years

Bloodhound

An excellent hunter, the bloodhound has been treasured for centuries. The loose skin on the head and around the neck and the deep wrinkles give this dog a humorous appearance despite its strongly built body.

Male: 25–27 in.
90–110 lbs.
....
Female: 23–25 in.
81–99 lbs.

F 10 months

M 5 years

Background Notes

The bloodhound has a considerable history, probably dating back to ancient Greece and Rome. In the early eighth century, a hunting dog at a monastery in the Belgian highlands was named after St. Huberts, the priest who cared for it. After its migration to and modification in England in the eleventh century, this breed was later renamed the bloodhound. The name is claimed to have come from its habit of chasing a wounded animal, but some say that it refers to a pure-blooded dog. Its outstanding ability as a scent hound, superior to any other hound, has made the bloodhound highly useful as a search dog in police investigations in the United States, where it is used to search for missing children, criminals, and lost campers. This dog always works on a lead and is never used to attack.

Key Characteristics

Powerful, sturdy, big in size, but graceful, the bloodhound has thin, loose, wrinkled skin; a deep chest; a firm abdomen; long, wrinkled, low-set pendant ears; dark hazel, yellow, or brown eyes matching the coat color; a long, beautiful tail that looks like an otter's; strong, heavy-boned front legs; and powerful hind legs. His short, smooth coat is black and tan, reddish brown, or either of these colors in various shades. Small white stars on the chest are permissible.

Sociable, friendly, and gentle, this dog is especially good with children and

M 5 years

bloodhound needs to walk a few miles every day. Be sure to use a strong lead, as this dog is extremely strong in pulling. It needs sufficient outdoor exercise as often as possible, always accompanied by people, in order to be a calm, gentle dog. Running for hours in a fenced space is also good.

Puppies and Training

Six to twelve puppies are born per litter. Newborns are dark black and have no wrinkles. Some turn light-colored as they mature. The bloodhound takes an extremely long time to mature: two years for a female and three for a male.

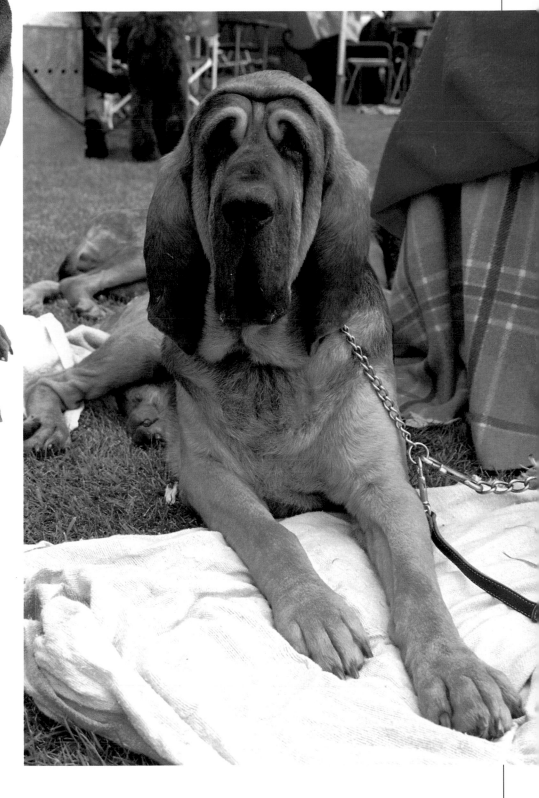

with other animals, though a stud dog may be aggressive or violent, especially with other male dogs. Though it can be somewhat stubborn, the bloodhound loves to fawn. It dribbles, but otherwise is a clean dog. This is not a dog for the city or a small space.

Care and Exercise

The coat has to be rubbed circularly to remove dead hair. Bathing is required only when the dog is dirty. The whiskers should be cut before a dog show. To prevent disease, the ears should be cleaned at least once a week. A consultation with a veterinarian is recommended if the dog develops unusual body odor. The nails should always be kept short, otherwise the leg joints could develop some abnormality. The

Borzoi

This breed was treasured by the great Russian writer Tolstoy and by Russian aristocrats. A tall, large dog with a streamlined body, the borzoi has a silky coat that gives it an aristocratic air.

F 1 year

Background Notes

The borzoi is claimed to be a cross between the long-extinct Lapp sled dog and the collie, and was developed at the end of the Middle Ages to hunt wolves and hares on the Russian plains. Known as the Russian wolfhound until 1936, it was renamed the borzoi, which means agility and speed in Russian.

This large, exotic breed quickly became famous, first among the women of the Russian aristocracy and later to the rest of the world through paintings and photographs. Bearing some resemblance to the greyhound, the borzoi is a sight hound capable of chasing its prey over a long distance. Used to hunt jackals in South Africa and coyotes in Canada, in North America this dog is popular in dog races that use a lure.

Key Characteristics

The borzoi has a streamlined body; a narrow thorax; a deep chest; well-developed hindquarters with a considerable angle between the thigh and hock, which provides flexibility; a strong, curved back, the sign of a fast runner; a lean, long face; dark eyes; a uniquely shaped muzzle; and a very long tail. The long silky coat is feathery on the chest, tail, and hindquarters. Any color is acceptable, though many are white based.

Sensitive, somewhat delicate, gentle, and playful, this dog loves to fawn and to play with adults and children. Although not quick to learn obedience, when trained it becomes a reliable dog. Besides being extremely expensive, the borzoi requires a great amount of exercise, making it an unsuitable dog for people who are inexperienced in handling dogs. The borzoi needs to be trained strictly, because it is somewhat stubborn. If there are other pet animals in the house, it is important to introduce this dog gradually.

Care and Exercise

No special care is required for this breed's coat; daily brushing is sufficient to keep it shiny. Daily exercise on a lead is necessary, and plenty of free exercise outdoors is highly desirable at least twice a week.

Puppies and Training

Litters may number more than six to seven puppies, but six to seven is average. The puppies grow fast, and too much exercise during puppyhood is undesirable. The amount of exercise should be gradually increased at one year of age, when running may begin.

M 2 years

Male: 28–34 in.
75–106 lbs.

Female: 26 in.
59–86 lbs.

F 1 year

Cirneco dell'Etna

The cirneco dell'Etna is a medium-sized hunter from Sicily, Italy, where it is still used to hunt hares and game birds in the area of Mount Etna. Fearless, tireless, and full of dignity, despite his size, this dog is popular worldwide as a dog who does not bark very much.

Background Notes

Indigenous to Sicily and developed only on that island, this dog is believed to have come from the greyhounds brought there three thousand years ago by the Phoenicians. An excellent hunter, it is also an excellent watchdog.

Key Characteristics

The cirneco dell'Etna has a muzzle like an ancient greyhound; big triangular prick ears; amber or gray slightly deep-set eyes; a liver nose; and a tail that hangs down like a saber when the dog is standing still. The coat is extremely short and tan in color, with white marking only on the chest.

Fearless, intelligent, dignified, loyal, tireless, and active, this multipurpose dog can serve as a hunter, guard dog, and family dog. Unlike other hunting dogs, it hardly barks during hunting.

Care and Exercise

Almost no coat care is required; an occasional massage with a towel will suffice. This dog requires a lot of daily exercise.

Puppies and Training

There are four to eight puppies per litter. This short-haired breed is naturally susceptible to the cold, and delivery during the cold season must be carefully conducted.

F 3 years

Male: 18–22 in.
22–26 lbs.
Female: 16–18 in.
18–22 lbs.

F 3 years

Deerhound

Modified from the ancient wolfhound to hunt deer, the deerhound is absolutely obedient to its master and very gentle with children. Of all the large breeds, this one makes the best-natured family dog.

Background Notes

Like its wolfhound ancestor, the deerhound was a large hunting dog indigenous to the Scottish highlands. The breed nearly died out by the end of the nineteenth century, but was brought back in this century by keen dog lovers.

Key Characteristics

A typical large greyhound type, the deerhound has a lean, long head; a pointed muzzle; small button ears; and a back that arches toward the loin, where it connects smoothly to the long tail. The coat is wiry on the body and long neck, silky on the jaws and ears. The coat is one color, preferably blue-gray, with light markings. The dog is absolutely obedient to its master and gentle with children.

Care and Exercise

The wiry coat should be brushed with a regular brush or a pin brush. This large breed needs a lot of exercise.

Puppies and Training

The eight to nine puppies in a litter weigh a little less than a pound at birth. It takes a male dog three years and a female two years to mature.

M 4 years

Male: 30–32 in.
86–110 lbs.
....
Female: 28 in.
75–95 lbs.

M 5 years

M 5 years

Dachshund

The dachshund is a long, low-bodied dog created to crawl into a burrow to hunt badger. This breed's unique appearance and cheerful nature have made it widely popular as a companion, a watchdog, and a family dog, although it was originally a hunter.

Background Notes

The ancestors of both the dachshund and the basset hound probably lived in Germany a few hundred years ago. The smaller one of these dogs was called the dachshund, implying that it was used for badger hunting (*Dachs* means badger and *Hund* means dog in German). Despite its small size, the dachshund dares to go into a burrow after martens and white weasels, and will attack much larger animals. Earlier in this century, the miniature dachshund was created to hunt hares. Most dachshunds are now bred as pets, though some in Europe, especially in Germany, are still used as hunters. The dachshund was given the nickname "sausage dog" after an American cartoon drawn early this century by Dud Hogan, who depicted a hot dog bun with a dachshund inside it instead of an ordinary sausage.

Male: 8–9 in.
11 lbs.

Female: 7–8 in.
11 lbs.

Miniature, smooth-haired, F 3 years

Key Characteristics

Classified into two variations by size, the standard and the miniature, the dachshund has a body twice as long as its height. The low, compact body is well fitted to go into a burrow. This dog has a wedge-shaped head; reddish brown or brownish black almond eyes; a long nose bridge; and long, wide pendant ears that are rounded at the tips. The coat comes in three variations: smooth, long, and wire-haired. The coat coloring includes red with tan or shades of yellow; black, chocolate, gray, or

Male: 9–11 in.
15 lbs.
Female: 8–9 in.
14 lbs.

Smooth-haired, M 3 years

Miniature, long-haired, M 2 years

Wire-haired,
M 2.5 years

Wire-haired,
M 2.5 years (left),
F 4 months (right)

white mixed with tan or black; and brown with gray or dark color markings. Humorous and playful, the dachshund is a good learner, a loyal companion, and an excellent guard dog.

Care and Exercise

The smooth-haired dachshund has little body odor and is easy to care for. Occasional but thorough rubbing of the whole body with a damp cloth will suffice. The long-haired dachshund needs to be brushed and combed daily, while the wire-haired needs professional trimming. It needs no special exercise, but it must never be allowed to jump down from a bed or a chair in order to avoid damaging its long back.

Puppies and Training

Each litter of three to four puppies is generally healthy and matures with no trouble.

Long-haired, M 2 years

Drever

An old hound from Sweden, the drever does not hesitate to attack large animals, although it is gentle, obedient to its master and good with children. Easy to care for because of its small size and short coat, the drever is suitable for a house pet.

Background Notes

Although much remains unknown about its origin, the drever is believed to have lived in Sweden for a long time, and was officially recognized in 1947. It was used to hunt hares, foxes, and even bears because of its strong body and fearless spirit. It would circle a bear, barking and jumping away if approached, until the hunter arrived. Though renowned in Sweden, this dog is uncommon elsewhere.

Key Characteristics

A small-sized hound, the drever has a lean head; gentle almond eyes; a white muzzle with a scissor bite; wide pendant ears of medium length; long, strong jaws; and a long tail that is not curled over the back. The thick, dense coat lies flat on the body and is slightly longer on the back and around the neck and buttocks. Any color is permissible, but some white is essential. Daring and fearless against any enemy or animals, the drever is very loyal to its master.

Care and Exercise

Brushing once or twice a month will suffice. A daily walk and plenty of exercise is required.

Puppies and Training

The four to eight puppies in each litter are delivered easily. The puppies are easy to raise, as they are healthy and friendly.

M 4 years

M 4 years

Male: 14 in.
33 lbs.
Female: 12–13 in.
29 lbs.

M 4 years

Elkhound

This breed's ancestor was a Scandinavian guard dog who protected villagers' livestock from wolves and bears. Compact and energetic, the elkhound has worked for a long time as a sleigh dog and as a hunter in the harsh climate of northern Europe.

Background Notes

Known also as the Norwegian elkhound, the elkhound has a history dating back six thousand years to the Viking era. It was introduced to America only in the early twentieth century.

Key Characteristics

Compact and squarely built, the elkhound has flexible, springy hindquarters; a V-shaped head; high-set prick ears; dark brown eyes; firmly closed lips and a scissor bite; and a tightly curled tail. The straight double coat is gray with black at the tip of the outer coat. Not large, but full of stamina, this dog has good scent and sight. Used mainly as a hunter, it is also suitable as a house pet and guard dog.

Care and Exercise

Regular combing and brushing is necessary, especially when the dog is shedding. This breed can adapt to a kennel or a house, as long as it is given a long walk on a leash every day.

Puppies and Training

Litters average seven puppies. Newborns are black, turning gray after one to two weeks. Puppies should be weaned five to six weeks after birth. Obedience training should start around the twelfth week.

M 3 years

M 3 years

M 1 year

Male: 20 in.
51 lbs.

Female: 20 in.
48 lbs.

Erdelyi Kopo

A cross between the indigenous dog of the Carpathians and the Polish hound, the Erdelyi kopo has an excellent sense of smell and direction. Obedient and quick to learn, it makes a good family dog.

Male: 21–25 in.
66–77 lbs.
....
Female: 21–25 in.
62–73 lbs.

Male: 18–20 in.
62–73 lbs.
....
Female: 18–20 in.
55–66 lbs.

M 6 years

M 6 years

Background Notes

The history of this breed dates back to the nineteenth century, when the Carpathians (the mountains in the east of Czechoslovakia and northern Romania) were under Magyar occupation. A Magyar dog crossed with an indigenous dog, further crossed with the Polish hound of east Europe, resulted in this breed, created for the unique climate and terrain of the Carpathians. The Erdelyi kopo is willing to hunt in forests, mountains, rivers, and in all weathers. The long-legged Erdelyi kopo is mainly used to hunt bear, deer, and large wildcats, and the short-legged to hunt foxes and hares.

Key Characteristics

Medium sized, the Erdelyi kopo comes in two types: the larger and long legged, and the smaller and short legged. It has a short, unpointed head without wrin-kles; somewhat obliquely placed dark brown eyes; a straight, thick nose bridge; very strong teeth; big pendant ears; firm paws full of elasticity and jumping strength; and a tail that hangs down when the dog is still and wags when it is hunting. The short coat lies flat on the body. The long-legged type is black and tan, with white markings on the forehead, chest, and tip of the feet and tail. The short-legged type is red-brown with white markings. Both types are fearless, obedient, loyal, intelligent, and very trainable.

Care and Exercise

An occasional brushing is all this dog needs. The coat will remain shiny if massaged with a chamois cloth. This breed needs a great deal of exercise.

Puppies and Training

The four to eight puppies per litter are gentle in nature and easy to raise.

Foxhound

A riding master and a pack of foxhounds create a lively hunting scene. The American foxhound, a relative of the English foxhound, is also an excellent field dog.

Background Notes

A cross between the hunting breed of the Normans and the English fox-hunting breed, the foxhound has been a much treasured house pet in England since the late Middle Ages. Once called the Talbot dog, it has been modified to suit the needs of hunters and the English climate, resulting in today's beautiful, skillful foxhound.

Key Characteristics

Beautifully built, the foxhound has a horizontal top line. The short, hard, dense coat is similar to that of other hounds in color and markings. The strong-willed English foxhound is an excellent field dog who hunts in a pack. The American foxhound, on the other hand, prefers to hunt alone. Gentle in nature, foxhounds make good family dogs. Provided with a good space for exercise, they can live in the city.

Care and Exercise

The coat should be massaged with a cloth or a gloved hand. If kept as a hunter, the foxhound needs a great amount of exercise. Dogs kept in a group of twenty to thirty tend to gain weight and require special attention to avoid it.

M 9 months

Puppies and Training

Five to seven puppies are born in a litter. Usually the mother has enough milk, and the puppies mature without any problems.

Male: 22–25 in.
66 lbs.
....
Female: 21–24 in.
62 lbs.

M 5 years

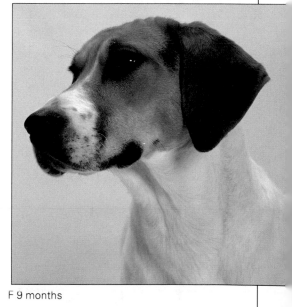

F 9 months

Greyhound

Dating back to ancient Greece, the muscular, streamlined greyhound is a well-known race dog today. Gentle and well mannered, it also makes a good family dog.

Background Notes

Well-known in ancient Greece and Egypt as an excellent sight hound, the greyhound was once called the gaze hound. A dog bearing striking resemblance to the greyhound in England in the early eighth century is on record.

F 4 years

F 5 years

Once used in all types of hunting, this breed became popular as a race dog with a reputation for being the fastest dog in the world. There are many theories about the origin of its name. One says that it is a contracted form of "degree hound," as it was once allowed to be possessed only by people with degrees. Others say that it derives from Greece. This dog was brought to the Atlantic coast of Europe by the Spanish around 1500.

Key Characteristics

The beautiful and graceful greyhound was built to race. It has a streamlined body beginning with the nose, ears, and arched neck to the loin and muscular hindquarters. While running, its long, thin tail works as a keel, and the ears are bent toward the neck. This dog has dark, shiny eyes. All colors are acceptable for the short, dense coat, including white and gray. Affectionate and sensitive, the greyhound is also competitive and strong willed, determined to win the race.

Tranquil at home, the greyhound is especially gentle with children and other dogs. It may become excited when approached by a small animal like a neighborhood cat. This dog needs a strictly controlled diet and a good deal of exercise, so it is an inappropriate breed for a busy dog owner.

Male: 28–30 in.
64–70 lbs.
....
Female: 27–29 in.
59–65 lbs.

Care and Exercise

The nails must be cut short regularly and the ears kept clean. Its environment should also be clean. Kept indoors, the greyhound tends to grow lazy and beefy. A strict diet and exercise on a leash as many hours as possible each day will prevent this from happening. Being run around a track by a professional trainer is also desirable.

Puppies and Training

Litters average ten to fifteen puppies. At delivery, the mother must be kept away from other animals so as to have enough rest. Human intervention is recommended if the delivery happens to be difficult. Male newborns weigh about one pound, and the tail may be damaged during delivery as it is very long. For best adjustment, puppies should be handled at an early age.

Hamilton Stovare

The Hamilton stovare has long worked in Sweden and other snowy Scandinavian countries as a bear and deer hunter. Due to its good nature, it is gaining popularity as a guard dog and a family dog. Short haired and medium sized, this dog is easy to look after.

M 8 years

Background Notes

Though theories vary about the origins of this breed, experts say that it was created from the Holstein beagle, Hanover beagle, Curlandian beagle, and foxhound, and named after Adolf Patrick Hamilton, its creator.

Key Characteristics

Muscular and sturdy, the Hamilton stovare has a lean, rectangular, chiseled head; a slightly arched skull; biggish black nostrils; a firm scissor bite; high-set hanging ears; gentle chestnut eyes; well-muscled long front legs that stretch straight from the shoulders down; and firm feet with thick, strong pads. The coat is thick, and the undercoat grows even thicker during winter. The coat color is black on the upper neck and back, chestnut on top of the head, and red on the rest of the body, with white on the legs, throat, chest, front half of muzzle, and tip of the tail.

Care and Exercise

An occasional massage with a towel is sufficient grooming. This breed is filled with stamina and loves to exercise. Gentle in nature, it makes a good walking companion.

M 8 years

Male: 20–23 in.
55 lbs.
....
Female: 18–22 in.
51 lbs.

Puppies and Training

There are four to ten puppies per litter. The mother and puppies are friendly, and the puppies are easy to raise.

M 8 years

Hungarian Greyhound

A hare and fox hunter with amazing speed, the Hungarian greyhound is also a racer who will chase a mechanical lure. Because of its good nature, it is gaining in popularity in Europe and elsewhere.

Background Notes

In the ninth century, when the Magyars invaded Transylvania, they brought along the ancestors of this dog. In the centuries that followed, these dogs were crossed with many others to create various types of greyhounds. Between the fifteenth and seventeenth centuries, these hounds were crossed further with the saluki, Afghan hound, and greyhounds of Turkish and Asian lineages, and in the nineteenth century, with the English greyhound to create today's Hungarian greyhound.

Key Characteristics

The Hungarian greyhound has a well-muscled arched loin; a lean head with a slight stop; a long, lean neck; ears that are laid back; a black nose; a thin long tail that turns slightly upwards; and lean, slim legs. The coat is extremely short and shiny. Coat colors include gray, black, brindle, dappled, and white, which is rare. Though not much of a scent hound, it is extremely fast. Gentle, loving, intelligent, friendly, and obedient to its master, it also makes a good guard dog.

Care and Exercise

The coat does not require much care. This dog should be exercised on a lead as much as possible.

Puppies and Training

The ten to fifteen puppies per litter should be handled at an early age so they will get used to people.

F 3.5 years

Male: 25–29 in.
59–68 lbs.
....
Female: 23–27 in.
48–57 lbs.

F 3.5 years (left), M 1 year (center), F 1 year (right)

Ibizan Hound

An ancient sight hound depicted on the tomb of Tutankhamen, the Ibizan hound has the ability to jump great heights, is agile, and now works as a scent hound and as a family dog.

Background Notes

This breed is said to have been used to hunt by the pharaohs of Egypt. Sculptures and paintings from ancient Egyptian tombs of around 3000 B.C. depict a dog bearing a striking resemblance to the Ibizan hound. This was discovered in 1922, when the tomb of Tutankhamen was excavated. In the eighth century B.C., Phoenician and Libyan merchants took this Egyptian dog on a ship to the present Spanish Balearic Islands, where it was named after the island of Ibiza. The islanders kept this dog away from other breeds and bred it for hunting hare. It was taken to the United States in 1956, and received official recognition by the American Kennel Club in 1979.

Key Characteristics

The Ibizan has a typical streamlined greyhound-type body, and the beautiful bearing of an ancient dog. Its body is also extremely sturdy, with a tucked-up abdomen; a long, narrow head; promi-

Male: 23–27 in.
51 lbs.
....
Female: 22–26 in.
42–48 lbs.

Rough, F 3.5 years

Smooth, M 3 years

Rough, F 3.5 years

nent erect ears set on level with amber or camel eyes; a pink nose; and a long tail that hangs naturally. The coat comes in two variations: rough and smooth. The coat color includes red, white, and red and white.

Agile and renowned for its distance vision, this dog does not weigh much, and is good-mannered and friendly with its family and other dogs. An obedient family dog, this is not a breed for a kennel, though it will adjust well to other environments. It is healthy and easy to raise.

Care and Exercise

The coat of this breed needs to be massaged thoroughly, followed by a light brushing and wiping with a damp cloth. The ears and nails must be checked occasionally. Drafts should be kept away from this dog's bed. Ordinary dog food is acceptable, but not cheap, low-quality food. An occasional long walk on a lead is required.

Puppies and Training

A litter of six to twelve puppies is delivered easily in most cases. Newborns weigh one pound on the average. If there are many puppies, a well-balanced weaning diet should be started in the third week. Handled at an early age, the puppies will grow accustomed to people. Firm training must be given, as they sometimes attack small animals like cats.

Smooth, F 2 years

Irish Wolfhound

The biggest dog breed, the Irish wolfhound can weigh about ninety pounds at six months of age. In late eighteenth century, it was used to hunt wolves and exterminated all the wolves in Ireland. Gentle in nature, this dog forms a good relationship with his master.

Background Notes

The national dog of Ireland, this breed was very popular among the nobility. Though the Irish wolfhound has been hunting wolves and other large animals since ancient times, details of its origin are unknown. In 1862, Capt. George Graham of the British Army tried to develop it as a rescue dog. The standard for this breed was established in 1885, and it was further developed to be the biggest dog. It was officially recognized by the American Kennel Club in 1950.

Key Characteristics

The Irish Wolfhound has a sturdy body that is longer than it is tall; an arched loin; a tucked-up abdomen; a deep chest, a long head with a slightly raised frontal bone; small ears that look like the greyhound's; dark eyes with little indentation between them; a long, moderately pointed muzzle; strong teeth with either a scissor or level bite; a long curved tail; well-boned straight front legs; and muscular hind legs. The rough, hard coat is wiry and long around the eyes and bottom jaw. Coloring includes gray, brindle, red, black, fawn, and white.

M 3 years

Male: 32–34 in.
119 lbs.
....
Female: 30 in.
106 lbs.

M 1 year

M 5 years

Tranquil in nature, this dog barks little, making it almost unfit as a watchdog. Its size, however, will scare away intruders. The Irish wolfhound is not a breed for inexperienced dog owners, as it is expensive and somewhat difficult to look after.

Care and Exercise

Daily brushing is sufficient if the dog is kept as a house pet. If kept as a show dog, dead hair must be removed and stripping is necessary. The ears need to be kept clean, and the nails must be kept short. The amount of exercise can be the same as for a small-sized dog, but this breed needs a big space to frolic in. It is not recommended that this dog be kept without a big yard and a high fence.

Puppies and Training

The record delivery is thirteen puppies, but the average litter is three to four. The puppies take twenty to twenty-four months to mature. While growing, they eat amazingly well, but once matured, the amount of food must be adjusted to their level of activity. Early handling by people and contact with other animals will keep puppies from being shy. In a home with children, this breed needs to be trained firmly to prevent it from acting wild.

F 3 years

Otterhound

Equipped with a water-repellent double coat and web feet, the otterhound loves water. Used to hunt otters, it is also an excellent gundog.

Background Notes

Though much remains unknown about the otterhound's ancestry, it is thought to have derived from the harrier and the water spaniel. There are two theories about its place of origin. One says that this breed was used to hunt otters in England during the reign of King Edward II (1307–27). The other says that this breed originated in France, as its appearance and double coat resemble those of the old French breed, the Wendy hound.

Key Characteristics

The Otterhound has webbed feet and a big head. A dog that is two feet tall should measure approximately one foot between the nose and the back of the skull. The outercoat is rough and crisp; the undercoat, woolly and water resistant. All coat colors are acceptable.

Generally cheerful and friendly, some of these dogs are stubborn. Energetic and willing to hunt, the otterhound is loyal to its master and makes a good guard dog.

Care and Exercise

The thick double coat needs a considerable amount of care. The otterhound loves to swim, which is convenient as swimming is good exercise. Fairly easy to look after, this dog will live for ten to twelve years.

Puppies and Training

There are seven to ten puppies per litter. The mother usually keeps calm and delivers the puppies without much trouble. Newborns weigh approximately one pound.

F 4 years

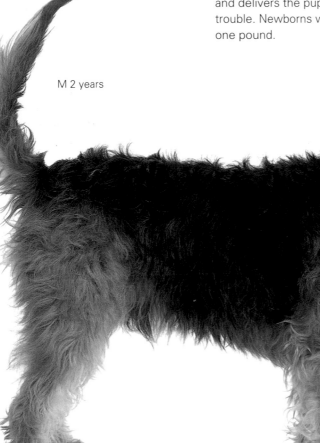

M 2 years

Male: 24–27 in.
75–114 lbs.
....
Female: 22–26 in.
64–99 lbs.

F 4 years

Petit Basset Griffon Vendeen

The smallest griffon Vendéen, this dog has great speed and is excellent at hunting hares, foxes, and deer. Very curious about its prey, it goes after it with enthusiasm.

Background Notes

The petit basset griffon Vendéen is thought to have originated from the griffon Vendéen. A scent hound rather than a sight hound, it is a reliable hunter still used for the task today.

Key Characteristics

The griffon Vendéen comes in four sizes, from big to small: grand griffon Vendéen, the briquet griffon Vendéen, the griffon Artois Vendéen, and the petit basset griffon Vendéen. All are good hunters. The petit basset griffon Vendéen has a long, narrow domed skull with a clearly defined stop; a long muzzle; big, dark eyes; a big, black

M 2 years

nose with open nostrils; narrow, thin ears that are set low on the head and fold inward; and a hanging tail that is thick at the base. The hard, rough coat is 1¼ to two inches in length. The coloring includes white with shades of orange and cream, and black and tan.

Fearless, full of stamina, and patient, this hard worker is loyal to its master, gentle and loving, and loves to fawn on its family. It is also suitable as a companion dog.

Care and Exercise

The hard coat requires brushing with a hard brush. Stronger than it looks, this breed requires a considerable amount of exercise, though speed is not particularly necessary.

Puppies and Training

The litters of from four to seven puppies are delivered easily. Puppies are very healthy and are easy to raise.

M 2 years

Male: 13–15 in.
24–35 lbs.
....
Female: 13–15 in.
24–35 lbs.

Pharaoh Hound

Like the Ibizan hound, the pharaoh hound is from ancient Egypt. Cheerful and gentle, it is very good with children. A newly recognized breed, this dog is quite rare.

M 4 years

Background Notes

Paintings in Egyptian tombs of 4000 B.C. depict dogs bearing a close resemblance to the pharaoh hound. It is said that several of these dogs were taken to Gozo, Malta, and Sicily by Phoenician merchants. On the island of Gozo the locals called this breed the rabbit dog. By 1968, eight pharaoh hounds had been exported to England and were recognized by the Kennel Club. This breed was not officially recognized in the United States until 1983.

and chest, and a fine white line in the center of the forehead.

Because of its strong hunting instinct, this dog will chase and catch neighbors' pet rabbits and cats. It is not a breed for apartments, but for suburban environments.

Care and Exercise

The coat has only to be brushed daily for a short time, and massaged with a rough cloth. Plenty of exercise on a leash and free outdoor exercise are recommended.

Puppies and Training

The litters of from three to seven puppies are easily delivered. The puppies grow fairly fast. They must be watched, as they often damage each other's tails while playing.

M 2 years

Key Characteristics

The pharaoh hound has a long, lean body; a slightly tucked-up abdomen; a flat, triangular head; big, high-set prick ears; amber eyes; a pinkish-brown nose; a foreface slightly longer than the skull; a long tail that curves when the dog is excited, but that is never curled over the back; and firmly knuckled feet like those of a cat. The short, shiny coat is rich tan with white on the tip of the tail, white star markings on the paws

Male: 23–25 in.
40–59 lbs.
....
Female: 21–24 in.
40–59 lbs.

M 4 years

Rhodesian Ridgeback

This extremely intelligent, all-weather breed is absolutely obedient to its master when properly trained.

F 7 years

M 1.5 years

Male: 25–27 in.
75 lbs.

Female: 24–26 in.
64 lbs.

Background Notes

Indigenous to southern Africa, the Rhodesian ridgeback is thought to be a cross between a Hottentot hunting dog and a dog in Cape Province. In 1876, it was taken to Rhodesia, where it became known as the African lion dog and was used by the settlers for hunting large animals. Exported to the United States in 1950, it was officially recognized by the American Kennel Club in 1955.

Key Characteristics

The Rhodesian ridgeback has an extremely strong, muscular body; a well-ribbed wide chest; a strong, muscular back that is slightly arched toward the buttocks; a big, wide head; drop ears tapering to a rounded point; dark amber eyes; a strong muzzle with a scissor or level bite; and a tail carried with a slight curve but not curled. The short, hard coat is dense, lying flat on the body. Very hard hair grows in a ridge along the spine. The coat colors are wheaten and red wheaten.

Care and Exercise

Provided with enough exercise, this dog needs no special care.

Puppies and Training

The litters of seven to eight puppies may sometimes be delivered with difficulty. Lack of obedience training makes this dog aggressive or nervous.

M 5 years

Saluki

An extremely old breed known since the Egyptian dynasty era, the saluki has worked for nomads hunting gazelles in Egypt, Arabia, and Persia. Slim and graceful, it is a great runner with inexhaustible stamina.

M 8 years

Background Notes

The saluki is said to have been highly valued by the pharaohs of ancient Egypt. This belief is based on a carving of a dog, which was excavated from nine-thousand-year-old Sumerian ruins, bearing a striking resemblance to the saluki. This breed was officially recognized by the American Kennel Club in 1927.

Key Characteristics

The healthy saluki should have ribs showing on its flanks. A streamlined greyhound type, it has a V-shaped head and big pendant ears. This breed has two coat types: a short coat all over, and a short coat with silky long feathering on the ears, tail, and legs. The coat coloring includes red and white, black and tan, white, fawn, cream, and gold.

Extremely strong-willed, intelligent, and alert, this dog is loyal and friendly to its family.

Male: 23–28 in.
44–55 lbs.
. . . .
Female: considerably shorter than male
31–44 lbs.

Care and Exercise

Daily brushing, however brief, is required. This dog's bed should be soft to avoid bedsores. A balanced diet and long hours of exercise are needed to prevent excess weight. Once this dog starts running, it has difficulty stopping, so it should always be exercised on a lead.

Puppies and Training

There are five to seven puppies in each litter. If handled at an early age, puppies will not grow nervous.

M 2 years

M 9 months

Sabueso Espanol

Thought to be the indigenous dog of Iberia, the sabueso español is a popular hunter of various kinds of game. With its strong body and great stamina, this dog is capable of working long hours regardless of the weather.

Background Notes

The sabueso español is said to be descended from a hound taken to Spain by the Phoenicians, and is of the same origin as other hounds widely distributed in Europe. It has lived in the Iberian Peninsula long enough to be acknowledged as an indigenous breed.

Key Characteristics

Despite its rather delicate looks, the sabueso español has a well-muscled, well-boned body; a longish head with a moderately domed skull; big nostrils with dark pigment; slightly hanging lips; big pendant ears; and a tail that hangs beyond the hock. The short coat is smooth and glossy, without feathering.

The coat color is red and white, or black and white. A variation of the sabueso español is slightly lighter, lower, and slimmer, with thin, elastic skin, and a dense, glossy coat. The coat color is red or black with white markings.

Loving, cheerful, good with children, and loyal to its master, this dog is wary of people it doesn't know.

M 3 years

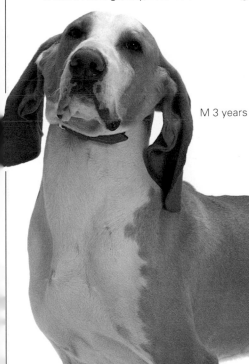

M 3 years

Care and Exercise

The short coat is easy to care for, needing only occasional brushing. This energetic dog needs plenty of exercise every day.

Puppies and Training

The four to eight puppies in each litter need firm obedience training.

Male: 20–22 in.
55 lbs.
....
Female: 19–20 in.
51 lbs.

Schweizer Laufhund

With an outstanding sense of smell among hounds, the Schweizer laufhund is very popular as a scent hound. It doesn't require a special diet, coat care, or exercise, and is gaining in popularity as a family dog.

Background Notes

This breed is claimed to descend from the hunting breeds brought to the Mediterranean islands and Nile basin by Phoenicians and Greeks before the Christian era. It is thought that these dogs were then taken from southern Europe to the English coast, from which they were introduced to Roman-occupied Switzerland. Because of its excellent sense of smell and fighting spirit, the Schweizer laufhund was once used to hunt bears.

Key Characteristics

Medium sized, the Schweizer laufhund has a slim, long body; a sharp, chiseled head; big black nostrils; gentle dark eyes; very long, cone-shaped pendant ears; a tail carried level with the back or hanging down in a slight curve; strong, heavy-boned legs; and firm feet with thick, springy pads. The short coat is hard and dense. The coat color is white with orange or yellow markings, or a solid color of red.

Peaceful, gentle, and very loyal to its master, this dog is also a determined and aggressive hunter.

F 1.5 years

Male: 18–21 in.
40–44 lbs.
....
Female: 18–21 in.
40–44 lbs.

Care and Exercise

Occasional brushing is all the grooming this breed needs. It loves and needs a lot of exercise.

Puppies and Training

There are from four to ten puppies in a litter. Though strong, they may need extra milk if the litter is large.

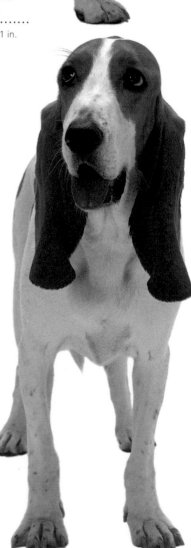

F 1.5 years

F 1.5 years

Tiroler Bracke

Despite its small size, the Tiroler bracke has a natural instinct for hunting, making it a good dog for inexperienced hunters. It is still a popular hunting dog in the severely cold Tirolean mountains.

Background Notes

Known also as the Tirolean hound, the Tiroler bracke was bred from the ancient Austrian hound and other hounds to hunt in winter in the Tirolean Alps. Its size makes it easy to take this dog hunting.

Key Characteristics

Medium boned, the Tiroler bracke has a slightly lean head with somewhat rounded forehead; wide, thin, flat ears; big dark eyes; a clearly defined stop; very strong teeth; and a long straight tail. The short coat is thick and hard. The coat color is red, or reddish yellow with white on the muzzle and around the jaws, chest, and the tip of the tail; tricolor is permissible.

Loving, calm, obedient, and alert to strangers, the Tiroler bracke is a good

M 3 years

M 3 years

watchdog and family dog. Brave and full of stamina, it follows its master's directions while hunting.

Care and Exercise

Light brushing with a natural-bristle brush is recommended. This dog needs a good deal of exercise, ideally in the mountains.

Puppies and Training

The litters of from four to eight puppies are strong and able to live in a cold climate.

Male: 16–19 in.
33–48 lbs.
....
Female: 16–19 in.
33–48 lbs.

M 3 years

Whippet

Galloping at great speed with its ears pulled back, the whippet looks like a horse being raced. Recently replaced by the greyhound on the race track, it is now mainly a family pet.

M 3 years

F 2 years

Background Notes

This dog is thought to have been bred 150 years ago by crossing the small-sized greyhound, various terriers, and the Italian greyhound. Originally, it was called the snap dog and was used to hunt rabbits and rats. Its great speed later gained it a place in England as a race dog. Because of this, Lancashire and Yorkshire miners nicknamed it the "poor man's racehorse."

Key Characteristics

Low in height and medium sized, or half the size of the greyhound, the whippet has a lean, streamlined body; powerfully arched hindquarters; a narrow, deep chest; a tucked-up abdomen; a rounded loin; round buttocks sloping smoothly onto the legs; a long back; muscled shoulders; a flat crown; well-balanced, long arched jaws; ears that pull back flat while the dog is galloping

Male: 19–22 in.
31 lbs.
....
Female: 18–21 in.
29 lbs.

and half erect when tensed; dark oval eyes; a long, tapering muzzle with a scissor bite and a strong lower jaw; muscular hindquarters with a sharp angle between the hock and thigh; straight, long front legs with strong pasterns; firm, thick pads with hard nails; and a long tail carried between the hind legs. The short coat is smooth and glossy. The coloring includes gray, tan, fawn, brindle and white, and various other colors.

Gentle, quiet, and intelligent, the whippet can live in a detached house or an apartment, both as a watchdog and a pet. Graceful and noble, this dog does not bark or howl, knows its place, and adapts to indoor life. It is not as deli-

F 2 years

cate as it looks and is easy to care for, though it must be kept away from cold.

Care and Exercise

The whippet needs hardly any coat care except for occasional massages with a damp cloth and bathing as necessary. Make sure to wipe this dog afterwards until completely dry. Exercises on a lead at least twice a day are necessary. If trained from an early age not to chase other animals, the whippet can be allowed to run in a big open space. Track running should be conducted by a professional trainer.

Puppies and Training

The litters of from four to eight puppies are generally delivered easily. The puppies mature very quickly.

Windhund

An excellent sight hound, the windhund has been used as a hunter in Poland for centuries. Gentle to its master and loving with children, this dog makes a good house pet.

Background Notes

The windhund was used in hawking by Polish aristocrats in the fourteenth century, when hunting on horseback was popular among the nobility. The high-speed windhund also chased both small and large animals such as wild

F 4 years

Male: 19–22 in.
31 lbs.
....
Female: 18–21 in.
29 lbs.

F 4 years

boar. This dog's ancestor is said to be a cross between the indigenous hunting breed and the Asian sight hound, further crossed with the English greyhound.

Key Characteristics

The windhund has a lean, balanced body built to run at a great speed; a high, angular, muscular back; an arched loin; a deep, wide chest; a firm, well-tucked-up abdomen; a long head of a moderate width with a flat crown and slight stop; small, smooth rose ears; dark, intelligent-looking eyes; and a scissor bite. The smooth coat lies flat on the body. Coloring includes white, black, parti-color and many others; brindle is not permissible.

Very energetic and extremely patient, this dog can be nervous, but is never aggressive.

Care and Exercise

Occasional massaging with a towel will suffice for coat care. However, the windhund needs a great deal of speedy exercise, such as galloping on a lead alongside a bicycle. During exercise, other dogs must be watched carefully.

Puppies and Training

The four to eight puppies per litter are easily delivered. The delivery room must be kept warm in winter. Handled at an early age, the puppies will grow to be friendly with people.

Scottish Terrier

Terrier Group

Airedale Terrier

Known as the "king of terriers," the Airedale terrier is the biggest of the terrier group and has been traditionally used as a hunting breed. It has also been used as a military dog and police dog.

Background Notes

Since the nineteenth century, the Airedale has worked to hunt birds, otters, and larger animals. Brave, agile, and active, it is a good swimmer, a trait inherited from its otterhound ancestry. Today the Airedale is a popular family dog all over the world.

Key Characteristics

Tallest of all the terriers, the Airedale terrier has long limbs, making it look muscular and square; small dark eyes; button ears; and a docked tail of moderate length that is carried gaily. It has a double coat that is generally hard and wiry, or sometimes straight or wavy. The coat color is tan with a black or grizzle patch covering the base of the neck and back like a saddle. Black mixed with red, or small white spots on the chest are permissible.

Good with children and very protective, this dog is a fine companion. The Airedale terrier adapts to any environment and likes a variety of activities.

Care and Exercise

The hard coat needs to be brushed and combed at least three times a week and requires trimming. Plucking and stripping are also needed for a show dog. Exercise must always be conducted on a lead. An encounter with a cat or another dog during a walk will agitate even a well-trained Airedale.

F 3 years

Puppies and Training

There are five to twelve puppies in a litter. Newborns are usually black, developing a second color as they mature. Most breeders repeatedly paste the ears to the skull to set the top line of the folded ears above the level of the skull as they mature. The growth of permanent teeth means that the puppy is mature. The owner's loving care and handling started at an early age are vital for an Airedale terrier to be healthy in body and mind. Thorough obedience training should also be given while the puppy is still very young.

F 3 years

Male: 23–24 in.
46–59 lbs.
....
Female: 21–23 in.
46–59 lbs.

F 3 years

American Staffordshire Terrier

Known also as the pit bull terrier, this heavily boned fighting dog was created in the nineteenth century. Though obedient to its master, this dog is always willing to fight, making him also suitable as a guard dog.

Background Notes

Created from the Staffordshire bull terrier and the bull terrier, this brave and powerful dog was modified and bred solely for fighting. It was first recognized by the United Kennel Club in 1898 as the American pit bull terrier.

In 1936 it was also recognized by the American Kennel Club as the Stafford terrier, and later in 1972 was officially renamed as the American Staffordshire terrier to distinguish him from the lighter-weight English Staffordshire bull terrier.

Key Characteristics

Muscular, the American Staffordshire terrier has heavily boned limbs; a powerful, wedge-shaped big head with a deep stop; round dark eyes set low in the skull; prick or half-rose ears, cropped or uncropped if they are short; and a tail that tapers to a fine point. The glossy coat is smooth. All coat colors are permissible except white. By United Kennel Club standards, markings of all colors are permissible. With a highly developed protection instinct, this breed sensitively responds to its master's mood. Obedience training is easily accepted by this dog.

Care and Exercise

The coat will stay healthy and glossy if brushed and massaged. Long walks and galloping on a lead are essential. This dog should always be on a lead or it will fight with other dogs.

Puppies and Training

There are five to ten puppies in a litter. Firm handling is needed to train them. The ears should be cropped by a veterinarian around the twelfth week.

M 3 years

Male: 17–19 in.
44 lbs.
....
Female: 15–18 in.
40 lbs.

F 6 months

M 11 months

Australian Terrier

This is one of the few non-English terriers. Created by Australian settlers, it is the smallest of the working terriers, and its unrefined, sweet appearance has gained it great popularity in the United States.

M 4 years

Male: 10 in.
12–14 lbs.
....
Female: 10 in.
12–14 lbs.

M 5.5 years

Background Notes

The Australian terrier was bred from the cairn, Dandie Dinmont, Irish, Yorkshire, and a few other terriers in Australia in the nineteenth century. This breed protected the settlers' properties and lives, and was highly prized. It made its first appearance in England in 1906, and was later officially recognized by the Kennel Club in 1933. The American Kennel Club also recognized this breed in 1960 after an enthusiastic campaign by Australian terrier supporters.

Key Characteristics

The Australian terrier has a body that is longer than it is tall; high-set ears; small dark eyes; and a docked tail. It has a harsh double coat with a ruff on the throat and a topknot. The coat color is either blue black or silver black with tan markings. Solid red or sand are also permissible.

Brave and alert, the Australian terrier makes a good guard dog. This breed is also sensible, thoughtful, and good with children.

Care and Exercise

The long hair on the ears should be pulled out and the hair on the legs removed or stripped to maintain a clean appearance of the coat. Two walks a day are required. Free exercise in a fenced area is ideal.

M 5.5 years

Puppies and Training

Litters average three to four puppies. Newborns are mostly black, developing adult coloration as they mature. The ears prick up between the sixth and eighth weeks. The tail should be docked within a week of birth.

Bedlington Terrier

Despite an elegant and sophisticated lamblike appearance, the Bedlington terrier is in fact an agile and aggressive dog created by miners.

M 4 years

Male: 16–17 in.
18–22 lbs.
....
Female: 15–16 in.
15–20 lbs.

Background Notes

The miners in North Umberland in northern England created the Bedlington terrier in the nineteenth century to hunt foxes and weasels. Later, this breed became very popular among poachers, then became a prize possession of aristocrats. Ironically, it was later used to hunt poachers. Claimed to be kin to the Dandie Dinmont terrier, the Bedlington is a cross between the scent-and-sight terrier and the chase hound, and is equipped with the abilities of the whippet. Its unique sheeplike appearance has always gained it a number of admirers.

Key Characteristics

The Bedlington terrier has a powerful body; a back with a beautifully arched top line; long limbs compared to other terriers; a wide head with a deep stop; low-set pendant ears; and eyes ranging from light to dark hazel. It has a fine,

F 2 years (left), F 2 years (center), M 4 years (right)

curly double coat of hard and soft hair. The coat color includes blue, liver, and sand often mixed with tan.

The Bedlington quickly responds to its master's mood and is highly trainable. Brave and equipped with an extremely high protective instinct, it makes a good guard dog. Loyal to its family, this dog is also popular as a domestic pet.

Care and Exercise

Regular trimming by an experienced professional is required to maintain this dog's peculiar lamblike appearance. The head needs trimming to give it a Roman-nose profile. The ears trimmed to leave tassles at the tips. The Bedlington should be groomed regularly with a slicker and a comb. This speedy dog must not be exercised without a lead unless it is in a fenced area, because if it sees a running dog or a cat it will give chase.

Puppies and Training

There are three to six puppies in a litter. Newborns are either black or dark brown, turning blue or liver respectively, before they are one year old. If

groomed from an early age, puppies will be accustomed to future trimming. Proper attention must be paid to this breed, as it tends to fight with other dogs.

Black Russian Terrier

Created in Russia, the black Russian terrier is a large, very strong hunting breed that will even go after a bear. This dog will gain more popularity in the future in Europe and the United States as it is recognized by the FCI (the French equivalent of the AKC).

Background Notes

The black Russian terrier was created by Russian breeders from the giant schnauzer crossed with the Airedale terrier and the Rottweiler. The giant schnauzer used to be called the Russian bear schnauzer in Russia, as it resembled the black Russian terrier. Although a popular house pet and guard dog in Moscow and the suburbs of St. Petersburg, the black Russian is not yet a very well-known breed in Europe.

Key Characteristics

Square and resembling the giant schnauzer, the black Russian terrier has a sturdy, well-boned muscular body; a flat skull with an unclear stop; and a muzzle pointed at the tip. The hard, slightly wavy coat is profuse and grows five to ten inches long, which is good for extremely cold weather. The hair on the forehead is longer, covering the face. The coat color is black or salt and pepper.

F 2 years

F 2 years

Male: 26–29 in.
70–81 lbs.
....
Female: 25–28 in.
66–77 lbs.

Sensitive, very intelligent, brave, daring to fight against much larger animals, this obedient and loyal breed is excellent as a guard dog or house pet.

Care and Exercise

The dense undercoat needs regular hard brushing and combing. A great deal of exercise is required every day.

Puppies and Training

There are four to eight relatively strong puppies in a litter. Handling from an early age is required. The tail should be docked within a week of birth.

F 2 years

Border Terrier

As its name implies, the Border terrier is from the border between Scotland and England, where it served farmers as a working terrier and guard dog. Its otterlike face and rough coat give this breed an unsophisticated, yet natural appearance.

Background Notes

The Border terrier was bred from a group of terriers known to have lived for centuries in the Cheviot Hills on the border of Scotland and England. It was much treasured by the local farmers for its talent at killing foxes and other animals who crept into the farmyard for livestock. In the United States an attempt is being made to create a new hunting dog from the Border terrier and other breeds.

Key Characteristics

The Border terrier is longer than it is tall, with a head resembling an otter's; small V-shaped drop ears; dark hazel eyes; a tail that is naturally short without being docked; and thick, loose skin. The coloring of its wiry coat includes red, grizzle and tan, blue and tan, and wheaten.

Assertive, strong-willed, and quick to learn obedience, this dog is affectionate with its family.

Care and Exercise

The coat should be trimmed on the head, legs, neck, and tip of tail, and the long hair removed. Active and hard-working, this dog needs to be given work to do, and should be exercised on a lead for long periods of time.

Puppies and Training

There are three to six puppies in a litter. All colors are permissible for newborns.

Male: 9–11 in.
13–15 lbs.
....
Female: 8–11 in.
11–14 lbs.

F 10 months

F 10 months

Bull Terrier

Its egg-shaped face and tiny eyes give the bull terrier a unique look. Despite its humorous appearance it was originally a fighting dog.

Male: 12 in.
24 lbs.
....
Female: 12 in.
24 lbs.

Miniature, F 9 months

Background Notes

The bull terrier was created in nineteenth-century England as a cross between the bulldog and the now-extinct white English terrier. Full of fire and courage, it was used in dogfights during the Victorian era, but dogfights were later banned by the Parliament. The popular white bull terrier appeared in 1860, slightly later than the colored bull terrier. Although first regarded as somewhat inferior to the colored dog, it later acquired fame in advertising and fashion.

Key Characteristics

Sturdy and muscular, the bull terrier has heavily boned short limbs; an egg-shaped head; prick ears; a black nose; a natural tail left undocked; and high-set, closely placed small eyes, a distinctive characteristic of this breed. The smooth coat lies flat on the body. The coat color is all white or white with red or brindle markings on head. Brindle or red bull terriers often have a white blaze or red on the chest, legs, and tip of the tail.

The bull terrier dedicates itself to pleasing its master and is full of love for people, even strangers. However, it should not be kept with other pets, as it may often fight with them. If not controlled, this dog can be extremely aggressive and dangerous to people. Strict training and sure, safe handling are essential for this breed.

Care and Exercise

The smooth, dense coat hardly needs trimming, but should be brushed twice a week with a rubber or natural-bristle brush, or gloves used for hounds. Bathe this dog as necessary; the white bull terrier may need to be bathed more often because its coat shows dirt more.

Male: 20–22 in.
44–55 lbs.
....
Female: 19–21 in.
44 lbs.

Standard, F 4 years

Exercise should be on a lead or in a fenced area. This dog must be watched carefully because it tends to fight with other dogs.

Puppies and Training

There are four to eight puppies in a litter. Their ears usually become erect at three or four months of age, but may stay down until the permanent teeth are fully grown in. Newborns have a pink nose, which turns black as they mature.

Bull Terrier, standard

Cairn Terrier

One of the oldest terriers, the cairn terrier is indigenous to the Isle of Skye in Scotland. It is an unpolished, yet strong, friendly, working dog.

Background Notes

The best-known cairn terrier may be as Toto in the *Wizard of Oz*. As is typical of this breed, Toto is loyal to Dorothy and bravely protects her from eerie monsters and flying monkeys. The cairn terrier was developed over centuries in the highlands of northwest Scotland. It is named after the Scottish cairns, heaps of stone used as memorials or landmarks, which are the preferred hideaways of small wild animals. This small-sized breed could squeeze itself into the cairns to exterminate rats, to the highlanders' great satisfaction. The cairn terrier was once crossed largely with the West Highland white terrier, as this dog was thought to be closely related to it, but the American Kennel Club prohibited this breeding in 1916.

F 1.5 years

Gentle and not aggressive under ordinary circumstances, intelligent and easily trained, this dog is eager to please people and good with children. Content in any environment, it is a good family dog. As with other terriers, males should not be kept together as they tend to fight.

Today these two dogs are considered to be completely separate breeds, though they have many characteristics in common.

Key Characteristics

The cairn terrier has a short, wide head; intelligent-looking dark eyes; and an erect tail that should not be docked. The shaggy double coat is water-repellent. Any coat colors permissible except white. General colors are red, blackish gray, sand, brindle, and silver.

F 8 months

M 3 years

Male: 10 in.
14 lbs.
....
Female: 9 in.
13 lbs.

Care and Exercise

The naturally shaggy coat takes very little grooming, though at least once a week it needs to be brushed and combed with a hard steel comb, including the underside of the tail. A wig brush will stimulate the coat and prevent matting. Check the eyes regularly and remove any dirt. Exercise this dog on a lead for long hours; otherwise let it play freely in a fenced-in yard. Because terriers like to dig, care must be taken to prevent this dog from escaping.

Puppies and Training

There are three to five puppies in a litter. All colors are permissible for newborns, because the cairn terrier changes colors as it matures, when it finally takes on adult coloration. Some adults have been known to change color as well. Puppies' ears prick up before eight to twelve months of age. Some ears will later drop, but usually they prick up again after permanent teeth have completely grown in.

Cesky Terrier

An extremely sturdy small terrier with a great reputation as a rat catcher in the former Czechoslovakia, the Cesky terrier is normally gentle, but is an aggressive hunter.

Background Notes

The Cesky terrier was created to catch rats and moles by a Czechoslovakian geneticist and breeder for Scotch terriers, Dr. Frantiesk Llorak.

Key Characteristics

The short-legged Cesky terrier has a long, sturdy body; muscular shoulders and thighs; long hanging ears touching the cheeks; gentle-looking moderately deep-set eyes; a well-developed jaw and nose; and a tail that is seven or eight inches long and is carried level with the back when the dog is excited. The coat is long, with whiskers, a beard, and eyebrows. The coat color is either blue gray or light coffee.

Merry, obedient and loyal to its master, this breed is a patient, fearless, and vigorous hunter. Properly trained, it makes a good playmate for children.

Care and Exercise

This breed needs regular trimming. Long hair should be combed frequently and carefully, and short hair needs to be brushed. For exercise, a short walk is enough, but lack of exercise will soon make this dog overweight.

Puppies and Training

There are three to six puppies per litter. The Cesky terrier mother is gentle and good with her puppies, taking good care of them. Newborns are dark colored and grow lighter as they mature.

F 1 year

Male: 11–14 in.
13–20 lbs.
....
Female: 11–14 in.
13–20 lbs.

F 1 year

Dandie Dinmont Terrier

The name comes from the main character in an English novel, *Guy Mannering*, written by Sir Walter Scott in 1814. The fluffy topknot is characteristic of this friendly, affectionate breed.

Male: 8–11 in.
18 lbs.
Female: 8–11 in.
18 lbs.

M 3 years

M 3 years

Background Notes

The Dandie Dinmont terrier is from the border between England and Scotland. Developed in England and the United States to hunt small animals, it was later used as an otter catcher by poachers and Gypsies.

Key Characteristics

Small-sized and short limbed, the Dandie Dinmont terrier has a big, oddly shaped head; hazel eyes; drop ears with fringes at the tips; and a short, curved tail. The coat is soft with a fluffy topknot. The coloring includes pepper, ranging from silver to blue black, and mustard, ranging from fawn to dark red.

Though a good family dog, the Dandie Dinmont terrier tends to be loyal only to its master. Determined and persistent, it is quite trainable.

Care and Exercise

Use a terrier palm brush or a pin brush for the coat at least three times a week. If excess hair is left unremoved, or if the coat is not well cared for, it will soon mat. Long hours of exercise on a lead will keep this dog healthy. Always put the Dandie Dinmont on a leash, or it may run away and never come back. Care must also be taken as this breed likes to dig and crawl under fences.

Puppies and Training

There are three to six puppies in a litter. Newborns are black or tan, turning pepper after six to eight months. A sable dog with a black mask will turn mustard. Puppies take approximately two years to mature.

Fox Terrier Smooth

Once a sporting breed used for fox hunting, this dog was modified in the late nineteenth century. It is a popular breed in the United Kingdom.

Background Notes

Even those uninterested in dogs will recognize this breed as the dog listening to "his master's voice" on a gramophone. The most widely recognized and most popular of all purebreds, the smooth fox terrier became known worldwide because it was taken to the British colonies by the English. First used by English horsemen as a sporting dog to hunt foxes, its talent as a trick dog was later recognized, and it is still used in circuses today. Until recently, the smooth and wire fox terriers were thought to be one breed with two coat variations, but today they are recognized as two separate breeds.

Key Characteristics

The smooth fox terrier has a compact, muscular body; button ears folded forward above the level of the skull; and a docked tail that is carried erect. The coat is short, smooth, flat, and dense. If the coat is not sufficiently cared for, longer hairs will grow on both sides of neck, back of legs, and tail. The coat color is mostly white with tan, black, or black and tan. The head is often black, with tan above the eyes and on the cheeks. A few dogs are all white. This extremely energetic dog is eager to go outdoors and will be happy as long as it has enough exercise. It barks at strangers and thus makes a good watchdog.

M 2 years

M 1 year

Puppies and Training

There are three to six puppies in a litter. The markings of newborns will remain the same as they mature. The tail should be docked within a week of birth.

Male: 13–16 in.
17–19 lbs.
. . . .
Female: 12–15 in.
14–17 lbs.

Care and Exercise

Use a natural bristle brush or hound gloves for brushing, then use a fine comb. If rubbed with a chamois cloth, the coat will stay glossy. Long hair can be removed with a stripping comb or a specially made razor. This energetic breed needs a great amount of exercise, a combination of walks on a lead and free exercise in an open space. It loves ball games and asks its master to repeat the game again and again. During exercise, pay attention that this dog does not attack other pets and dogs or wander off.

M 3 years

Fox Terrier Wire

A traditional English breed created as a fox hunter, this dog has an older history than the smooth fox terrier and appeared in a dog show for the first time in 1872. It reached a peak of popularity in the 1920s.

Background Notes

Like the smooth fox terrier, the wire fox terrier is a recognized breed in many countries and was also used to hunt foxes while accompanying horsemen. The best known of this breed is Asta in the movie version of Dashiell Hammett's detective story, *The Thin Man*. The charming shape and showmanship of this dog caused it to be known as "the chorus girl" of the dog world. The wire fox terrier, along with the smooth fox terrier, has been awarded the best-in-show prize more frequently than any other breed.

Key Characteristics

Squarely built, the wire fox terrier has a long rectangular head, button ears, and an erect tail. The wiry double coat is hard and wavy, with longer hair on the eyebrows, muzzle, legs, and chest. White predominates, with black, tan, or black and tan markings. All white is not disqualified, though it is rare. A tan head with black button markings is also permissible.

This breed likes to act in a pack, and is sociable and eager to please people. Agile and a frequent barker, it makes a good watchdog, though it is often distracted by other dogs and cats and starts chasing them. Males have a tendency to be aggressive toward other males.

Male: 15 in.
15–18 lbs.

Female: 14 in.
15 lbs.

M 4 years

M 10 months

Care and Exercise

This breed needs regular brushing with a natural-bristle brush, hound gloves, or a comb. A show dog needs to be hand plucked and stripped to keep a good coat color and texture. Palm pads for terriers are useful. A pet dog with no prospect of dog shows is probably better off being clipped. The wire fox terrier needs a great amount of exercise to stay healthy. Appropriate exercise is a combination of walks on a lead, ball games, and other vigorous activities.

M 10 months

Puppies and Training

Generally there are three to six puppies in a litter, but often there are more or fewer. Newborns with a predominantly black head turn a beautiful tan before one year of age. The wire fox terrier should be trained firmly to respond quickly to simple commands such as "Come," "Sit," "Stay," and "No."

German Hunting Terrier

The German hunting terrier is an all-around hunter of animals, ranging from rats to boars, both on land and in water. This dog's somewhat stubborn and persistent nature makes it a good watchdog. As it is small, it may be kept in the city.

M

Background Notes

Created in early eighteenth-century Germany from the fox terrier, the German hunting terrier resembles the rough-coated Irish terrier. Willing to retrieve even in water, it will also jump into the burrows of foxes and hares with great speed and attack wild boars fiercely.

Key Characteristics

The German hunting terrier has a powerful skull that is well balanced by its cheeks; strong jaws and teeth; high-set V-shaped ears hanging on the sides of the head; dark, small, slightly deep-set eyes; straight front legs; and a tail that is carried almost erect. The coat comes in two variations: smooth and wire. The coat colors are mainly black and tan, black, and dark brown.

Courageous, aggressive toward other animals, loyal only to its master, this breed makes a good watchdog and guard dog.

Care and Exercise

This dog needs only occasional brushing. An agile terrier who loves to exercise, it occasionally needs to run freely in a big exercise area.

Puppies and Training

The litters of from three to seven puppies are easily delivered. Most German hunting terriers are aloof with strangers, so the mother is best kept alone during delivery. Puppies' tails should be docked within a week of birth.

Male: 16 in.
20–22 lbs.
....
Female: 16 in.
17–19 lbs.

M

F (left), M (right)

Glen of Imaal Terrier

This dog became popular in Europe after being seen in a dog show in Ireland. Brave and intelligent, it is a spiritual breed with the characteristic terrier willingness to accept any challenge.

F 1 year

Background Notes

The Glen of Imaal terrier made its first public appearance in an Irish dog show in 1933, where it drew the attention of dog-lovers who later brought it to other parts of Europe. Brought to the United States only in 1968, this dog's reputation as a rat catcher as well as its attractive appearance and ability to catch foxes and badgers gained it great popularity. Today it is more of a house pet than a hunter.

Key Characteristics

Small and compact, the Glen of Imaal terrier resembles the Welsh corgi. It has a short, cute tail; legs that are short for its body length; and brown eyes, the charm of this breed. The hard coat comes in wheaten, blue, gray, and brindle.

Aggressive toward other dogs and animals and with the very strong character of terriers, it is also an obedient and reliable family dog and watchdog.

Care and Exercise

The harsh coat rarely mats, requiring only occasional brushing. Use a comb where the hair is long. Regular trimming is required. An energetic breed, this dog loves to run without a lead in a big open space.

F 1 year

Puppies and Training

There is an average of three to six relatively strong puppies per litter. Tails should be docked within one week of birth.

Male: 14 in.
31–35 lbs.
....
Female: 12 in.
31 lbs.

F 1 year

Irish Terrier

Loyal to all members of its family, the Irish terrier accomplishes its tasks with determination and will face any difficulty to guard its family.

F 3 years

Background Notes

The Irish terrier has been a working farm dog and guard dog in Ireland for centuries. An all-around breed, it was used to guard the home, to accompany its master everywhere, and to look after children. It is believed that the Irish terrier became so popular because of its devotion and importance to its family.

Key Characteristics

Squarely built, the Irish terrier resembles the fox terrier, but is taller. It has a rectangular head; button ears; small dark eyes with a sensitive expression; and an erect docked tail. It is much lighter in weight than it looks. The double coat is wiry and dense. No locks or curls are permissible. Coloring includes all solid colors ranging from light red to wheaten. Small white patches on the chest are undesirable.

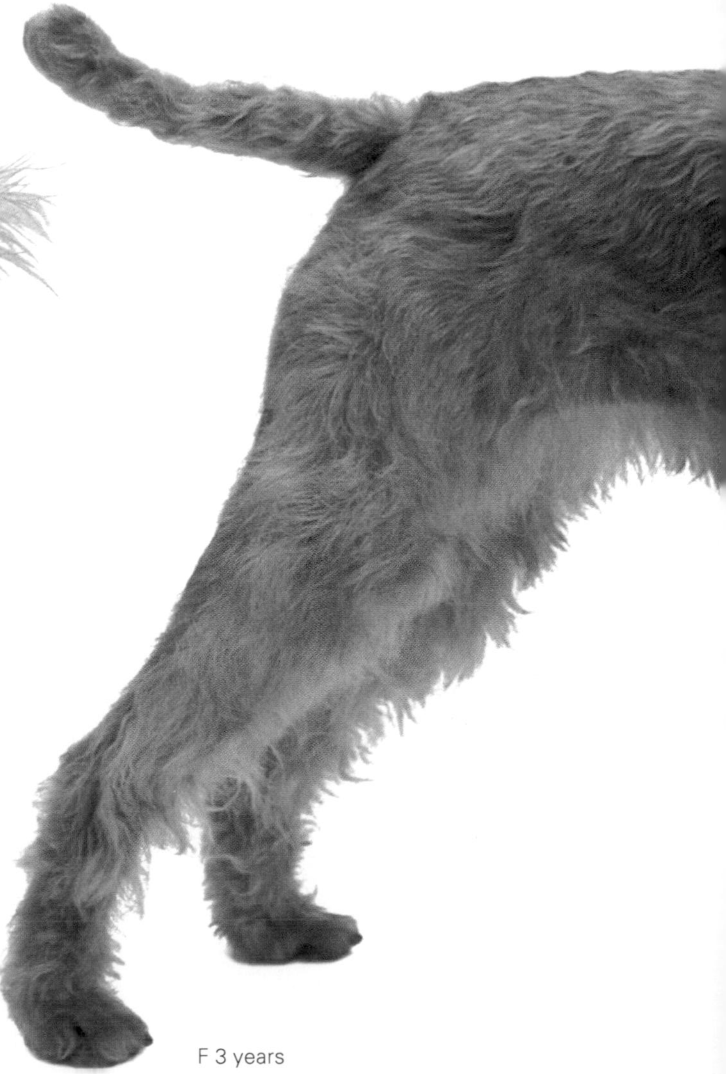

F 3 years

Male: 18 in.
26 lbs.
....
Female: 18 in.
24 lbs.

Brave and protective, this dog adapts to any environment, but male dogs may fight if kept together.

Care and Exercise

The more frequently it is groomed, the more beautiful the coat will be. Except

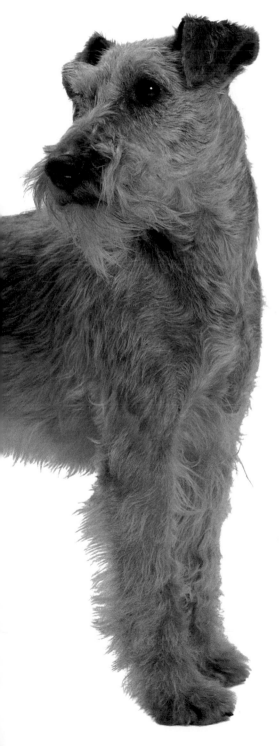

F 3 years

for regular brushing and combing, this dog is easy to look after. Frequent plucking will enhance the coat color. Bathing is necessary only when other measures fail to keep the dog clean. Its pads should be kept free of corns. This active breed needs a lot of exercise, preferably a combination of long walks on a lead and free running in a fenced area.

Puppies and Training

There are four to eight puppies in a litter. Some newborns have a few black hairs, but these will vanish before they mature. Firm handling of this dog is necessary, and small children will find it beyond control. If trained at an early age, it will become a family dog.

Jack Russell Terrier

A small but ideal hunter, the Jack Russell terrier is an agile, patient, and brave dog, and is prized by hunters. Friendly with its family, devoted and loyal to its master, it is fearless and extremely alert to intruders.

this breed soon gained popularity among European hunters and horsemen. In 1990, the Kennel Club set standards for this breed, followed by the FCI, who set provisional standards for it. The American Kennel Club has not set standards for this breed.

Key Characteristics

The Jack Russell terrier has a deep chest; a straight, rather short, a slightly arched back; a flat, moderately wide head with a slight stop; slightly deep-set dark almond eyes; small high-set V-shaped drop ears that are folded forward; a black nose; and powerful jaws with a scissor bite. Its general appearance resembles the fox terrier, though the Jack Russell terrier has

Rough, M 1 year

Smooth, M 6 years

Broken, F 3 years

Background Notes

The Jack Russell terrier was created by Rev. Jack Russell of Devon, England, in 1870 after a series of modifications. One of the first members of the Kennel Club, and also a well-known judge and breeder, Russell aimed to create a small, agile, brave terrier, who was good at hunting small animals like foxes and raccoons. He crossed a few working terriers with dogs that looked like the wire fox terrier, having a white base and head with markings. Reverend Russell's death in 1883 threatened the Jack Russell terrier with oblivion, but

shorter limbs. The coat comes in three types: smooth, broken, and rough. Coat colors are tricolor and predominantly white with lemon, tan, or black markings on the head, muzzle, and loins. The Parson Jack Russell terrier is slightly longer limbed. It was officially recognized recently.

Care and Exercise

The coat needs regular brushing, and careful combing is needed where it is long. This dog needs sufficient exercise every day. It loves to run freely in a big open space.

Smooth, M 6 years

Male: 9–11 in.
11–13 lbs.
. . . .
Female: 9–11 in.
11–13 lbs.

Puppies and Training

The litters of four to eight puppies are easily delivered. The puppies are strong and easy to raise.

Broken, M 4 years

Male: 12–14 in.
11–13 lbs.
. . . .
Female: 12–14 in.
11–13 lbs.

Parson Jack Russell Terrier, F 4 years

Kerry Blue Terrier

The national dog of Ireland, also known as the Irish Blue, this breed has been much treasured as a hunter, sheepdog, police dog, and domestic watchdog. It has rich long hair on its face and a curly gray coat.

M 3 years

Background Notes

The Kerry blue terrier, as its name implies, is an indigenous dog of Kerry, in the southwest of Ireland. It became popular in the nineteenth century, when its admirers began promoting this breed, trimming it to look its best, and emphasizing the dog's many talents.

Key Characteristics

Built squarely and resembling the fox terrier, this dog has button ears; small dark eyes; a strong, well-balanced body; and a docked tail that is carried erect. Unlike most terriers, it is single coated. The soft, silky coat is dense and wavy. Coloring includes light silver

M 2 years

Male: 18–20 in.
33–40 lbs.
....
Female: 1/–19 in.
29–35 lbs.

gray and all blues ranging from midnight blue to slate blue. Darker patches are found on the head, legs, and tail.

Sociable and gentle with people, this breed stays young at heart and acts like a puppy with its master even in old age. Very protective, it makes an excellent guard dog who will never give up in a fight. Male dogs are better kept apart.

Care and Exercise

The coat needs to be groomed with a steel comb and a slicker brush at least every other day. It should be clipped with scissors and a clipper, and the dog should be bathed every month. This breed does not shed hair and has no body odor. Long walks on a lead and vigorous games will keep it strong and spirited. This dog must be watched while off a lead.

Puppies and Training

There are four to eight puppies in a litter. Newborns are black first and then turn red, brown, or gray; they will turn Kerry blue at 1½ years of age. The right balance in obedience training is very important. The owner must be patient and firm with this dog, but training that is too strict may discourage it.

M 3 years

Lakeland Terrier

This breed goes back for centuries, but its present style was fixed at the beginning of this century. Although its V-shaped drop ears are cute, this is a confident, fearless dog.

Background Notes

Closely related to the Border, Bedling-ton, and Dandie Dinmont terriers, the Lakeland terrier comes from the Lake District of northern England, where it has been modified over a long time as a digging and hunting dog. Unlike other terriers, it was used to hunt foxes and other wild animals preying on livestock.

The Lakeland's brave behavior brought it fame as a dog of indomitable spirit. Early this century, a club was founded by its admirers to promote this breed. The Lakeland terrier was officially rec-ognized in England in 1921, and in the United States in 1934. Around that time it was given the nickname "Lakie," and was perfected as a show dog.

Key Characteristics

Small and squarely built, resembling the wire fox terrier, the Lakeland terrier has a small, short head; dark eyes; and short, erect button ears. The coat is double, with a soft undercoat and a dense, curly outer coat. Coloring in-cludes blue, black, liver, black and tan, blue and tan, red, grizzle, grizzle and tan, and wheaten.

Active, cheerful, and extremely ener-getic, this dog loves to exercise with its master, hence it suits young people. Friendly with all, the Lakeland is intelli-gent and alert. Because it has a habit of barking frequently, it makes a good watchdog. Male dogs should be kept apart to prevent fighting.

Care and Exercise

The soft undercoat and wiry outer coat need a good brushing at least three times a week. Occasional bathing will prevent the coat from becoming too dry. This dog needs long periods of exercise on a lead, or without a lead in a securely fenced area. It must be watched as it will fight with other dogs.

Male: 14–15 in.
18 lbs.
Female: 14 in.
17 lbs.

M 11 months

Puppies and Training

There are three to five puppies in a litter. Newborns have soft, curly hair that falls out and is replaced with adult hair. The coat color changes from dark to light, then to limpid. This change of color begins around the saddle, and continues until the puppy is fully mature.

F 2 years

Manchester Terrier

A terrier of considerable antiquity, the elegantly built Manchester terrier was bred as a
hare and vermin hunter. Its
glossy smooth coat does not
resemble that of a terrier.

Background Notes

One of the oldest of terriers, this dog's
ancestry dates back to before the
sixteenth century. It was supposedly
crossed with a sporting terrier, the
whippet, and the greyhound during the
nineteenth century. The name comes
from the city of Manchester, England,
which established a breeding center to
maintain this dog.

Male: 16 in.
18 lbs.
....
Female: 15 in.
17 lbs.

F 2 years

F 9 months

Key Characteristics

This breed comes in two size variations: the standard Manchester terrier from the terrier group and the toy Manchester terrier from the toy group. It has a back that is slightly arched at the loin; a long, narrow head without a stop; ears that are no longer cropped; and a whiplike tail of moderate length. The coat is thick, dense, glossy, and smooth. The coat color is black and tan. The division between colors should be clearly defined, and white is not desirable. More than half of the body surface being white is cause for disqualification for a show. This dog is cheerful, good-mannered, and clean. Warm hearted, sensitive to its master's moods, and brave, it makes a good guard dog and house pet. Though adaptable and friendly with people, it is unwilling to live with other pets.

Care and Exercise

The Manchester terrier likes to be kept clean and needs brushing at least three times a week. It should be bathed occasionally. A daily hour-long walk on a lead is advisable.

Puppies and Training

The two to four puppies per litter are born the same color they will be as adults. Their ears should not be cropped.

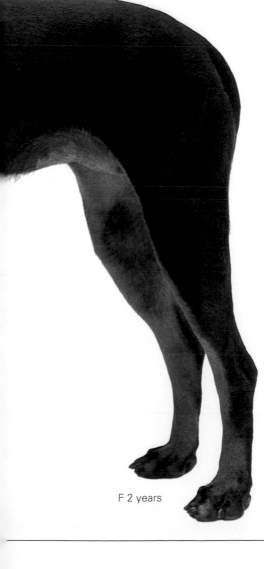

F 2 years

F 1 year

Norfolk Terrier

The Norfolk terrier's medium-sized drop ears are rounded at the tips, unlike the Norwich terrier's prick ears. Although independent, this dog loves the companionship of people and is good with children and other pets.

M 5 years

Background Notes

The Norfolk were bred in Cambridge, Market Harborough, and Norwich, England, in the early twentieth century. Originally a hunter, it was officially recognized in 1932. The Norwich and Norfolk terriers were considered the same breed until 1964, when the Kennel Club classified them as two different breeds because of the different configuration of their ears. This classification was accepted in the United States in 1979.

Key Characteristics

Compact and low, the Norfolk terrier has a short back; short legs; small drop ears whose rounded tips touch the cheeks; a docked tail; and dark eyes with black rims. It has a hard, curly double coat. Eyebrows, whiskers, and a mane around the neck and chest are desirable. The coloring includes red, wheaten, black and tan, and grizzle, in all shades. White patches are undesirable.

M 5 years

Care and Exercise

This breed often develops skin allergies, which can be prevented by frequent brushing. It needs long walks on a lead.

Puppies and Training

Litters average three puppies. Handling at an early age is desirable to prevent them from being afraid of people.

Male: 10 in.
11–13 lbs.

Female: 9–10 in.
10–12 lbs.

M 5 years

Norwich Terrier

Bred for hunting vermin, this terrier is widely popular because it is loyal and easy to look after. The Norwich was recently recognized as a separate breed from its cousin, the Norfolk terrier, who looks exactly like the Norwich except for the ears.

M 4 years

M 4 years

Male: 10 in.
11–13 lbs.
....
Female: 9–10 in.
10–12 lbs.

eyebrows, and a manelike chest and neck. Coloring includes red, wheaten, black and tan, and grizzle. White markings on the chest are undesirable.

One of the best-looking breeds, the Norwich terrier fits into any environment and gets along well with people and other pets.

Background Notes

The Norwich terrier and the Norfolk terrier come from the same ancestors and the same region and were bred for the same purpose. They were separately recognized first by the Kennel Club in 1964, and then by the American Kennel Club in 1979, and have since been pursuing different careers. The Norwich terrier has won a number of awards in recent American and English dog shows. Though now widely popular, it retains the unspoiled characteristics of its ancestors.

Key Characteristics

Compact and short legged, the Norwich terrier has black or dark green eyes. Its erect ears with pointed tips distinguish it from the Norfolk terrier. The tail should be docked. The hard coat is double, short, and wiry. The coat is longer on the head with whiskers,

Care and Exercise

Trimming of the long hair on the ears, legs, and the tail required to keep this dog neat looking. It should be brushed and combed two to three times a week. A long daily walk on a lead is advisable. This breed is sometimes a little too adventurous and may run away. Keep the Norwich in a securely fenced area, and take care to prevent it from digging out under the fence.

Puppies and Training

The average litter is three puppies. Their ears prick up six to eight weeks after birth.

M 3 years

Scottish Terrier

Known as the "Scottie," the Scottish terrier is from Aberdeen, Scotland, and was once called the Aberdeen terrier. Proud and stubborn, it is an independent one-person dog, devoted to its master alone.

Background Notes

The history of the Scottish terrier is said to go back several centuries. Though there are many theories about its origin, it is probable that its ancestors include all other Highland terriers (Dandie Dinmont, Skye, Cairn, West Highland, and so on), as there was a great deal of interbreeding of terriers in the past. The Scottish terrier comes from the rocky area of Aberdeen, and was bred to hunt foxes and weasels hiding in their burrows.

F 1 year

M 2 years

Much of its fame is due to Fala, the beloved Scottish terrier owned by President Franklin D. Roosevelt.

Key Characteristics

The Scottish terrier has a compact, strong body; short legs; a moderately long head; prick ears; brown or black eyes; and a naturally erect tail. The double coat is wiry, and the dog has thick whiskers and eyebrows. The coat colors are brindle, and black and wheaten. Small markings on the chest are permissible.

The breed can be extremely stubborn and proud, as though it were a much larger dog. Because of this, the Scottish terrier can only live with someone who truly loves it and is tolerant of its faults.

Male: 10 in.
19–22 lbs.
....
Female: 10 in.
18–21 lbs.

Care and Exercise

To look its best, this breed needs to be plucked and stripped. A hard natural-bristle brush, a pin brush, and a steel comb are recommended. Combing is necessary at least three times a week. Show dogs should be professionally groomed, while pets only need to be clipped. This dog should be exercised on a lead or in a fenced area where it cannot dig out and run away.

Puppies and Training

There are three to five puppies in a litter. The ears usually prick up by the eighth week, but may remain bent until the permanent teeth are completely grown in. Otherwise, they can be taped up. The coat color changes occasionally before they mature. Obedience training is necessary, but make sure not to use harsh words during training. A well-trained dog will stay out of trouble.

M 2 years

Skye Terrier

The dog's long coat covers not only its face but the outline of its body. For centuries the Skye terrier's appearance and loving nature have made it universally beloved.

Background Notes

One of the oldest terriers, the Skye terrier first appeared in *Of Englishe Dogges,* written in the sixteenth century by the famous Dr. Caius. According to this book, the Skye terrier, which "by reason of the length of heare, makes showe neither of face nor of body," was born on the "barbarous borders fro' the uttermost countryes northward." From that time, it has been known as a persistent enemy to all vermin. Originally from the Hebrides, mainly the Isle of Skye, west of Scotland, this dog was brought from there to England, where it was found to be a unique pet as well as an attractive show dog. One of its keen admirers was Queen Victoria. Boss, her favorite pet Skye terrier, was painted by Sir Edwin Landseer. This breed became a favorite of people of all classes, and has gained great popularity over the last two hundred years.

M 5 years

Male: 10 in.
24 lbs.
....
Female: 9 in.
22 lbs.

F 10 months

Key Characteristics

Small in size, the Skye terrier has a fairly long body; short legs; jaws powerful enough to be used as a weapon; brown eyes; and a tail left undocked and long. The majority of Skye terriers are prick-eared, but some have drop ears. The double coat is about one foot long and often reaches the ground hanging on both sides and parting from the nose to the base of the tail. The undercoat is soft and woolly, the outer coat hard and straight. Coloring includes black, blue, cream, fawn, various shades of gray, and silver platinum. Black points on the ears, muzzle, and tip of tail are desirable.

F 4 years

F 10 months

Agile, reserved, introverted, but alert to strangers, the Skye is protective toward its family and an excellent watchdog. Although sometimes stubborn, it is a friendly and sweet house pet with its family and master.

Care and Exercise

This breed hardly needs trimming, but requires daily brushing and combing with a good pin brush and metal comb. Some people use knitting pins to part the hair neatly. The inside of the ears and the skin must be kept clean, and the back of the tail should be kept clean to prevent skin disease. Properly groomed, this dog does not need many baths. It should be exercised on a lead for a long time, or allowed to run until tired in a fenced area. The Skye must always be watched while it is exercising or it may run away. It is essential to keep this terrier healthy both in body and spirit.

Puppies and Training

Litters average three to six puppies, and never more than nine. The ears usually prick up within three months of birth. The coat often changes color before the puppies are mature.

Soft-coated Wheaten Terrier

An all-round, medium-sized terrier who has lived in Ireland for over two hundred years, the soft-coated wheaten is friendly, cheerful, and now widely popular in the United States.

Background Notes

Like other Irish terriers, the soft-coated wheaten terrier was bred as an all-round sheepdog, and is probably a descendant of the Kerry blue terriers. First officially recognized in 1937 in Ireland, and in 1943 in England, it was taken to the United States in 1946, but did not receive recognition from the American Kennel Club until 1973.

Key Characteristics

Sturdy and resembling the Kerry blue terrier, the soft-coated wheaten has a wider and shorter head; button ears; small hazel or brown eyes; and a docked tail. The coat is soft and wavy. The fringe on the ears should be removed, but overall trimming is necessary only for show dogs. The coat color is light wheaten. A darker shade on the ears and muzzle is permissible.

This dog is gentle, kinder, and less aggressive than other terriers. A good companion to children, adults, and other pets, always cheerful, energetic and alert, the wheaten also makes an excellent guard dog. Because it is eager to please people, it is easy to train.

Care and Exercise

This breed's coat stays clean and free from matting if it is groomed and combed frequently. It should be brushed and combed at least three times a week with a good, long-tooth steel comb and a wire slicker brush. Do not pluck, but trim the hair with thinning shears. Check the foot pads and between the toes for any odd bits or matting, and keep the hair on the tail short for reasons of hygiene. A long walk on a lead is ideal for this breed; this will keep the

M 3 years

M 2 years

dog healthy and close to its master. If you are unable to walk the dog, let it run in a fenced yard. The wheaten loves retrieval exercises.

Male: 18 in.
40 lbs.
....
Female: 18 in.
33 lbs.

Puppies and Training

There are five to six puppies in a litter. The color ranges from red to wheaten, with a black mask. Puppies are darker colored at birth and gradually turn lighter.

M 3 years

M 8 months

Sealyham Terrier

The secret of the Sealyham's popularity in the United States and England lies in its sophisticated appearance and noble face enhanced by its beautiful white coat. A relatively new working dog, it was bred one hundred years ago for hunting purposes.

M 6 months

Background Notes

This breed was created in the late nineteenth century by Capt. John Edwardes, and was named after Edwardes's estate in Sealyham, Haverfordwest, Wales. The Sealyham's courage in attacking animals that would scare off other dogs shows that its ancestry includes fox, bull, and Dandie Dinmont terriers.

Key Characteristics

Although resembling the wire fox terrier, this dog is heavier and shorter legged. Compact and muscular, it has a rectangular head; button ears; long whiskers; unparted eyebrows; and dark eyes. The harsh, wiry coat is generally white, with tan, lemon, and badger markings.

While playful, eager to please, and sociable, the Sealyham is also an excellent guard dog.

Care and Exercise

If groomed at least twice a week, the coat will be free from matting. Exercising the dog on a lead for long hours will help create a healthy character.

Puppies and Training

The three to six puppies in a litter have the same markings as do adults.

M 6 months

M 6 months

Male: 11 in.
20 lbs.
....
Female: 10 in.
18 lbs.

Staffordshire Bull Terrier

The Staffordshire bull terrier was originally bred and developed as a fighting dog. Although dogfights were banned in England over 150 years ago, this dog retains the fighting traits of bravery, patience, and stamina.

Background Notes

This breed was very popular in early-nineteenth-century England. In 1835 the British government banned dogfights and appealed to dogfight fans to enjoy this breed in the show ring instead.

Key Characteristics

The Staffordshire bull terrier has a strong, muscular back and neck; heavily boned legs set wide apart; a wedge-shaped head with a clearly defined stop; rose ears or half-prick ears; dark eyes; and a tail of medium length. The smooth coat is white, blue, or brindle with or without white. Black and tan, liver, or white covering more than 80 percent of the body surface is undesirable.

Kind and especially good with children, this dog must be watched around strangers or other animals.

Male: 14–16 in.
24–37 lbs.
Female: 14–16 in.
24–37 lbs.

M 4 years

Care and Exercise

If brushed with a hard natural-bristle brush and massaged with a chamois cloth, the coat will gleam and shine. The American Kennel Club prohibits the trimming and removal of whiskers. A good amount of walking on a lead will keep this dog muscular. For the safety of others it should only run freely in protected areas.

Puppies and Training

There are four to six puppies in a litter. They should live in individual kennels so that they do not fight.

F 3 years

M 4 years

West Highland White Terrier

An elegant-looking terrier with a beautiful, shiny white coat, this agile dog is very charming but full of fighting spirit, and must be restrained when around other dogs.

Background Notes

Known as "Westie," the West Highland white terrier comes from the terrier family that includes the Cairn and Scottish terriers. These dogs were once variations of one breed, but as breeding progressed, they became separate breeds. In the past, the white puppies of the cairn terrier were disqualified, but later they were often recognized as Westies. The West Highland white terrier was officially recognized in the United States in 1908 and has become exceedingly popular since the 1960s. Today, it is one of the most popular terriers. The West Highland ranks the best of all terriers as a hunter of small animals.

Key Characteristics

The West Highland white terrier has a compact body; a short, wide head; not-

F 5 years

Male: 11 in.
20 lbs.
....
Female: 10 in.
18 lbs.

F 4 years

F 3 years

too-short legs compared to the Scottish or Dandie Dinmont terrier; firmly erect small pointed ears; medium-sized dark sparkling eyes full of curiosity; a black nose; and a tail, not to be docked, that is carried erect. The hard double coat is two inches long. The coat is thick on the head and face, and short on the neck and shoulders. Only a pure white coat is permissible.

The merriest, most optimistic, and most sociable of all the indigenous terriers of Scotland, this dog is at ease in any environment and makes a wonderful family pet, though it does not get along well with other pets. The West Highland makes an excellent guard dog, as it is observant and alert.

Care and Exercise

This breed needs grooming two to three times a week, and also requires careful trimming at regular intervals. A show dog needs to be plucked and stripped as well. A pet needs only to be clipped and trimmed with scissors, if the owner so desires. The coat on the underside of the tail should be trimmed for reasons of hygiene. Bathing is required once a month. The dog should be walked on a lead, or allowed to play retrieving games in a big safe area, both for as long as possible. If without a lead, the West Highland must be watched carefully and the exercise area must be escape proof. Pulling a lead directly above this dog's head will upset the animal and cause it to bark excessively.

Puppies and Training

Two to five puppies are born in each litter. Their size varies greatly, from small to medium. The nose and foot pads are pink at birth, but soon turn black. The ears prick up before the eighth week.

M 3 years

Welsh Terrier

Looking like a small Airedale terrier, the Welsh terrier loves companionship. Comical and eager to please, it makes not only an endearing pet but an agile, brave watchdog.

Background Notes

The Welsh terrier's ancestors are believed to have lived in Wales several centuries ago. This dog was bred to protect livestock and crops from foxes, weasels, hares, and rats by crawling underground to catch them. It first appeared in an American dog show about one hundred years ago.

Key Characteristics

The Welsh terrier has a long skull, dark hazel eyes set fairly wide apart, button ears, and an erect tail. The hard, thick coat is wiry. Reddish tan predominates, with either black or grizzle on the back of the ears and on the lower neck, loin, and upper side of the tail.

Care and Exercise

A pet needs only clipping, while a show dog requires hand stripping. If carefully brushed at least three times a week, the Welsh terrier will retain its tailored look. One bath a month is enough. This breed loves to be with people, and enjoys long hours of walking on a lead and playing retrieving.

Puppies and Training

The three to six puppies per litter are born mostly solid black, which fades rapidly. The typical blanket markings appear three to four months after birth.

M 4.5 years

Male: 15 in.
20 lbs.
....
Female: 14 in.
18 lbs.

M 4.5 years

Pomeranian

Toy Group

Affenpinscher

An old breed from Germany, the affenpinscher ("monkey terrier") has a comical face a little like a monkey's. Extremely intelligent and affectionate with people, this dog is highly popular as a house pet.

Background Notes

The affenpinscher was well known throughout Europe by the seventeenth century. Some say that it is the ancestor of the Brussels griffon, although there is no proof of this. Considering their similarities, however, it is possible that they are related. The affenpinscher was once a prized possession of royalty.

Key Characteristics

Big black eyes, whiskers, and a fringe on the jaw give this dog a monkeylike appearance. It also has a short forehead; slightly undershot jaws; ears that need cropping and a tail that needs docking. The rough, hard coat is short on the loins, longer on the head and legs.

M 1 year

M 7 months

Black is desirable, but black with tan, red, gray, or other colors is permissible.

Playful, loving, intelligent, and easy to train, the affenpinscher is a good watchdog.

Care and Exercise

This dog should be brushed two to three times a week. Exercise should consist of a walk on a lead once or twice a day, or free exercise in a secure area. Outdoor activities should be avoided in rain or cold.

Puppies and Training

A litter of two to three puppies is delivered approximately sixty-three days after mating. Born very small and black, they change color as they mature.

Male: 10 in.
7 lbs.
....
Female: 10 in.
7 lbs.

M 1 year

Australian Silky Terrier

Active and patient with children, the Australian silky terrier is an ideal house pet for a city dweller. This dog looks like the Yorkshire terrier, but it is slightly larger, with a shorter coat.

short hair on the face, ears, knees, and from the hocks down. The hair should be parted onto both sides of the body from the head to the base of the tail. Coloring is tan and all shades of blue.

A strong sense of territory often makes this terrier aggressive toward strangers and other pets.

Care and Exercise

The coat will become tangled if not brushed daily and shampooed weekly.

More active than other toy dogs, this terrier needs to be exercised sufficiently on a lead or freely exercised in a secure open area. Obedience training is essential.

Puppies and Training

The three to five puppies per litter mature in 1½ to two years, and live for ten to twelve years.

Male: 9–10 in.
8–10 lbs.
....
Female: 9–10 in.
8–10 lbs.

M 2 years

Background Notes

This breed was created in Sydney, Australia, from the Australian terrier and the Yorkshire terrier, and was once called the Sydney terrier. It was popular both as a city pet and as a ratter for chickens, ducks, geese, and turkeys. Exported to the United States in the 1950s, it was officially recognized by the American Kennel Club in 1959.

Key Characteristics

The Australian silky terrier has a low body that is longer than it is tall; a straight back; a V-shaped, moderately long head; a flat skull; V-shaped prick ears set a little apart; small, dark, intelligent-looking eyes; and a docked tail. Its gorgeous, silky hair is fairly long, with plenty of hair on the crown and

M 2 years

Bichon Frise

Depicted in Goya's paintings, the bichon frise was once a much-loved possession of noblewomen because of its pretentious gait and fluffy white coat. *Bichon frisé* means "curly-haired puppy."

Background Notes

Dogs of the bichon type have been known since the Middle Ages in Mediterranean lands, and it is certain that this breed's ancestor is either the barbet or the water spaniel. The bichon frise's friendly and attractive character was much appreciated, and the dog was often taken on a voyage by sailors

Male: 9–11 in.
7–11 lbs.
....
Female: 9–11 in.
7–11 lbs.

M 1 year

F 2 years

as an item for trade. It is said that this breed was brought to Europe from the Canary Island of Tenerife by an Italian tourist in the fourteenth century. Bred to be smaller in sixteenth-century France, it enjoyed favor with both French and Italian aristocratic women as an expensive, cuddly white dog. It later became popular in English palaces during the reign of Henry II. By the end of the nineteenth century, however, the bichon frise was a common village dog. After World War I, a group of fanatical fans revived this dog's popularity in France by establishing clear lines of breeding. In 1933, it was officially named the bichon frise and was recognized by the French Kennel Club the following year. In 1956, it was brought to the United States by the French and was recognized by the American Kennel Club as a non-sporting breed.

Key Characteristics

The bichon frise is a small breed resembling the poodle. It has a body that is longer than it is tall; a head in proportion to its body size; big brown or black eyes; and a prominent, round black nose. The double coat is rich and silky. The coarse and curly outcoat must measure two inches or longer. The undercoat is short and soft.

Smooth, flowing hair, hangs from the ears and tail. The coat color is white, or white with cream, apricot, or gray. Clearly defined markings and a black coat are undesirable.

Loving, playful, and obedient to its family, this dog is good with children and other pets and makes a wonderful, well-mannered companion.

Care and Exercise

If carefully groomed, the coat will remain fluffy and elegant. It should be brushed daily for at least half an hour. A show dog should also be groomed with a powder puff. As for exercise, this breed will be happy just playing indoors.

Puppies and Training

The three to five puppies per litter are six months old before developing adult coloration and take longer to mature than other breeds. Handling at an early age is recommended.

F 2 years

M 4 years

Brussels Griffon

This old breed from Belgium worked as a ratter at farms and stables and was originally called the stable griffon. It was imported to England and America in the 1880s. This dog's protruding jaws and rich whiskers give it a humorous, sweet look.

Male: 8 in.
8–10 lbs.
....
Female: 8 in.
9–10 lbs.

Rough, M 9 months

Rough, F 2 years

Rough, M 2 years

Background Notes

The Brussels griffon has been known as an energetic little dog in Belgium since the fifteenth century. Some believe that the affenpinscher, Yorkshire terrier, pug, black and tan terrier, and ruby spaniel were its ancestors, though details are not known. Today this dog is both a companion and a watchdog. It received official recognition in 1883 from the Belgian Kennel Club, and was exported to England and America in the mid-1880s.

Key Characteristics

The Brussels griffon has a small, firm, strong body; a wide, deep chest; a short back; well-developed hindquarters; straight front limbs; strong hind legs; a slightly arched, powerful neck; an extremely short nose; a wide muzzle that arches slightly upwards; a slightly protruding lower jaw that makes the dog look assertive; big black-rimmed black eyes with a sharp expression; high-set ears; that are left natural or cropped; and a tail that is docked short. The coat comes in two variations: a straight, hard, and smooth coat, and a long, hard, wiry rough coat similar to that of the affenpinscher. The coat color is either reddish brown or black with reddish brown. Solid black is permitted.

Cheerful, independent, and persistent, this dog is a great bluffer who will blatantly bark at a dog ten times its size.

Care and Exercise

The smooth coat needs little grooming, at the most brushing twice a week. The rough coat has to be hand stripped by a professional groomer. It can be clipped, but this may often eliminate its rough feel. This dog does not like to be confined in a small place. It likes to play freely and without supervision, and should be allowed to run in a big fenced area.

Puppies and Training

Females become pregnant irregularly. A litter of one to three puppies is delivered with difficulty, because they have big heads. Newborns are small, and only 60 percent survive after two to four weeks. This breed lives for eight to ten years. The Brussels griffon is often stubborn and hard to train. A potential owner should be loving and tolerant.

Smooth, M 3 years

Cavalier King Charles Spaniel

This dog's origin goes back to the King Charles spaniel, the much-loved possession of English kings in the seventeenth century, who was mostly kept indoors as a "carpet dog." This breed, however, was created in the nineteenth century to be kept in a kennel.

F 4 years

Key Characteristics

Sturdy and slightly bigger than the King Charles spaniel, the cavalier has a graceful carriage; well-laid-back shoulders; a straight back; a firm, powerful loin; a cone-shaped muzzle; a flat skull; big, dark round but not prominent eyes set wide apart; a shallow stop; biggish open nostrils; high-set long pendant ears; straight front legs; muscular hind legs; a tail that is often docked, but never more than a third of the whole length; and an elegant and powerful gait. The long, silky coat may be wavy, but fringe and curl are undesirable. Rich feathering is found on the ears, front chest, and legs. Like the King Charles spaniel, the coloring includes black and tan, ruby, blenheim (gold), and tricolor. This dog is extremely merry, active, and fearless. Loving with its family, especially children, it makes a good companion for children and elderly people to walk with.

Background Notes

By the early 1800s, the King Charles spaniel, an old breed, had lost much of its original character; its muzzle, for instance, was much shorter. It was also declining in popularity. This situation drove a group of enthusiastic admirers to try to revive the original sturdy spaniel. The King Charles spaniel was once a highly popular dog in the seventeenth century kept by both King Charles I and II. King Charles II was so keen on this animal that Samuel Pepys, a then naval officer, said that all he saw at the palace was "the King's foolish indulgence in this dog, paying no attention to his work."

The name cavalier, meaning a medieval knight, refers to its breeders' hope to revive the King Charles spaniel that had existed in the Middle Ages. Despite its popularity in England, ranking second in the toy group to the Yorkshire terrier, the cavalier King Charles spaniel is still rarely sighted in America, and has not yet received recognition from the American Kennel Club.

M 5 years

Care and Exercise

The long coat, especially on the ears, has to be combed, and the rest of the body has to be brushed. This dog loves exercise, but only short walks.

Puppies and Training

The two to six puppies per litter are relatively strong and playful.

Male: 12–13 in.
10–19 lbs.
....
Female: 12–13 in.
10–19 lbs.

M 10 months

Chihuahua

The smallest dog in the world, the chihuahua has an "apple-dome" head and charming big ears. Although its origins remain debatable, it was probably used in religious rituals as a sacred animal in Mexico and other South American countries.

Background Notes

The Chihuahua was discovered in Mexico in 1850. The breed as we know it today is said to have been bred from small dogs known among the Toltecs of Mexico in the ninth century. Experts claim that the Aztecs who conquered the Toltecs crossed the Chinese crested dog and the Techichi, a small, hairless Asian dog brought to Mexico, to create the Chihuahua. Others say that its ancestor was a Spanish dog that accompanied Hernando Cortez and his army during their invasion of Mexico in 1519. A Mexican Indian legend states that this small dog was a highly important religious object. Archaeologists in Mexico and South America have found bones of similar dogs buried with their master. The blue-coated dog was supposed to be sacred, while the red-coated was sacrificed on the bier during its master's cremation. These dogs' souls were thought to travel afterlife, carrying their masters' sins with them. The Chihuahua was recognized by the American Kennel Club in 1904.

Key Characteristics

The Chihuahua has a firm, compact body that is slightly longer than it is tall; a short, straight back; a well-developed chest; a well-rounded apple-domed skull with or without a *molera* (a small opening in the top part of the skull due to the failure of ossification); big dark or ruby eyes that are set apart; a small, slightly pointed nose with a clearly defined nose bridge; big flaring ears that are erect when tense, normally set

Long, M 1 year

Long, M 1 year

Long, F 1 year

Smooth, F 1 year

Male: 5 in.
2–4 lbs.
....
Female: 5 in.
2–4 lbs.

at 45-degree angle; and a sickle tail of moderate length. The Chihuahua comes in two coat variations: smooth, a soft, flat coat with fringe on the neck; and long (rough), a soft coat with fringe on the ears and feathering on the neck and tail. Both varieties have under-coats. The coat color ranges from sand white to blue, in all combinations. Black with tan markings is permissible. The nose color should harmonize with the coat, except for blonde, and the darker, the more desirable.

Long, M 5 years

Long, M 2 years

Long, F 3 months

Care and Exercise

Both the smooth and the long have to be brushed at least twice a week with a soft, medium-length bristled brush. The ears, nails, and teeth must be cared for every week, and baths given as necessary. A minimum amount of exercise is required for this breed. The Chihuahua is happy as long as it can walk freely indoors. Extreme heat and cold are to be avoided.

Puppies and Training

The one to four puppies per litter are often delivered with great difficulty. They need to be kept warm, with a heating pad wrapped in a towel or a blanket. These puppies take a short time to mature.

Smooth, M 10 months

This dog is loving toward other Chihuahuas and family, but reserved with people it doesn't know. It loves to be the center of attention. The Chihuahua is curious, whimsical, and has a tendency to be nervous. It likes to stay clean at all times.

Smooth, M 4 years

Coton de Tulear

The coton de Tulear loves to accompany its family everywhere, even to the sea where it shows off its swimming ability. Small but equipped with great stamina, this dog can follow its master on horseback over a long distance.

M 4 years

Background Notes

This breed's history dates back several centuries, when it lived as a house pet in the city of Tulear in southern Madagascar. The FCI granted it recognition in 1970, and in the following year it was brought to the United States, where it has recently attracted a number of admirers.

Key Characteristics

As its name implies, the small and compact coton de Tulear has a coat that feels like cotton. The single coat is long and profuse and mostly white with slightly yellowish markings on the head, ears, and loin. Loving and friendly with its family, but alert to strangers, this dog is an excellent house pet. Though loyal and obedient, it has a merry, happy-go-lucky nature.

Care and Exercise

The soft coat tends to mat and needs to be combed two to three times a week. However, this dog needs less coat care than a Maltese. For exercise, it needs only a walk.

Puppies and Training

There are two to four puppies in a litter. The hair on mother's chest must be cut short before delivery.

M 4 years

Male: 12 in.
9 lbs.

Female: 12 in.
9 lbs.

Chinese Crested Dog

With a hairless body and a crest of hair reminiscent of a Chinese pig-tail, this unique dog has other peculiarities; for example, many do not have a complete set of teeth. It is said to be one of the ancestors of the Chihuahua.

F 1 year

Background Notes

All of the hairless breeds have considerable histories, and their origins are debatable. Some say that they come from China or Turkey, and others say that they are from Africa or Mexico. Obviously, this breed does not adapt to

Male: 12 in.
11 lbs.
....
Female: 12 in.
11 lbs.

a cold area, and this leads us to believe that its origins lie perhaps in Central Africa or Mexico. However, hairless mutation can occur elsewhere in the world, to dogs as well as to cats. This breed was officially recognized in 1883, but the recognition was later canceled, as no one registered it afterwards. It is still rare worldwide.

Key Characteristics

Small in size, the Chinese crested dog has well-laid-back shoulders; a straight back; a moderately long, slightly round skull with a slightly pronounced stop; a fairly long muzzle; dark eyes set wide apart; big erect ears either with or without fringe; hare feet; and a tail carried over the back. Some lack a few teeth, though the cause is unknown. The coat comes in two variations: hairless and powder puff. The hairless has no coat except for its characteristic crest, socks, and a plume on the tail. The skin is supple and smooth. The coat may be any color or combination of colors, though darker skin is desirable.

Merry, loving, friendly with its family and never aggressive toward children

M 2 years

Powder puff, M 2 years (left), M 11 months (right)

or other animals, this dog is never noisy and makes a good house pet and a companion, though it may be somewhat proud and a little reserved.

Care and Exercise

This dog obviously needs no coat care, but it does need skin care as the skin is rather fragile. If it seems dry, rub some cream into the skin. Outdoor exercise should take place only during the warm season and the dog should be kept inside during cold weather.

Puppies and Training

There are two to four puppies per litter, either with or without hair. The puppies tend to be weak and susceptible to the cold.

Powder puff, M 11 months

Italian Greyhound

This is a breed of considerable antiquity and, as Renaissance paintings show, was widely popular in Italy in the sixteenth century. Smallest of all hounds, it has been much prized by royalty and nobility.

Male: 12–15 in.
6–10 lbs.
....
Female: 12–15 in.
6–10 lbs.

M 2 years

F 2 years

F 4 years

F 2 years

Care and Exercise

The coat needs to be brushed and then massaged with a damp towel twice a week. This dog should be bathed only occasionally. It does not need much vigorous exercise, but should be walked twice daily. Like other hounds, it will run at full speed when given a chance. Remember always to exercise this dog on a lead.

Puppies and Training

The litters of three to five puppies are easily delivered. Newborns are very small and weak. White puppies remain unchanged until they mature, but others will change colors.

Background Notes

The greyhound is known to have been in Egypt, where the Italian greyhound is thought to have come from, a few thousand years before the Christian era. A chained skeleton of this breed has been found in the remains of Pompeii, Italy. This dog enjoyed much popularity in the medieval era among European royalty, reaching its height in Renaissance Italy. Many aristocrats were portrayed with their beloved Italian greyhounds by famous artists.

Key Characteristics

The Italian greyhound has a small, beautiful, slender body; a back that curves downwards; a deep, narrow chest; a tucked-up abdomen; long, straight limbs; a long, narrow head; an elegantly arched neck; dark, shiny eyes; small rose ears, an extremely lean long muzzle with a slightly pronounced stop; and a fairly long tail that is carried low. The coat is short, thin, smooth, and glossy. The coloring includes fawn, red, gray, blue, cream, and may be either with or without white. All markings are permissible except brindle, black, tan, and blue tan.

Loving and playful with its family, this dog is reserved with strangers. The owner should be gentle, because this dog can be quite sensitive to harsh words and behavior. It prefers resting in a warm, comfortable place and doesn't care for excessive physical attention.

Japanese Chin

From ancient Korea, this exotic dog was highly treasured by the imperial family and aristocrats of Japan. Big, protruding, set-apart eyes are the most charming characteristic of this breed.

Background Notes

The first dog from Japan to be recognized worldwide, the chin was brought to Japan in 730 A.D., in the Nara period, as a gift to Emperor Seimu. The *kentoshi,* Japanese government officers who were sent to China for research, also brought back a few chins. This breed had been modified, and by the Edo period, it was a much-prized possession of the *daimyos* (regional lords) and the shogun's ladies. Its popularity later spread among common people, too. Known at the time as the Japanese

M 3 years

Male: 9 in.
7 lbs.
....
Female: 9 in.
7 lbs.

spaniel, the chin was taken to England and the United States by Admiral Perry in the mid-1800s. Later on, export of this dog to America was restricted, and consequently, it became more popular in England. It was recently renamed the Japanese chin, since it is not at all related to the spaniel family.

Key Characteristics

The Japanese chin has a compact, firm, square body; a big, wide head; a short muzzle; big round black eyes set wide apart; small hanging V-shaped ears; and a high-set tail carried over the back. The long coat is straight and silky. The whole body is covered with this profuse coat except for the face, with collarlike feathering around neck. The ears, thighs, and tail are also feathered. This dog has hare feet, and preferably

M 2 years

M 2 years

long brushlike hair between the toes. The coat color is black and white, and red and white (the red includes sable, brindle, shades of lemon orange). The nose should be the same color as the markings.

Gentle, nervous, stubborn, and proud, this dog is fond of children but dislikes to be treated roughly. Not active, it fits into any environment, is good mannered, and likes to be kept clean.

Care and Exercise

The long coat needs light brushing and special care to prevent matting, and shampooing as necessary. The chin likes to run and play, but it needs no outdoor activity as long as it exercises freely indoors.

Puppies and Training

Litters of one to three puppies, often of different colors, are delivered sometimes with difficulty. Newborns need a good deal of care until the second or third week, then mature quickly.

M 2 years

Japanese Terrier

This squarely built dog was once known as the mikado terrier or the short-haired terrier. Its firm body and black face are characteristic of this breed. It moves with great agility.

Background Notes

This terrier is a cross between a small indigenous dog of Japan and a smooth fox terrier who was brought from Holland to Nagasaki in the 1700s. It was modified as a cuddly dog and moved from the Kyushu area, where Nagasaki is situated, to the Kansai area. In the early Showa period, the Japanese Terrier Club was founded, set standards, and began registration for this breed.

Key Characteristics

With a smart, compact build, the Japanese terrier has a moderately narrow flat skull of approximately the same length as the muzzle; a stop that is not clearly defined; cheeks that are thinly fleshed and without marked cheekbones; lobe-shaped or rose ears; a scissor bite; dark eyes; a black nose; and a docked tail. The coat is extremely short, smooth, and shiny. The coat color is white with black and tan markings.

Agile, cheerful, and alert, it makes an excellent watchdog.

Care and Exercise

The extremely short coat requires only light massaging with a soft brush or towel. For exercise, this dog will be happy indoors as long as it is free. Extremely susceptible to cold, this dog should be kept indoors on cold days. Careful temperature control of its environment is also recommended.

Puppies and Training

There are two to four puppies in a litter. They should be kept warm if delivered in the cold season. Strangers should be kept away from the delivery area. Puppies' tails are to be docked within one week of birth.

F 2 years

Male: 12–13 in.
11 lbs.
....
Female: 12–13 in.
11 lbs.

F 3 months

F 3 months

King Charles Spaniel

Amiable, cheerful, and gentle in nature, the King Charles spaniel is loving and friendly with children and other dogs. It is also agile and brave, and makes an excellent watchdog. It fits into any environment.

loin; a big round head; a nose that points upwards; big dark eyes set wide apart, with a clearly defined stop in between; an angular muzzle without the tongue sticking out; low-set ears with plenty of fringe; and a tail that is either docked or left long. The long coat is soft and wavy. The coloring includes black and tan, tricolor, chestnut, ruby, blenheim, and so on.

Care and Exercise

The King Charles should be brushed every day so that its coat does not tangle. Bathe it every week, making sure that shampoo does not get inside the eyes and ears. This dog does not require long exercise. Bushes and shrubs should be avoided, or the coat will get dirty and tangled.

Puppies and Training

The litters of two to four puppies often are delivered with difficulty. The puppies grow fast and mature in two years.

Male: 8–12 in.
4–12 lbs.
....
Female: 9–11 in.
4–12 lbs.

F 3 years

Background Notes

This dog has been a prize possession of English royalty for over three hundred years. It was a favorite of King Charles I and especially Charles II, who, in the seventeenth century, issued a law that a transit tax could not be imposed on his dog. The origins of this breed are uncertain. Some say that it has the blood of the short-muzzled dogs from Japan or China, and that it was not originally English. Those short-muzzled dogs are thought to be a cross between the springer spaniel and other small cocker types. Although its ancestors were hunters, it has become a prized pet dog.

Key Characteristics

Large for a member of the toy group, the King Charles spaniel has a compact, short body; a well-developed chest and

M 2 years

Lowchen

The Lowchen has a uniquely trimmed body, and looks somewhat like a small lion. Used in France for a many years as a watchdog, today it is gaining international popularity. This extremely loving dog is protective toward its family.

Background Notes

A small breed from southern Europe, its history probably dates back several centuries. In a Goya painting of a duchess of Arabia, a Lowchen appears in the tapestry behind her. Today this dog is found everywhere in Europe and is attracting many American admirers as well.

Key Characteristics

The Lowchen has a small, short body; a short head with a wide skull; pendant ears; round, gentle-looking dark eyes; a dark nose; and a tail of medium length. The long, wavy coat is trimmed like that of the toy poodle. Single colors like white, black, and lemon are desirable, but markings are permissible.

Cheerful, loving, and absolutely obedient to its master, this brave dog makes a good watchdog despite its small size. The Lowchen is extremely intelligent and good at learning.

Care and Exercise

The coat should be combed carefully every day to prevent matting. Regular trimming also is required. If given long walks, this breed will be happy even in a small space.

Puppies and Training

The three to six puppies per litter are relatively strong and easy to raise.

Male: 8–14 in.
4–9 lbs.
Female: 8–14 in.
4–9 lbs.

M 3 years

Mexican Hairless

This old indigenous breed of Mexico is hairless and susceptible to cold, but is stronger than it looks. Requiring no coat care, it makes a good house pet and watchdog.

Background Notes

The Mexican hairless is said to have been much valued food for Mexican Indians long before the Spanish invasion. Having a body temperature of 40°F, it was also popular as a natural heater. This breed made its way from Mexico to other South American countries, and later became known worldwide. In the nineteenth century, it was used widely as a guard dog. The Mexican hairless received official recognition from the American Kennel Club in 1959.

Key Characteristics

This dog has a flexible, straight back; a slightly arched neck; a wide skull; bat ears about four inches in length; medium-sized almond eyes ranging in color from black to yellow; a long, tapering muzzle; and a long smooth tail. There is a slight coat on the top part of the head, but the rest of the body must be hairless. The skin is soft, smooth, and reddish gray. Dogs with darker skin must have a black nose; others should have a pink or brown nose. Cheerful and friendly with its family, this dog is not aggressive but makes a good watchdog.

Care and Exercise

The Mexican hairless needs only gentle rubbing with a dry towel. It needs a moderate amount of exercise. When taking it outdoors, remember that this dog is susceptible to cold.

Puppies and Exercise

The three to six puppies per litter are born pink, and acquire adult coloration around one year of age. Delivery is relatively easy, but the puppies will require special measures against cold.

Standard, M 6 years

Male: 12–20 in.
20–31 lbs.

Female: 12–20 in.
20–31 lbs.

(Standard)

Male: 10–12 in.
11 lbs.

Female: 9–11 in.
10 lbs.

(Toy)

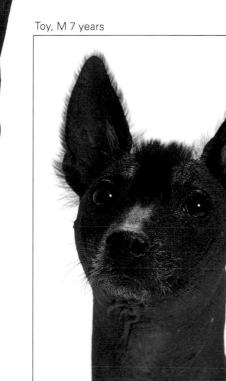

Toy, M 7 years

Maltese

An old breed known since 1500 B.C., the Maltese has shiny, lively, big black eyes and a gorgeous coat. A prince of the dog world, this dog has never been short of admiration.

Background Notes

The Maltese is claimed to have been brought to Malta from Asia Minor by Phoenician immigrants in 1500 B.C. It is likely that contemporary people were fascinated by it, as Greek and Roman art and documents depict very similar little white dogs. The Maltese also accompanied sailors as a pet on long journeys. During the reign of Queen Elizabeth I, it enjoyed popularity among women in the royal court and was priced at several thousand dollars. The Maltese is thought to be related to the spaniel family, not the terriers.

Key Characteristics

Extremely small, the Maltese has a level back; a short body; a slightly rounded head; black-rimmed dark eyes set close together; feathered drop ears; a black nose; and a high-set tail covered with a lot of long coat and carried over the back. The silky, long

M 5 years

single coat reaches the ground. The coat color is pure white, and light fawn or lemon ears are undesirable.

Cheerful, active, merry, and extroverted, this dog loves companionship. Although it dislikes to be forced to do anything, it is patient and never short-tempered.

Care and Exercise

This breed needs elaborate coat care. It must be shampooed at least once a week, especially around the eyes and mouth. Regular daily brushing is essential. If it is brushed while dirty, the coat will be damaged. A show dog can have a topknot, with or without ribbons. A pet can be trimmed, though this might not make it look its best. This dog requires only playing indoors for exercise. It must stay indoors on extremely hot or cold days and should never be allowed to play outdoors in bad weather. All short toy dogs are easily affected by the weather.

Puppies and Training

There are two to four puppies in a litter. Some have light fawn markings around the ears, which will vanish at two to four months. The rims of eyes and nose grow darker as the puppies mature. The Maltese lives for nine to ten years.

F 1 year

Male: 8–10 in.
4–7 lbs.
....
Female: 8–10 in.
4–7 lbs.

F 2 years

Miniature Pinscher

Known fondly as "minipin," this dog was hardly known outside Germany until 1920. The ancestor is the klein pinscher from Scandinavia, which was made smaller a few centuries ago. The miniature pinscher is widely popular as a watchdog and a house pet.

F 4 years

Male: 10–12 in.
10 lbs.
....
Female: 10–12 in.
9 lbs.

F 8 months

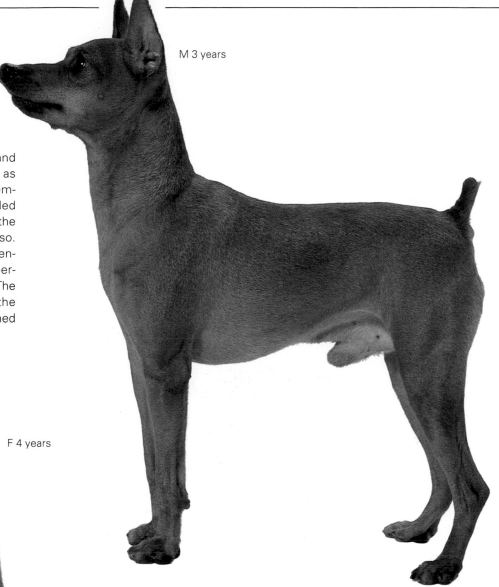

M 3 years

F 4 years

Background Notes

This breed originated in Germany and has worked there as a ratter and as a good barking watchdog. Its resemblance to the Doberman pinscher led many to believe that its ancestry is the miniature doberman, but that is not so. The miniature pinscher is a few centuries older than the miniature doberman, and they are not related at all. The miniature pinscher traveled to the United States in 1920, and soon gained much popularity as a house pet and a watchdog, with its beautiful body shape and intelligent, fearless character. A club was established in 1925 and the dog's current name was established. It is also called the Zwerg ("dwarf") pinscher in Germany and other countries.

Key Characteristics

The miniature pinscher has a well-balanced angular body; a deep chest; a firm back slightly sloping toward the rear; straight front legs of moderate length; well-muscled hind legs; a V-shaped head; small tight cheeks and lips; dark brown or black almond eyes set wide apart; erect ears that are either cropped or uncropped; and a high-set tail that is docked at an early age. The coat is smooth and glossy. Coloring includes red, black with tan markings, or chocolate with rust markings. The nose color is black except for a chocolate nose for chocolate dogs.

This breed walks carrying its front legs high in a precise hackney gait.

Active, cheerful, and spirited, the miniature pinscher makes a good playmate for children. Loving toward its family, but self-possessed, it hates to be fussed over. Fearless and confident, it makes an excellent guard dog and easily fits into any environment.

Care and Exercise

The coat should be brushed and massaged with a damp cloth once or twice a week. The nails and ears must be checked at least once a week. This energetic breed needs a daily walk on a lead, or short hours of free exercise in a safe area.

Puppies and Training

There are two to four puppies in a litter. They become very active at three to four weeks and take two years to mature. This breed lives ten to eleven years.

Papillon

This dog's patterned face and ears, which look like the spread wings of a butterfly, gave it its name, which means butterfly in French. The papillon fits into any environment and loves to play with other pets. Though sensitive, it also loves to fawn on its master.

Background Notes

This dog's ancestor was one of the "dwarf spaniels" that were highly popular among the French upper class in the sixteenth century. History tells us that Madame Pompadour and Marie Antoinette also loved this small but smart dog. The papillon, also known as the butterfly spaniel, made its way from France to England, then to the United States, where it was officially recognized by the American Kennel Club in 1935.

Key Characteristics

It is desirable for this dog's body length to slightly exceed its height, and the back top line should be level. The papillon has straight, slender legs; a small rounded skull; biggish dark almond eyes with black rims; a black, rounded nose that is flat at the tip, a pointed muzzle that is considerably narrower than the skull; and a high-set tail, with plenty of feathering, arched over the back like a squirrel's. The ears, without doubt the characteristic of this breed,

M 3 years

Male: 8–11 in.
10 lbs.

Female: 9–11 in.
8 lbs.

are wide, big, and carried like the spread wings of a butterfly, fringed at the tips. The ears come in two variations: prick ears, or papillon; and drop ears, or phalene. The silky, shiny coat is long on the chest, back of the front legs, and tail. The hind legs are beautifully coated, as if the dog were dressed in riding breeches. There is no undercoat, despite the abundant flowing outercoat. The only recognized coloring is particolor: ideally, base white with black or brown markings on the top part of the head, ears, and around the eyes. All white dogs and dogs with no white are disqualified to show.

Merry, cheerful, and agile, the papillon is always curious about its surroundings and is assertive and brave despite its size.

Care and Exercise

The coat needs to be lightly brushed twice a week, and no trimming is necessary. The dog should be bathed two to three times each month, using a baby shampoo and drying the coat speedily and thoroughly afterwards. For exercise, the papillon needs only to be left free indoors. It loves exercise and plays a lot with other pets.

M 3 years

Puppies and Training

The two to four puppies per litter should be kept warm for two to four weeks after birth. They usually have the same patterned ears as their parents. It will be clear from the time of delivery whether they are papillons or phalenes. Their life span is ten to twelve years.

F 8 months

Phalene, M 3 years

Peruvian Hairless

This rare hairless breed is loving and gentle with its family and friendly with other pets. A good house pet, the Peruvian hairless is also a good watchdog, as it is alert and nervous toward strangers.

Background Notes

A breed of considerable antiquity, this dog dates back to the Incan Empire in Peru. In today's Peru, however, only a very small number of Peruvian hairlesses are being bred, and those only for purposes of genetic research. This dog was officially recognized by the FCI

Medium, M 2 years

Medium, M 2 years

Male: 16–20 in.
18–26 lbs.
....
Female: 16–20 in.
18–26 lbs.

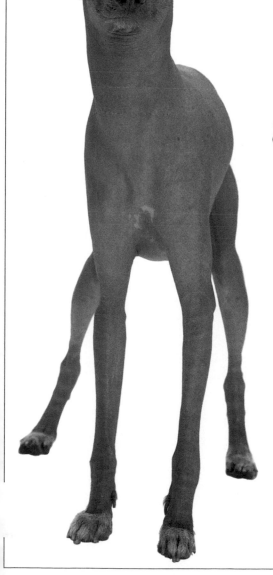

in 1985 after enthusiastic breeding and campaigning by German dog-lovers.

Key Characteristics

The Peruvian hairless comes in three sizes: large, medium, and miniature. All of them have a strong body; a wide skull; a long muzzle; big ears bent forward at the tips; and small almond eyes. Some dog lack a few teeth, consequently sticking out the tip of the tongue. The dog is hairless all over, with a small amount of hair on top of the head, the rims of ears, feet, and the tip of the tail. It has dark skin and a dark nose.

Care and Exercise

This breed needs to be massaged well with a dry towel. It is susceptible to cold.

Puppies and Training

There are two to five puppies in a litter. The mother and puppies both have weak skin and need special skin care.

Medium, M 2 years

Pekingese

Once known as the lion dog for its shiny golden mane and sturdy frame, or the sleeve dog because its admirers always kept the dog inside their sleeves, the Pekingese was once a sacred dog of the Tang Dynasty. Though small, it is a dignified and aristocratic dog.

Background Notes

The origins of this breed can be traced back to records from the Tang Dynasty (A.D. 618 to 906), but it may date back even further. The Pekingese was so treasured as a sacred animal that anyone who stole one from the palace would be executed. In the mid-nineteenth century, an English officer brought home five to six Pekingese who had been abandoned in the palace of Hsi Tai Hou during the Opium War. The Pekingese

M 2 years

Male: 9 in.
13 lbs.
....
Female: 8 in.
11 lbs.

F 11 months

F 7 months

was officially recognized by the American Kennel Club in 1909, and now enjoys an international reputation as one of the most popular toy dogs.

Key Characteristics

Thickset, the Pekingese has slightly bowed forelegs; a big, wide head; heart-shaped ears set apart, with fringe reaching below the muzzle; a short nose; big, round dark eyes; a wrinkled short muzzle; and a high-set tail carried over the back. The coat is long and straight, with an undercoat; feathering on the neck, legs, tail, and toes; and an abundant, flowing lionlike mane on the neck. Coloring includes all colors, such as black, red, fawn, black and tan, sable, white, bridle, and parti-color. A black mask extending to the ears and eyes is desirable.

Despite its sweet looks, this dog is independent, assertive, and stubborn. Possessive of its master, it has a strong sense of territory and is cool to people it doesn't know.

Care and Exercise

The Pekingese needs to be brushed at least three times every week. Shampooing should be avoided because it damages the coat. Clean the coat with cornstarch or baby powder, then dampen it with a little spray of water. This breed needs no trimming, but its eyes need to be cared for every day, with an eye ointment, if necessary. The Pekingese will be happy as long as it is free indoors; it needs no additional exercise. Young dogs, however, should be given some outdoor activities.

Puppies and Training

The litters of two to four puppies are often delivered with great difficulty. They have a life span of ten to twelve years.

M 8 months

Pomeranian

The ancestors of this expensive but popular toy dog were large northern sleigh dogs and dogs used to herd livestock. Its size was reduced in England, and its style was established in the United States.

Background Notes

The reduction in size of these once-large dogs began in Pomerania in Eastern Europe, hence their name. Its ancestors are thought to include the Samoyed, Norwegian elkhound, chow chow, and Arctic dogs of the spitz family. The popularity of small dogs in eighteenth-century England promoted breeding of small dogs, and this dog was modified from twenty-eight pounds to four pounds. The Pomeranian was much loved by Queen Victoria. In 1900, it was officially recognized in the United States.

Key Characteristics

The tiny Pomeranian has a short body; a back with a level top line; a deep and wide chest; a V-shaped head; a wide, slightly prominent forehead; dark almond eyes; prick ears; a clearly defined stop; a tight muzzle; and a high-set tail that turns over back. It is double coated. The outer coat is harsh, the undercoat soft and fluffy. The legs and tail are richly feathered, and the chest is frilled. Coloring includes all single colors such as black, brown, chocolate, red, orange,

Male: 7 in.
3–7 lbs.
....
Female: 7 in.
3–7 lbs.

M 10 months

F 10 months

F 2.5 years

cream, and white. Shading of coat color with sable or black is permissible. The nose is black.

Intelligent, agile, cheerful, and friendly, the Pomeranian is also curious, slightly noisy, and easily excited. Despite its size, it is a brave watchdog. Proud but obedient to its master, this is a good companion dog who adjusts to any environment or weather.

Care and Exercise

Show dogs require a great amount of care. Daily brushing keeps the coat long and plentiful. Sprinkle a small amount of baby powder on the coat, and spray it a little with water before brushing. During summer shedding, shampooing is best avoided to keep the coat undamaged. Look after the teeth weekly, and the eyes daily. This breed requires a minimum amount of exercise.

Puppies and Training

There are one to three puppies in a litter. Their coat colors change before they mature at one to 1½ years of age. Full coats grow in at age two. The Pomeranian has a life span of nine to eleven years. This breed is patient, making it easy to train.

Pug

The pug's deeply wrinkled face gave it its name, which means clenched fist in Latin. The sturdy body is well balanced with the large, solid head. Cheerful and mischievous, the pug is known as the clown of the toy group.

Background Notes

The pug is said to date to 400 B.C. China. Once the pet of Tibetan monks, it became the mascot of the House of Orange in Holland, in the sixteenth century, after a pug warned the Dutch Prince of Orange of the approaching Spanish invaders. Though the pug was popular throughout Europe in the late 1700s, it nearly went to the point of extinction in the nineteenth century. It regained its popularity later in the United States.

Key Characteristics

Stubby and muscular, the pug has a wide chest; straight, extremely strong front legs; well-muscled hind legs; a big, dignified head; a slightly arched thick-set neck; a black mask; a wrinkled forehead; big round eyes with a gentle expression; a short black nose bridge; a short, angular muzzle; small, high-set, thinly fleshed button ears or rose ears; and a tail that curls in two tight loops over the hip. The coat is short, soft, and dense. Coloring includes black, silver, fawn, and apricot fawn. If fawn, it is desirable to have a trace of black line extending from the occiput to the tail.

The pug makes a grunting nasal noise, somewhat like a pig, to communicate with people. It also snores in its sleep! This dog is always sociable and plays joyfully with its human companions. Though quick to learn, it is a somewhat self-reliant dog who reacts to its master's commands when it chooses to.

F 2 years

M 3.5 years

Care and Exercise

This breed sheds a lot of hair and needs to be brushed at least twice every week. Shampoo it as necessary. The stop at the muzzle base must always

Male: 10–11 in.
13–18 lbs.
....
Female: 10–11 in.
13–18 lbs.

M 1 year

be clean and dry. The eyes should be washed every other day. Unless forced not to, the pug has a tendency to be a picky eater. It needs a lot more exercise than other toy dogs. During the hot season, its respiration should be checked to make sure it is normal.

Puppies and Training

Delivery of the two to five puppies per litter can be difficult. Puppies take two to three years to mature, and live nine to eleven years.

Shih Tzu

Shih tzu means lion in Chinese, and refers to this dog's flowing manelike coat. Carrying its tail high and walking in proudly, the shih tzu has an aristocratic air. Joyful and active, it is widely popular in Japan as a house pet.

Background Notes

The shih tzu is supposed to have come from Tibet and to be related to the Pekingese, though much of its ancestry remains unknown. With its small size and long coat, it attracted a number of admirers in the Chinese court of the seventh century, where it made numerous appearances in paintings and sculptures and was one of the most favored house pets. In the 1930s, it was exported to England, and then, after World War II, was taken to the United States by military officers going home. This dog was recognized by the American Kennel Club in 1969. Since then, it has been extremely popular.

Male: 8–11 in.
8–13 lbs.

Female: 8–11 in.
8–15 lbs.

M 1 year

M 1 year

Key Characteristics

Small in size, the shih tzu's body length slightly exceeds its height. It has a broad body; a back with a level top line; a deep chest; moderately big and firm feet; a wide, rounded head; an angular, unwrinkled muzzle with a clearly defined stop; big, round, expressive dark eyes; large hanging ears; and a high-set tail carried over the back. The abundant, flowing coat is dense and reaches the ground. A wavy undercoat is permissible. The pug has long whiskers. All coat colors are permissible. The nose is black, but a liver nose is permissible for liver-colored dogs.

This dog is gentle and gets along well with children as long as it is treated carefully. The size and temperament of this breed make it an ideal house pet even in an urban high rise.

Care and Exercise

A show dog takes weekly brushing. The coat should be dried thoroughly with a hair drier after shampooing. The hair on top of the head should be tied with a ribbon or rubber band, so that the eyes do not get irritated. The ears must be checked every week. This breed requires a minimum amount of exercise. It loves to play outdoors, but a show dog must be kept indoors so that its long coat remains undamaged. For the best presentation in a show, a fully grown coat will be best protected if its tip is wrapped in paper.

Puppies and Training

The two to four puppies per litter are sometimes delivered with great difficulty. Their colors change after birth. They mature in one to 2½ years.

M 1 year

Toy Manchester Terrier

As its name implies, the toy Manchester terrier's ancestor is the Manchester terrier. In the nineteenth century, the Manchester terrier was reduced in size by selective breeding to create this breed, which easily adapts to living in an apartment with or without another dog.

M 4 years

Care and Exercise

The coat has to be brushed twice a week with a hard natural-bristle brush. Exercising in a small area or long walks are permissible, but free running is really ideal.

Puppies and Training

The three to five puppies in a litter grow fast and mature in a year.

Male: 10–12 in.
7–11 lbs.
....
Female: 10–12 in.
7–11 lbs.

F 4 years

Background Notes

The Manchester terrier, also known as the black and tan terrier, has lived in England for centuries. The toy Manchester, known in England as the English toy terrier, was created from this breed after small pet terriers became fashionable.

Key Characteristics

This dog has a short body of medium length; a slightly arched back; a narrow, deep chest; a narrow V-shaped head; prick ears with pointed tips; a level or scissor bite; and a whiplike tail that tapers toward the tip and is carried, straight down. The short coat is thick, smooth, and glossy. The coat color is black, with mahogany and tan markings. White is undesirable.

Intelligent, curious, active, and often aggressive toward other animals, the toy Manchester also makes a good watchdog.

M 4 years

Yorkshire Terrier

A "moving jewel" with a flowing silky coat, the Yorkshire terrier enjoys great international popularity. With its dainty big eyes and active character, it has always been a popular dog, though its history dates back only about one hundred years.

Background Notes

Developed in Victorian times in Yorkshire, England, this dog was created from the Manchester terrier, Skye terrier, Maltese, and other breeds as a ratter. The Yorkshire terrier was introduced to the United States in 1878. The compact size, sweet expression, and cheerful character of this dog had a wide appeal, and the "Yorkie" is now the most popular breed of toy dogs.

Key Characteristics

Compact and well balanced, the Yorkshire terrier has a back with level top line; a small head with a rather flat crown; small V-shaped erect ears; sparkling, medium-sized dark eyes with black rims; a black nose; and a tail that is docked to medium length. The glossy, abundant coat, which lies close to the body, is straight and reaches the ground. It is parted from head to tail. The coat color is steel blue on the back and tail, gold on the head, chest, and feet. The Yorkshire is very affectionate and loves its master's company; left

M 4 years

alone in the house, however, it might destroy things out of loneliness. This dog is best for someone who wants a constant companion. Handled with care, it is good with children and other animals. Intelligent, quick to learn, and very trainable, the Yorkshire makes a good guard dog despite its size.

Male: 6–7 in.
3–7 lbs.
Female: 6–7 in.
3–7 lbs.

F 11 years

F 11 years

Care and Exercise

If brushed daily and groomed regularly by a professional, the coat will stay in good condition. The long topknot is usually tied with a ribbon at the top of the head. Shampoo this dog carefully, making sure that it doesn't get cold, and dry it speedily with a hair drier. The Yorkshire needs no special exercise as long as it is free indoors. It is susceptible to cold and bad weather.

Puppies and Training

Usually there are three puppies in a litter. If the mother is small, she might have great difficulty in delivering. Newborns are black, with tan on the eyebrows, tip of the jaws, chest, and feet. They mature in two years.

Miniature Poodle

Non-Sporting Group

Bulldog

Popularly known as the national symbol of Great Britain, this rather stout, blocky dog was originally created to bait bulls. The bulldog has had its ups and downs in both popularity and notoriety, but has evolved into a loving and almost gentle, although at times stubborn, household pet.

M 2 years

Background Notes

Considering its size, this breed was once quite savage, for it was used to bite a chained bull's nose to incite it to fight. Many fighting dogs were probably involved in its development in Britain, including the mastiff. The bulldog was later used for dogfighting when bullfighting came to be considered inhumane and was banned. After dogfights were also banned in 1835, this dog's ferocity was eliminated through selective breeding, though its appearance was retained.

Key Characteristics

Heavy, stout limbed, low set, and powerful, the English bulldog is capable of great bursts of speed. It has broad shoulders; especially muscular hindquarters; a quite large head; a very short pug face; a big, prominent undershot lower jaw; round cheeks; thick, broad flews (chops) extending well below the sides of the lower jaw; dewlaps from head to chest to form two large wrinkles; small rose-shaped high-set ears; medium-sized round very dark eyes; a large, broad, deep-set black nose; and a short thick-based tapered tail

M 5 years

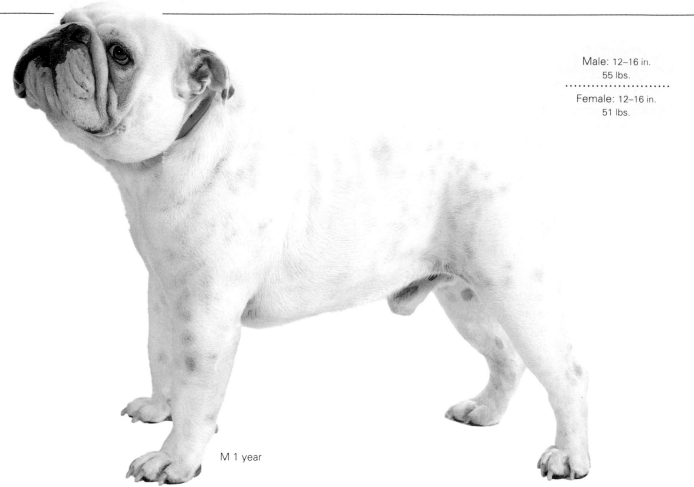

Male: 12–16 in.
55 lbs.
....
Female: 12–16 in.
51 lbs.

M 1 year

that hangs low and is either straight or curled. The coat should be short, smooth, fine in texture, flat lying, and glossy. The color should be uniform, brindle, solid white, red, fawn, or pie-bald. Brown and liver are undesirable.

Superbly compatible with children, this breed is quite pacific, kind, calm, friendly, and cheerful, yet it has a digni-fied demeanor overall.

Care and Exercise

This dog needs only regular brushing with a rough cloth and minimal exer-cise. As it is sensitive to excessive exercise and heat, it's best to keep this dog cool and well-ventilated. It is best to segregate this dog during feeding time as it tends to be possessive about its food, and thus aggressive toward nearby dogs and animals.

Puppies and Training

The average of four puppies per litter have comparatively large heads and are generally delivered by cesarean sec-tion. The color at birth is essentially that of an adult. Bulldog puppies are relatively easy to train and raise.

M 2 years

Boston Terrier

This short, compact American breed has a gentle, loving disposition that has given it a reputation as a first-class household pet and companion.

Background Notes

Descended from the bulldog and bull terrier, the Boston terrier is one of the few American breeds.

Key Characteristics

Compact and angular, the Boston terrier has a square, flat-topped, wrinkle-free head; a short, wide muzzle; large dark round eyes set far apart; small erect ears; and a short straight or screw tail. The short glossy coat is preferably brindle and white, but black and white is permissible. A white muzzle band, a blaze between the eyes and on the forechest, a white collar, and white on the forelegs and below the hocks are desirable.

Cheerful, intelligent, and lively, it will become a member of the family, and is good with other pets and children.

F 2 years

Male: 10–16 in.
11–24 lbs.
....
Female: 10–16 in.
11–24 lbs.

Care and Exercise

Easily cared for, this breed requires only a regular strong massage with a rough cloth, an occasional bath, and brief daily exercise.

Puppies and Training

Passage through the birth canal by the three to four puppies per litter is at best difficult, so they are usually delivered by cesarean section.

M 3 years

Canaan Dog

Generally considered to be the national dog of Israel, this medium-sized breed of great antiquity has a strong defensive instinct.

M 8 years

Background Notes

Indigenous to Canaan, these dogs were domesticated by the local tribes for guarding flocks of sheep and goats against predators and thieves. Now used as a watchdog and sheep dog, the Canaan dog has also served as a guard dog and messenger for the Israeli military.

Key Characteristics

The Canaan dog is medium-sized with a sturdy body; a straight top line; round catlike feet with thick pads; a blunt wedge-shaped head; a scissor bite; prick ears set low, making the head seem wider than it is; and a bushy tail set high and curled up over the back. This breed has a medium-length outer coat and an undercoat that varies with the season. Feathering is abundant, and a mane is preferable for males. Acceptable coloring includes all colors except for gray, brindle, and tricolor.

Agile, alert, and with acute senses, the Canaan dog is instinctively aggressive and distrustful of strangers.

Care and Exercise

This breed requires only weekly brushing. Vigorous daily exercise on a lead is necessary, but speed is not an essential part of this routine.

Puppies and Training

A litter consists of four to six strong puppies that retain an instinctive wildness and defensiveness, thus needing strong training from an early age.

Male: 20–24 in.
44–66 lbs.

Female: 19–23 in.
40–53 lbs.

M 9 years

Chow Chow

With a distinctive blue-black tongue and an unusual stilted gait, this quite aloof, beautiful dog was once a sporting favorite of Chinese emperors. Its history goes back over two thousand years, although its origins are clouded in mystery.

Background Notes

Among the oldest of domesticated dog breeds, the chow chow is said to date back to 150 B.C. Some say it is related to the Akita and Samoyed. With its heavy coat, it is most likely of quite northern, possibly Arctic, origin, and was taken to Mongolia, Siberia, and China, where it was used as a sleigh

F 2 months

Male: 19–22 in.
44–66 lbs.
....
Female: 18–20 in.
35–55 lbs.

F 1 year

F 1.5 years

stubborn, as well as being unpredictable toward other animals.

Care and Exercise

Grooming twice a week, using a brush for the outercoat and a rake comb for the undercoat, should help keep the dog from matting. When kept indoors, this dog tends to become lazy, so to help maintain its active nature, it should be given a fair amount of outdoor exercise.

Puppies and Training

The big-headed puppies, usually three to six per litter, make natural birth difficult, so they are generally delivered by cesarean section. Toilet training should begin around the eighth week, and obedience training should be started as early as possible to get the puppies used to people and to help curb their independent nature.

dog. For centuries the chow chow was used in China as a sporting and guard dog, as well as a source for hides and as a delicacy for the table. The seventh-century Tang emperor is said to have had a kennel of more than twenty-five hundred pairs of chow chows. In early 1880s, the first chow chows were exported to England. It made its first appearance in an American dog show in 1890, and is now a very popular breed in the United States. The breed's name is actually English, coming from the term used by British sailors for their cargo of Chinese bric-a-brac.

Key Characteristics

Compact, powerful, and squarely built, the chow chow has heavily muscled shoulders; a deep, broad chest; a full, powerful neck; a big broad head that is flat on top; a short, wide muzzle; a large black nose; egg-shaped dark eyes; and small round-tipped erect ears. It is double-coated. Any solid color is acceptable for the brushlike coat.

A guard dog by nature, the chow chow is intelligent and loving around its family, but it can also be arrogant and

M 7 months

Dalmatian

Though its origins are debatable, the Dalmatian is an old breed. This dog has a rhythmical gait and a very chic appearance, being spotted with black or liver. It was much loved by the upper classes of the nineteenth century.

M 2 years

Background Notes

The place and date of origin of the Dalmatian are greatly disputed, but, the present name and breed comes from Dalmatia, a region on the Adriatic Sea north of Albania. Having done duty as a military sentinel, a shepherd, a retriever, a ratter, a bird dog, and in packs as a boar and stag hunter, the Dalmatian is a fast, strong, and intelligent breed best known as a coach dog that ran alongside horse-drawn carriages and fire wagons. It has also performed admirably on the stage, in circuses, and as a firehouse mascot.

Key Characteristics

The Dalmatian has a powerful back with a level, slightly arched top line; muscular shoulders; a deep but not too wide chest; an elegantly long neck; a moderately long, flat, wide skull; round eyes that may be dark black, brown, or blue (in black-spotted dogs) or light brown, gold, or dark blue (in liver-spotted dogs); moderately sized drop ears; and a long gradually tapering tail

Male: 23–24 in.
48–64 lbs.
....
Female: 22–23 in.
48–55 lbs.

M 5 years

F 2 years

reaching to the hocks. The coat should be short, hard, dense, and glossy, with a pure white ground and round, clearly defined either black or liver in color and about the size of a silver dollar.

An excellent companion dog or household pet, the Dalmatian is outgoing and friendly, but is sometimes aloof with strangers and a bit unpredictable around other dogs.

Care and Exercise

Little grooming is necessary; however, daily brushing helps keep shedding under control. An extremely active breed, the Dalmatian needs and loves a great deal of exercise, lengthy running being ideal.

Puppies and Training

When the eight to ten puppies per litter are born, they are white, the spots gradually appearing after ten to fourteen days. Puppies need to be taught to be quiet and not shy away from strangers. They become quick learners and willing participants in training as they mature.

Eurasier

Among the newest of the spitz-type breeds, the Eurasier is quite strong, courageous, and responsible, yet sociable. It is both an excellent guard dog and a highly popular household pet in its native Germany.

Background Notes

Created in the 1960s by Julius Wipfel, a breeder from Weinheim, Germany, who wished to produce an ideal sturdy medium-sized pet. The offspring from a cross between a male chow chow and a female Keeshond were bred with a Samoyed to produce the starting stock.

Key Characteristics

The Eurasier is a spitz-like dog because like a spitz, it has chow chow lineage. It has a firm body with a straight, level top line; straight forelegs; a wedge-shaped head with a flat skull and a clearly defined stop; almond-shaped dark eyes; small triangular erect ears; and a high-set tail curled up over the back. Its dense coat is longer around the neck and on the tail and thighs, and should be solid-colored red, orange, wolf gray, or black.

The Eurasier can be trained easily as a companion dog. Sociable and gentle, obedient to its family, it can serve as a fearless guard, and even as a hunter.

Care and Exercise

The dense undercoat needs occasional brushing with a moderately hard brush, and the outer coat needs combing. One daily walk is sufficient exercise.

Puppies and Training

The mother is quite loving, and the three to six strong puppies per litter may be birthed and raised without intervention. For the best obedience response, training of the puppies should begin early.

Male: 20–24 in.
40–70 lbs.
....
Female: 20–24 in.
40–70 lbs.

F 8 months

F 8 months

French Bulldog

This breed, with its very distinctive bat ears and flat skull, was initially a bull baiter, but became a fashionable, devoted pet.

M 4 years

M 2 years

black nose; an undershot square lower jaw; and moderately sized round eyes set wide apart and deep. The coat should be short, smooth, fine textured, and lustrous, and may be colored any shade of brindle, white, fawn, and brindle and white. This very adaptable house pet is a devoted one-person dog.

Care and Exercise

Only a daily rubdown with a rough cloth is needed and, although the dog is fairly active, not very much exercise is needed. Clean, quiet, and well suited to city life, the French bulldog may be kept indoors, if care is taken that the room is well ventilated and never too hot.

Puppies and Training

As with other bulldogs, delivery is generally by cesarean section, but the two to five puppies per litter are quite strong.

Background Notes

Experts' opinions are divided about the origin of the French bulldog. One theory is that its ancestors were dogs exported from England; another is that its ancestors were French. It is quite likely that the truth lies somewhere in between: its ancestor was probably the English bulldog, who made its way to France in the seventeenth century, where it was bred by Parisians for fighting.

Key Characteristics

The French bulldog has a short body; a roach back tapering toward the tail; a broad, deep chest; straight muscular forelegs that are slightly shorter than the hind legs; a large square head that is flat between the wide-apart bat ears and domed at the forehead; a broad, deep, muzzle; an extremely short wide

Male: 12 in.
18–22 lbs.
....
Female: 12 in.
18–22 lbs.

M 2 years (left), F 2 years (right)

Finnish Spitz

This breed has a coat somewhat like a cross between that of a chow chow and a fox. Because of its unique appearance and its ability to hunt, the Finnish spitz has gained great popularity in its homeland.

Background Notes

The breed standards for this dog were set in Finland in 1812. Once used by the Lapps to hunt bear and elk, today it is used as a bird dog. Because it needs experienced handling, the number of

M 3 years

Male: 17–20 in.
51–59 lbs.
....
Female: 16–18 in.
46–55 lbs.

registered dogs has declined some-what in recent years.

Key Characteristics

The Finnish spitz has a deep chest; a well tucked-up abdomen; a pointed muzzle; erect ears; short muscular jaws; dark eyes with a sweet expression; and a loosely curled tail carried on the back. The short, straight coat is brownish red or yellowish red with white markings on chest and toes. Active, friendly, gentle, faithful, and brave, this brisk-moving dog is very loyal to its master, but it can be aggressive with other dogs and animals.

Care and Exercise

This breed requires no special care apart from thorough brushing every four to five days. It is happy with a short daily walk, but delights to run freely in the mountains or in a field.

Puppies and Training

The three to six puppies per litter are usually easily delivered. Puppies should have as much contact with people as possible.

F 2 years

F 4 years

German Spitz

Available in three sizes, this spitz breed has enjoyed popularity in its native Germany, but remains little known elsewhere. It is used today as a sheepdog.

F 1 year

M 4 years

Background Notes

The German spitz is said to descend from the Samoyeds that accompanied the Vikings as they moved across northern Europe. These dogs formed the rootstock of the many spitz types that became sheepdogs throughout the Continent. The German spitz was developed in northern Germany and the Netherlands during the Middle Ages. The three sizes differ only in height: large (up to 20 inches), middle (14½ inches), and small (11 inches).

Key Characteristics

The German spitz has a wedge-shaped head; triangular erect ears with pointed tips; and a tail curled up over the back. The thick double coat is long and spiky, the undercoat thick and dense. Coloring includes black brown, chocolate, red, orange, cream, orange sable, wolf sable, beaver, blue, white, parti-color, black-tan, and so on.

This dog is happy, independent, intelligent, active, and ever alert, but it also can be yappy and distrustful of strangers.

Care and Exercise

Thorough grooming is necessary to maintain this dog's long coat. The outer coat should be combed with a rough comb, taking care not to pull out the hair, and the undercoat should simply be brushed. Not much regular exercise is required as long as the dog can play freely indoors.

Puppies and Training

The two to four puppies per litter mature quickly, and the ears, lying flat at birth, prick up between eight to twelve weeks of age.

Male: 11–20 in.
22–44 lbs.
....
Female: 11–20 in.
22–44 lbs.

F 10 months

Italian Volpino

Popular in its native Italy, this attractive, delicate, but brave breed of spitz has a dainty expression and a graceful carriage, and makes a good watchdog.

Background Notes

As with many of the other spitz types, the origin of this breed is lost in history. Despite its similarity to the German spitz and Pomeranian, this breed has slightly larger ears and eyes, and a rounded skull. It is known in Tuscany as the Florence spitz, and in Rome as the cane de Quirinale.

Male: 11–12 in.
11 lbs.
....
Female: 9–11 in.
10 lbs.

F 1 year

Key Characteristics

Compact and foxlike, the Italian volpino has a V-shaped head; small dark eyes; triangular prick ears; and a bushy tail curled up over the back. Its thick, somewhat harsh long outercoat should be spiky, and longest around the neck, loin, and tail; and white, red, or honey in color.

Intelligent, merry, agile, and fearless, this dog is quite obedient, loyal, and affectionate to its master.

Care and Exercise

Though long, the straight coat requires only periodic grooming with a moderately hard brush. Short daily walks are all that is needed for exercise.

Puppies and Training

The mother is well able to care for the two to five puppies per litter with no assistance. Training is also easy.

F 1 year

Japanese Spitz

Pure, snow white, and unique among Japan's dogs as a spitz type with its characteristic pointed muzzle, this very popular companion dog is gaining a following worldwide.

This dog has acute senses and is intelligent, merry, and friendly with children, as well as being loyal to its master.

Care and Exercise

Occasional brushing is all that's necessary, except during the shedding season, when dead hair should be combed out. If the dog lives indoors a daily walk will be appreciated.

Puppies and Training

The three to six puppies born in a litter are strong and easily trained.

M 4.5 years

Male: 12–15 in.
15–22 lbs.
....
Female: 12–15 in.
13–20 lbs.

Background Notes

This dog is a relatively new breed. It is said that two pure white Samoyed females imported from Canada by a Tokyo breeder in the early 1900s were crossed with offspring of pure white dogs, also from imported stock, being bred in Nagoya. By around 1955, the Japanese spitz had become the most popular breed in the country. It was the first dog to receive official recognition in Japan as a purebred.

Key Characteristics

Well balanced, beautiful, and noble, the Japanese spitz has a pointed muzzle; a small round black nose; firm, tightly closed black lips; a scissor bite; dark almond eyes with black rims; and small triangular prick ears. It is double-coated, except for the short hair on the face, ears, muzzle, tips of the forelegs, and below the hocks, with feathering also from the neck to the chest and the tail. Only a solid, pure white coat is acceptable.

M 6 years

Keeshond

Also known as the Dutch barge dog, this ideal family pet and watchdog has been well loved in its native land for over two hundred years.

Background Notes

Probably developed from northern sleigh dogs, this breed was well established throughout the Netherlands by the late eighteenth century. Kees de Gyselaer of Dordrecht, the leader of the Patriots, owned a dog he called Kees who became the party's mascot, the dog of the people. When the Patriots lost, the breed's popularity went into a dramatic decline. Never bred to be working dogs, Keeshonds have served solely as loyal, devoted companion dogs.

Key Characteristics

The foxlike Keeshond has a short, compact body that is about as tall as it is long; a wedge-shaped head; dark brown almond-shaped eyes; small high-set triangular prick ears; and a tightly curled tail carried over the back. The outercoat should be abundant, spiky, long, and straight, and the undercoat must be thick and soft like down. The undercoat is light gray or cream, the outercoat black and gray with black tips. There are spectacle markings around the eyes.

Gentle, affectionate, and always friendly, especially with children, the Keeshond is considered by many to be the perfect house pet.

F 4 years

Male: 18 in.
40 lbs.
....
Female: 17 in.
35 lbs.

Care and Exercise

Brushing twice a week for about forty-five minutes is recommended to help keep the abundant coat mat-free. Bathing should be avoided unless absolutely necessary, as it tends to soften the hair. This breed adapts well to city life.

Puppies and Training

The three to eight puppies per litter are born black or seal brown, lightening to an off-white or cream in four months. Markings appear between five months and 1½ years.

F 4 years

Kromfohrlander

A sweet, intelligent, obedient companion dog with a humorous expression and a moderately long coat, this breed fits into any environment and is well suited even for small apartments.

Background Notes

The Kromfohrlander is believed to have originated in Germany in the nineteenth century as a cross between an English griffon and a fox terrier. An alert, affectionate companion and watchdog, it can be found with three types of coat, as shown here. This dog's appealing expression makes it hard for anyone to resist giving it a hug.

are undesirable. Loyal and loving to its master, the Kromfohrlander accepts all challenges with enthusiasm.

Care and Exercise

Easily cared for, this breed requires only a weekly brushing and a daily walk.

Wire Short, M 4 years

Male: 15–18 in.
26 lbs.
....
Female: 15–18 in.
26 lbs.

Long, M 4 years

Key Characteristics

Small and compact, the Kromfohrlander has straight forelegs; a lean V-shaped head; a big black nose; a scissor or level bite; dark oval eyes; triangular round-tipped drop ears lying close to the head; an arched neck; and a slightly curved moderately long tail that is carried high. The coat comes in three variations: long, wire short (slightly hard short hair), and wire (medium-length hair). All have a white ground with light chestnut markings; black markings

Puppies and Training

The three to five strong puppies per litter are delivered without difficulty, and can be easily raised. This breed's natural curiosity makes training them quite simple.

Wire, F 1.5 years

Lhasa Apso

The Lhasa apso has a history of more than thirteen hundred years as a guard dog for the chambers of Tibetan monasteries, with its luxuriously long coat acting as insulation against the harsh climate of the Himalayas. This hardy, very alert dog makes a dedicated companion.

Background Notes

The oldest and most popular of the four breeds indigenous to Tibet, the origin of this dog is unclear. It has been widely kept as a pet and sentinel not only in the lamaseries, but also in the homes of the common people as it is believed to receive people's souls at the moment of their deaths, and hence has received much respect. Prized also for its very keen sense of hearing, it was given as a special gift by the Dalai Lama, and was presented to several Chinese emperors. First shown in a dog show in London in 1929, it quickly

F 3 years

gained a following, being officially recognized by the Kennel Club in 1933, and the American Kennel Club in 1935.

Key Characteristics

The Lhasa apso has a compact body with its length exceeding its height; a somewhat narrow skull; a medium-length muzzle; a black nose; medium-sized dark brown oval eyes with a good fall over them; and a well-feathered high-set tail carried in a screw high over the back. Its very abundant, long, heavy, straight coat should be neither soft nor silky. The head, body, and legs are completely covered, and the coat on face forms whiskers and a beard. Coloring includes gold, sand, honey, dark grizzle, slate, smoke, black, or parti-color; however, gold or lion is most desirable, with dark tips to the ears and beard.

A loving, playful dog with its master, wary of and aloof around strangers, not generous with children as it dislikes abuse or lack of respect and can be short-tempered.

Male: 10–11 in.
15 lbs.

Female: 9–10 in.
13 lbs.

M 4 months

Care and Exercise

This dog requires a considerable amount of coat care, including daily brushing and thorough grooming twice a week for at least an hour, starting from when the dog reaches eight to ten weeks old. Quite active, this breed also requires a moderate amount of regular daily exercise either indoors or out.

Puppies and Training

The four to five puppies per litter are usually born slightly darker than an adult. They are easily trained, and obedience lessons should begin at six weeks of age.

M 3 years

Poodle

Long considered the national dog of France, this elegant breed is available in three sizes, and has enjoyed worldwide popularity on a scale equaled by no other.

Background Notes

Believed to have originated in either Germany or Russia, the standard (largest type) poodle was used mainly as a water retriever; the word poodle comes from the German *pudelin* for the splash made by an oar hitting water. In Russia, this dog was also used to pull milk carts. The standard poodle made its way to France, where it was bred down to produce the toy poodle, which quickly became a prized pet of eighteenth-century European

Male: 11–15 in.
7–13 lbs.
....
Female: 11–15 in.
7–13 lbs.

Standard, M 2 years

Male: 15 in.
13–22 lbs.
....
Female: 15 in.
13–22 lbs.

aristocracy. The sporting clip method of trimming the coat was originally used to facilitate swimming, but fancier clips, such as the lion, soon became the fashion. Extremely intelligent and quick to mimic and learn, this breed also became a mainstay of vaudeville acts and traveling circuses.

clip (for dogs under one year of age), the sporting English saddle clip, and the Continental clip.

All poodles are loyal, playful, and at times exuberant, but the standard is also brave and unconcerned about trivialities, whereas the miniature and toy tend to be a bit picky and excitable, and thus are not well suited to be around small children.

Care and Exercise

The coat grows rapidly and has to be shampooed and brushed for two to five hours every week, and should be professionally trimmed, shaved, and clipped every three to six weeks beginning when the dog is 3½ weeks old. The ears and teeth need to be regularly

Toy, F 8 years

Male: 10 in.
4–7 lbs.
....
Female: 10 in.
4–7 lbs.

Miniature, M 3 years

Key Characteristics

Varying only by size, all three types of poodle are squarely built, move very proudly, and have a short back; a deep chest; broad muscular loins; a moderately round skull; a long straight muzzle with a clearly defined stop; long, wide, pendant ears hanging close to the face; and a high-set docked tail held straight and erect. The dense, harsh coat can be any solid color, such as black, white, café au lait, brown, silver, gray, or blue. Show trimming variations are the puppy

Standard, F 5 years

M 2 years

F 3 years

checked and cleaned. All poodle sizes adapt well to city life. This breed is active irrespective of place, but much of its exercise should be indoors.

Puppies and Training

Litters number three to eight puppies for standard and miniatures, two to five for toys, with the coat changing color until it becomes full at about two years. Obedience training should begin at six months of age.

Schipperke

Despite its small size, this sturdy, speedy, generally long-lived Belgian dog makes a great family pet as it is extremely good with children, and often acts as their guardian.

Background Notes

This diminutive Flemish dog was developed in Flanders by breeding down the black Leauvenaar sheepdog. It was once principally a barge watchdog, and in fact the name schipperke means "little captain" in Flemish. A workers' companion until 1885, this breed became a fashionable pet of the upper class when the Belgian queen saw one and acquired it at a show in Brussels. It first reached the United States in 1888.

Key Characteristics

The schipperke has a short, straight, powerful back; slightly arched jaws; a round loin; a deep, broad neck; a broad, foxy face; narrowed round eyes; high-set triangular small prick ears; dark brown oval eyes; a small black nose; a medium-sized muzzle; and a docked tail. It is double-coated, with a short, dense undercoat and a slightly harsh outer coat. Solid black is desirable, but other solid colors are permissible.

Curious about everything in its surroundings, the schipperke is lively, alert, and at times independent. Always reserved and wary of strangers, this dog makes a brave, dedicated watchdog and an aggressive ratter.

M 5 years

Care and Exercise

This breed is easily cared for, needing only a quick brushing twice a week and a regular brisk walk.

Puppies and Training

The training of the three to seven puppies per litter must start within six months of age to get them used to obeying commands and being around people.

Male: 12 in.
18 lbs.
·····················
Female: 12 in.
18 lbs.

F 7 months

Schnauzer

Although these three popular dogs are quite distinct in size and use, they share the same name, general build, characteristic long bushy eyebrows, distinguished mutton chops, and harsh wiry coat.

Background Notes

Created in Germany, the standard is the oldest type of schnauzer, and the one from which the other two were derived. This dog was bred as a hunter for rats and weasels, but its all-around abilities made it valued as a water-bird dog, guard dog, and house pet. The miniature schnauzer has worked as a guard dog for farmyards and stables. The giant schnauzer, equipped with an excellent sense of smell, was produced for use as a drover, and later worked as a police dog as well.

Key Characteristics

Robust, squarely built, well boned, and muscular, schnauzers have high-set V-shaped drop ears that are usually cropped to form an erect triangle; profuse eyebrows; whiskers; and a moderately high-set tail that is docked short. The miniature has a compact, powerful body; the standard, a sturdy, heavy-boned angular body; and the giant, a large, powerful body. The dense, harsh coat is double, consisting of a wiry outer coat and a soft, short undercoat.

Miniature, M 1 year

The standard and the giant should be either pepper or black. The miniature should be either black and silver, black and tan, or solid colors. Tan shades are permissible. The miniature is friendly with people, but alert, and it barks well. The standard is brave, obedient, agile, active, and highly trainable. Male dogs

Male: 12–14 in.
11–18 lbs.
....
Female: 12–14 in.
11–18 lbs.

Miniature, M 3 years

Standard, M 3 years

can be aggressive toward other animals. The giant has acute senses and is gentle, friendly with its family and children, and fearless.

Care and Exercise

Grooming requires daily brushing, combing, and some stripping of dead and split hair, with special attention being paid to areas where the hair is long. All three types like to run at a fast pace on a lead, and should occasionally be allowed to exercise freely in a big open space.

Puppies and Training

Although the mother is somewhat nervous, she is good at rearing her litter of puppies, which will number three to six for miniatures, four to nine for standards, and five to eight for giants. If desired, the ears should be cropped between the eighth and twelfth weeks.

Male: 18–20 in.
26–40 lbs.
....
Female: 17–19 in.
22–33 lbs.

Male: 25–27 in.
75–95 lbs.
....
Female: 23–25 in.
66–88 lbs.

Giant, F 3 years

Shar Pei

This dog's name roughly translates to "draping sandpaperlike skin" in Chinese, referring to the unique coat that makes this merry, independent, loving dog falsely appear sad.

Background Notes

Though it is believed to have originated in China, little is known about this breed's lineage. Some say that Tibetan mastiff ancestry is likely, as this dog once weighed up to 140 pounds, and common lineage with the chow chow is suggested because only these two breeds have a blue-black tongue. This dog guarded sheep and other livestock, as well as being used for dogfighting. It also once served as food for the table. Its listing in the 1978 *Guinness Book of Records* as the world's rarest breed made the shar pei known worldwide. Today it is bred as a unique house pet.

Key Characteristics

Compact, powerfully active, and squarely built, the shar pei has a short back with a slightly concave top line; a broad, deep chest; heavily boned straight forelegs; muscular, somewhat angular hindquarters; hind dewclaws that are removed; hare feet with thick, springy pads; fine wrinkles on the face, forming dewlaps; a rather large head with a broad, flat skull and moderate stop; a characteristically rather long, broad, square muzzle; a large, wide nose, preferably black; a scissor bite; medium-sized dark almond-shaped eyes lying forward on the skull; and small, high-set triangular ears. The loose, heavily wrin-

M 5 years

kled skin should have a harsh, straight, brushlike coat, and be a solid color such as black, red, fawn, cream, and so on. White markings are undesirable.

Highly affectionate, but calmly disposed, the shar pei loves to play with children and makes a good house pet and guard dog.

M 1 year

Male: 18–20 in.
40–51 lbs.
....
Female: 16–18 in.
35–44 lbs.

Care and Exercise

Because of this breed's loose skin, starting from puppyhood the coat, including the face, needs to be brushed with a stiff brush and strongly massaged with a towel. Regular daily exercise on a lead should emphasize pulling, but not necessarily speed.

Puppies and Training

Each litter consists of four to six strong puppies, which should have regular contact with people as early as possible.

F 5 years

M 7 months

Tibetan Spaniel

With its sweet, loving nature, this ancient breed, indigenous to the Himalayas, has found a favored place as a companion dog and pet in many homes throughout the world.

M 7 months

M 3 years

Male: 10 in.
9–15 lbs.
....
Female: 10 in.
9–15 lbs.

Background Notes

The origin of this breed can be traced back at least one thousand years. It acted as a prayer dog, spinning fortune wheels in lamaseries to select a small bit of parchment on which one's fate had been written. Around 1800, it was introduced to England, where it was selectively modified to make the muzzle longer, to better distinguish it from the Pekingese.

Key Characteristics

With a body length slightly exceeding its height, the Tibetan spaniel has a relatively small head; a slightly domed skull; a medium-length muzzle; a slightly undershot mouth; and a high-set well-plumed tail curled over the back. Its silky double coat is long on the ears and the back of the front legs. All colors are permissible.

Cheerful, sociable, but aloof with strangers, this dog can be quite fearless and assertive despite its small size.

Care and Exercise

The Tibetan spaniel needs brushing two or three times a week. It is very active, and daily walking and running are necessary.

Puppies and Training

A litter numbers two to four puppies. As this breed can be stubborn, obedience training should be begun at an early age.

F, M, M, F, M (from left), all 6 months

Tibetan Terrier

Bred by Tibetan lamas and local villagers for almost two millennia, the English name of this dog is misleading as it has no terrier traits or blood. This exceptionally hardy, very compact, sheepdoglike breed is a very affectionate, always-willing-to-please companion that loves traveling.

Background Notes

A small breed long treasured by Tibetan lamas and monks, the Tibetan terrier was often presented as a gift to show one's respect for and gratefulness to special friends, as well as to bring them luck in the future. It was never sold, as "selling luck" might tempt fate negatively, or cross bred, as this would dilute one's good fortune.

Key Characteristics

The Tibetan terrier has a very compact, powerful body; a marked stop in front of the eyes and a medium-length high-set tail curled over the back. The thick double coat is long on the head and legs with a short "beard" under the chin. Any color except chocolate or liver is acceptable.

Highly energetic, intelligent, and adaptable, but at times a bit shy and reserved, especially around strangers, this dog is a devoted follower willing to take part in family activities.

Care and Exercise

Keep the coat tangle-free by brushing it for one hour twice a week and giving the dog regular baths. Although this breed adapts well to city life, it still needs plenty of exercise.

Puppies and Training

There are five to eight puppies in a litter. Those born white will remain so, but light-colored ones will eventually turn gold, brindle, or silver.

M 2 years

Male: 14–16 in.
18–31 lbs.

Female: 14–16 in.
15–29 lbs.

M 2 years

Glossary

Aka Meaning red in Japanese, this Japanese Kennel Club term refers to coat colors in native breeds ranging from light tan to Tosa brown.

Aka-goma Japanese Kennel Club term, meaning red sesame, for the coat of Japanese breeds having black peppering on a red ground.

Aka-tora Meaning red tiger in Japanese, this Japanese Kennel Club term refers to a black-striped brindle pattern on a red ground in native breeds.

Albino A dog with an uncommon recessive trait inhibiting melanin formation, thus causing it to have a white or ivory coat and pink or blue eyes.

Almond eye An elongated-appearing eye, due to tissue surrounding the eye (see page 29).

Apple head A very rounded, domelike skull top (see page 29). See, for example, the Chihuahua.

Apricot A Japanese Kennel Club term for a reddish yellow coat (see page 31).

ASCOB An abbreviation meaning a coat of Any Solid Color Other than Black, although a small amount of white on the chest and/or throat (other locations are disqualifiers) or tan points are allowable.

Bat ear A rounded, broad-based erect ear, as in bulldogs (see page 29).

Beaver A Japanese Kennel Club term for a coat somewhat deeper than fawn.

Belton A Kennel Club term for the ticking or roaning pattern of intermingled color and white hairs found in English setters (named for a village in Northumberland). Variations include blue (black and white), tricolor (blue with tan), orange, lemon, and liver belton (see page 32).

Bird dog A sporting breed developed to hunt game birds.

Biscuit A Japanese Kennel Club term for an almost cream, light fawn coat.

Bite The relative positioning of the upper and lower sets of teeth when the mouth is closed; types include scissor, level, undershot, and overshot.

Black mask A Japanese Kennel Club term for a lower face and muzzle that are both black (see page 32).

Black muzzle Only the muzzle, not the face, is black.

Black and tan A black coat highlighted by a combination of tan markings on the sides of the muzzle, or on the throat, and lower limbs, plus small ones above the eyes and around the anus (see page 32).

Blanket A solid coat color that extends from the neck to the tail along the back and upper part of the sides.

Blaze A central facial white stripe usually running between the eyes (see page 32).

Blenheim The Kennel Club term for the well-distributed chestnut-red patches on a pearly white ground pattern found in cavalier and King Charles spaniels, and the Japanese chin.

Blocky head A squarish, cubelike head as in the Boston terrier (see page 29).

Blue An inherited dilution of a black coat color caused by a recessive which shows phenotypically as blue (see page 31).

Blue black Hair with a blue base and black tip (see page 31).

Bobtail Used as both a pseudonym for the Old English sheepdog and for a dog that naturally lacks a tail or has one docked very short (see page 30).

Body length The horizontal distance from the anterior portion of the breastbone (prosternum) to the posterior portion of the pelvic girdle (see page 28).

Breeder Generally a person who breeds dogs, but under many kennel club rules usually specifically referring to the owner of the dam (even if it has been hired for mating) when the litter was whelped.

Brindle A fine, even mixture of black hairs and those of a lighter color such as tan, gold, brown, or gray, usually expressed as a striped, tigerlike coat such as is found in boxers (see page 32).

Broken up face A receding nose, together with a deep stop, wrinkle, and undershot jaw such as is found in bulldogs and Pekingese (see page 29).

Bronze A copperish-colored coat (see page 32).

Button ear A folded down ear that lies close to the skull so that it covers the orifice as in the bullmastiff (see page 29).

Café au lait Japanese Kennel Club term for coffee with cream-colored coat.

Camel Japanese Kennel Club term for a coat the color of this desert animal.

Chestnut Japanese Kennel Club term for a medium-brown coat color (see page 31).

China eye Usually a clear blue eye, but sometimes a flecked or spotted light blue or whitish eye such as is found in a blue merle collie (see page 29).

Chocolate Japanese Kennel Club term for coat colors ranging from dark fawn to brown (see page 31).

Circular eye A round eye such as is found in the smooth fox terrier (see page 29).

Clip A coat trimming that produces a styled cut such as the "lion cut" in poodles.

Coat The hair covering a dog; may be either single or double.

Collar Markings, usually white, found around the neck.

Companion dog A canine that has earned a specified score at a number of kennel club–licensed obedience trials, and has thus been awarded the CD suffix to be used with the dog's name.

Crank tail A tight tail shaped like a crank that is carried down (see page 31).

Cream A light yellow coat.

Cropping A method (cutting or trimming) for inducing the ears to stand erect; not permitted by the Kennel Club.

Culottes Longer hair on the back of the thighs that give a dog a "baggy trousers" look, such as in the schipperke.

Curled tail A tightly curled (single or double) tail held close to the back or buttocks, although the tip may be held high.

Dapple An inherited coat coloring determined by a single or multiple dominant gene that is expressed as a mottled or variegated pattern as in the dachshund (see page 32).

Dewlap Rather loose, pendulous skin under the throat and/or neck, as in the boxer and basset hound (see page 28).

Dewclaw A functionless, vestigial fifth digit on the inside of the leg in dogs (see page 28).

Dish-faced A foreface (from the stop to the nose tip) that forms a slightly concave profile, as in the pointer.

Dock To amputate the greater part of the tail to make it short.

Dog show A national-kennel-club-sanctioned championship competition that may be for all breeds or for a single breed (the latter is called a specialty show).

Domed head A convex evenly rounded (vs. flat) top skull (see page 29). See, for example, the American cocker spaniel.

Double coat A coat that has both an outer layer of hair resistant to weather and an inner layer of softer hair for warmth and waterproofing.

Down-faced A muzzle that inclines downwards from the top of the skull to the tip of the nose (see page 29), as in the bull terrier.

Drop ear An ear that is folded forward partly, or completely over the ear opening (see page 30).

Dudley nose A flesh-colored or pink nose; a disqualification point in many breeds of show dogs such as in the Boston terrier.

Ear guide dog A canine that is specially trained to guide the deaf.

Even bite The condition in which the front teeth (upper and lower incisors) meet with no overlap when the mouth is closed.

Fawn A light brown or red-yellow color with a hue of medium brilliance (see page 32).

Feathering Patches of longer hairs on the ends of the ears, legs, tail, or body.

Flag A long tail with feathering that is usually carried high (see page 30).

Four-eyed A Japanese Kennel Club term for dogs with small tan markings above the eyes.

Full coat A coat that has attained mature length and quantity.

Golden A coat color akin to that of a lion.

Goma Meaning sesame in Japanese, this Association for the Conservation of Japanese Breeds term is a contrasting-color peppering of which there are four types (*aka-goma, goma, kuro-goma, shiro-goma*) in native Japanese dogs.

Grizzle A roan pattern that is usually a mixture of black, bluish-gray, iron-gray, or red hairs with white hairs.

Groom The act of brushing, combing, or trimming a dog's coat.

Guard dog A canine trained for such sentry duty as watching over big farms, factories, and warehouses and alerting owners when strangers appear.

Guard hairs Generally stiff hairs that are longer and smoother than that of the undercoat through which they grow and which they conceal.

Guide dog A canine specially trained to lead and act as eyes for the blind. Females of the German shepherd and Labrador retriever are most suited.

Gundog A specially trained canine or representative breed able to work with its master in finding and retrieving live or shot game.

Half-prick ear Also called semi-prick ear, this Japanese Kennel Club term refers to ears that bend forward at one-third the distance from the tip, as found in collies and sheepdogs (see page 29).

Handler The person controlling a dog in the show ring or field trial; if receiving a fee for this service, this person is called a professional handler.

Hand-pluck To pluck an undercoat with fingertips.

Harlequin A coat pattern of usually black or blue patches on a white ground as is found in Great Danes (see page 32).

Haw A third eyelid or nictitating membrane found in the inside corner of the eye in some breeds (see page 29). See, for example, the bloodhound, St. Bernard, and clumber spaniel.

Height Sometimes referred to as shoulder height, this vertical measurement is taken from the withers to the ground (see page 28).

Hock Essentially the dog's true heel, composed of the tarsus, or the collection of bones of the hind leg forming the joint between the lower thigh and the metatarsus (see page 28).

Honey The Japanese Kennel Club term for a light yellow/red coat such as is found in the Lhasa apso.

Hook tail A tail that is carried down, but with the tip curled upwards (see page 30).

Hound A dog developed for hunting by scent or sight.

Hound-marked A coat coloration composed of tan and/or black patches usually on the head, back, legs, and tail, on a generally white ground (see page 32). See, for example, the beagle.

Hunting dog A grouping that includes both gundogs that hunt game and hounds that hunt other animals.

Kink tail A bent tail caused by a malformation of the caudal vertebrae (see page 31).

Kuro Meaning black in Japanese, this Japanese Kennel Club term refers to the black coat sprinkled with light fawn hairs found in some local breeds.

Kuro-goma This Japanese Kennel Club term meaning black sesame refers to the coat of Japanese breeds having a blacker peppering than the more common *goma*, and thus a darker overall appearance.

Kuro-tora Meaning black tiger in Japanese, this Japanese Kennel Club term refers to a black-striped brindle pattern on a dark ground in native breeds.

Lead Commonly called a leash, this can be a strap, cord, chain, and so on, attached to a collar or harness for restraining or leading a dog.

Lemon Japanese Kennel Club terminology for a coat ranging from lemon yellow to orange yellow.

Level bite The condition in which the front teeth (upper and lower incisors) meet exactly edge to edge with no overlap when the mouth is closed.

Lion color A tawny coat such as is found in Ibizan hounds.

Liver A deep brown (see page 31).

Lobe-shaped ear The Japanese Kennel Club term for slightly folded, bamboo-leaf-like ears set at the back of the head (see page 30).

Mahogany The Japanese Kennel Club term for a chestnut red, almost reddish fawn coat such as in Irish setters (see page 31).

Mahogany tan Japanese Kennel Club's term for a reddish fawn coat sprinkled with yellow.

Mahogany brindle A brindle pattern on a mahogany ground.

Mane An abundance of long hair found on the nape and sides of the neck.

Marking A small patch of contrastingly colored hairs, usually on the head or body.

Mask A fore face that is darkly shaded such as in the mastiff, boxer, and Pekingese (see page 32).

Mat A rather firm corded coat such as is found in the puli and Komondor.

Merle A mottled or variegated coloring, determined by a single or multiple dominant gene, such as is found in the collie (see page 32).

Molera A malformation exhibited as a small opening at the top part of the head due to incomplete, imperfect, or abnormal ossification of the skull. See, for example, the Chihuahua.

Muzzle The foreface, consisting of the nasal bone, nostrils, jaws, and head in front of the eyes.

Nose bridge The straight or arched upper side of the muzzle from the stop to the nose.

Orange The Japanese Kennel Club term for a range of light, reddish tan colored coats (see page 31).

Otter tail A round, tapering tail that is thick at the root, with the hair parted or divided on the underside, and not extending below the hock (see page 30). See, for example, the Labrador retriever.

Oval eye An egg-shaped or oval eye as is found in poodles (see page 29).

Pad A tough, thickened skin projection on the underside of the feet that serves as a shock absorber.

Parent club A nationally recognized club that sets standards for a specific breed.

Parti-color A coat with a variegated patchwork of two or more colors (see page 32). See, for example, the spaniel.

Pastern Known technically as the megacarpus, this is the region of the foreleg between the carpus or wrist and the digits (see page 28).

Pedigree A recorded, usually written, record of at least three generations of a dog's ancestry.

Penciling Black lines that divide tan coloring on the toes, such as found in the Manchester terrier (see page 32).

Peppering A salt and pepper mixture of black and white hairs such as is found in some schnauzers (see page 32).

Pied A coat composed of relatively large unequally proportioned patches of two or more colors, one usually being white.

Pluck To remove hairs from the overcoat using either one's fingertips or a stripper.

Plume As the name implies, a long fringe of hair that hangs from the tail (see page 30).

Point The stance taken by a hunting dog (hound or gundog) when it stands still to indicate the presence and position of game.

Point of shoulder The joint on the body where the upper leg meets the scapula (see page 28).

Point of the hock The outer angle of the hock.

Points Small patches of a contrasting color, usually white, black or tan, on the face, ears, legs, and tail.

Police dog A canine specially trained for working with the police.

Pompon The round tuft of hair left on the end of the tail when the coat is clipped, as on poodles.

Powder puff A small dog with a great deal of feathering, such as in the Chinese crested dog.

Prick ear A usually pointed ear, carried fully erect (see page 29).

Prominent eye A big, round, projecting eye such as found in chins and pugs (see page 29).

Pup Officially a dog less than one year (twelve months) old.

Puppy clip A cut style used for poodles of nine to twelve months old, in which the hairs on the face, feet, and tail root are clipped, leaving the long hairs elsewhere.

Rat tail A tapered tail that is thick at the root, and partially or completely devoid of hair, such as in the Irish water spaniel (see page 30).

Red A coat of reddish orange, from light or yellow red to stag red (see page 31).

Red fawn Japanese Kennel Club's term for a dark reddish gold coat.

Register A record filed with the national kennel club of a dog's breeding particulars.

Ring tail An almost fully circular tail that is carried up (see page 30).

Roan A fine mixture of colored hairs intermingled with white hairs such as is found in English cocker spaniels; usually used with an adjective to note the predominate color; for example, blue roan, orange roan, lemon roan, liver roan (see page 32).

Roman nose A nose with a bridge so comparatively high as to form a slightly convex line from the forehead to the nose tip. See, for example, the borzoi.

Rose ear A small drop ear, as seen in bulldogs, that folds over and back, revealing the burr (see page 30).

Ruff A growth of longer, thicker hair around the neck.

Rough coat A usually medium to long coarse overcoat.

Ruby The Japanese Kennel Club term for the dark red chestnut coat found in King Charles spaniels.

Sable An inherited coat color of black-tipped hairs on a basically silver, gray, gold, fawn, or brown ground (see page 32).

Saddle A black marking shaped and placed as named.

Salt and Pepper An alternate name for peppering (see page 32).

Sashi-o A Japanese term meaning sickle tail; however, it refers to one that is carried slightly forward and lower than normal (see page 30).

Scent hound A breed of hunting dog that tracks animals by smell, such as the beagle, elkhound, dachshund, foxhound, and otterhound.

Scissor bite As the name implies, a strong jaw in which the inner surface of the upper teeth comes down perfectly next to the outer surface of the lower teeth when the mouth is closed.

Screw tail A naturally short tail that is shaped like a compressed corkscrew (see page 31). See, for example, the bulldog.

Semi-pricked ear A usually pointed ear, carried erect, but with just the tip bending forward (see page 29).

Shade Gradated hair that is generally whitish at the base and colored toward the tip.

Shiro-goma A Japanese Kennel Club term, meaning white sesame, for the coat of Japanese breeds having black peppering on a white ground.

Sickle tail A tail that is carried up and out in a semicircle (see page 30).

Sight hound Also known as a gaze hound, this is a breed of hunting dog, such as a greyhound, borzoi, or Irish wolfhound, that runs or courses game animals by sight rather than scent.

Silky coat Another name for a glossy coat composed of hairs that are long, fine, and soft to the touch.

Silver A coat that is slightly grayish silver.

Silver gray A gray coat that has a slightly silver cast.

Skull The head bones, but this term usually refers to the part of the head from the stop to the occiput. There are three types: the long skull as in the borzoi; the short skull as in the pug, Boston terrier, and Pekingese; and the medium-length skull as in the beagle and setter.

Slate blue A dark, grayish blue coat (see page 31).

Smoke A coat that is a smoky, or sometimes slightly bluish gray.

Smooth coat A close-lying body covering completely composed of short hairs.

Snippyface A pointed, weak muzzle that lacks depth and breadth.

Socks Slightly longer hair on a dog's feet up to the pasterns and/or dewclaws.

Solid or self color A coat completely of one color.

Spectacles As the name implies, a shading or dark marking, shaped and situated like eyeglasses. See, for example, the Keeshond.

Spotted Coin-sized black or liver patches sprinkled all over a white body, such as in the Dalmatian.

Squirrel tail A curved tail that is carried up and forward (see page 30). See, for example, the papillon.

Stag red Japanese Kennel Club term for a reddish coat colored similar to that of an adult male deer.

Steel blue A non-silvery, dark grayish blue coat (see page 31).

Stern Usually referring to the tail of a sporting dog or hound (see page 30).

Stop The point at which the nasal bones and cranium meet, marked by a step up from the muzzle to the skull or an indentation between the eyes.

Stripper A special tool with teeth and a handle, designed for plucking hair from a dog.

Tassel Feathering on the ears, such as in the Bedlington terrier.

Thumb marks Black spots on or near the pastern, such as are usually found on the Manchester terrier.

Ticked A white coat sparsely covered with small patches of black, flecked, or colored hairs.

Tiger brindle Japanese Kennel Club term for a black-striped pattern on a gold ground coat (see page 32).

Topknot A tuft of longer hair on the top of the head.

Tora-ge Meaning tiger-haired, this is the general Japanese Kennel Club term for Japanese breeds with a brindle-patterned coat (see also *aka-tora* and *kuro-tora*).

Triangular eye An eye with a three-cornered appearance created by the surrounding tissue, such as in the Afghan hound (see page 29).

Tricolor A coat of three distinct colors, usually white, black, and tan.

Trim To groom a dog's coat by plucking or clipping.

Trot A rhythmic, two-beat gait in which the diagonally opposite feet (for example, the right hind and the left front) strike the ground together.

Tulip ear A rather wide ear carried erect and somewhat forward with the edges curving slightly inward (see page 29).

Turn-up An upturned foreface or underjaw, such as in the bulldog.

Undercoat A dense, soft, short coat concealed by a longer topcoat.

Undershot A bite in which the incisors of the lower jaw overlap or project beyond the front teeth of the upper jaw when the mouth is closed.

Urajiro This Japanese Kennel Club term meaning white rear, this refers to the almost pure white underside of a dog, from the chin to the neck, chest, abdomen, limbs, and tail in Japanese breeds.

Walleye Also known as fisheye, glass eye, or pearl eye, this type of eye has a pale bluish, whitish, or colorless iris (see page 29). See, for example, the Great Dane (Harlequin).

Wheaten A pale yellow or fawn-colored coat (see page 31).

Whip tail A tapered tail that is carried stiffly and, straight out as in the Dalmatian (see page 30).

Whiskers Rather long sensory organs appearing as hairs on the sides of the muzzle and sometimes on the underjaw. See, for example, the Brussels griffon.

White A coat color ranging from pure to smoky white.

Wire-haired A harsh, crisp, wiry textured coat that serves as protection against bad weather and enemies.

Withers The point just behind the neck from which the dog's body height is measured (see page 28).

Yellow Japanese Kennel Club term for a coat color that is between fox and light brown.

Index

Photo by Ray Paulsen

Tetsu Yamazaki

Born in Tokyo in 1949, photographer Tetsu Yamazaki graduated from Tama School of Art, then studied with noted photographer Yukichi Watanabe. Working as a freelance photographer and author and specializing in animal photography, he has traveled throughout Japan and abroad. His animal subjects instinctively sense his love of four-legged creatures and quickly become relaxed. This has led to the establishment of an unusual level of rapport that he is able to capture and communicate on film. These striking pictures have helped to establish his reputation as one of today's leading photographers of dogs and cats. Among his published works, including photographs in magazines, books, and calendars, is *Legacy of the Cat* (Chronicle Books, 1990).

Toyoharu Kojima

Born in Tokyo in 1933, author Toyoharu Kojima, currently an auditor of the Japan Kennel Club and a director of the West Tokyo Dog Club, has been actively involved in dog circles for well over thirty years. In addition to serving as a Japanese Kennel Club–sanctioned, international all-breed judge at hundreds of dog shows throughout Japan, he has attended numerous international shows, including Westminster, Crufts, and the Australia National. Respected throughout the international dog world, Toyoharu Kojima is also an avid cat specialist.